Best Love to All is an account of the experiences of the author's grandfather as a young officer on the Western Front with the Liverpool Pals. Based on his unpublished letters and diaries, it covers his participation in the battles of Arras and Ypres in 1917, with the Fifth and Second Armies during the great German Spring Offensive of 1918, and in Brussels after the armistice. Eric Rigby-Jones is one of the many unsung heroes of the war and, were it not for his own account, his bravery would now be forgotten. He was awarded the Military Cross and Bar for his actions on the first and last days of the Spring Offensive. Invalided home, he was presented with his medals by the King at Buckingham Palace a week after his 21st birthday. Eric would go on to become a leading industrialist in Ireland after the war, founding his company, Irish Ropes, in the disused British cavalry barracks in Newbridge, Co Kildare in 1933.

The book is well-researched and draws heavily on battalion war diaries and other memoirs. Unlike many books based on personal diaries it sets Eric's own detailed, vivid, and often humorous accounts within their broader military, political and social context, and highlights the many close ties that bound the officers and men of the Liverpool Pals together. It also introduces a wide range of characters including Lord Derby, the Secretary of State of War and 'King of Lancashire', who was instrumental in creating the Pals; his younger brother, Brigadier Stanley, who commanded them; Johnny Douglas, the England cricket captain, who was Eric's battalion commander; Brigadier Robert White, who sent Eric on a suicide mission in March 1918 and who had been tried and jailed for his part in the Jameson Raid in 1895; and Aidan Chavasse, the youngest son of the Bishop of Liverpool and brother of the double VC-winner, Noel Chavasse, who was killed during a Pals trench raid at Ypres.

The book is aimed at the general reader and will appeal in particular to those who are interested in the history of Liverpool and the Pals battalions and in Eric s later career. However it also includes new details and perspectives, as in Eric's own account of the German spring offensive, which will make it of interest to the specialist reader. The book is well-illustrated and includes numerous photographs and documents from the author's family albums as well as his own photographs of the battlefields where his grandfather fought.

John Rigby-Jones was educated at Sherborne School and read classics at Oriel College, Oxford. After qualifying as a chartered accountant in 1980 he worked in the private healthcare sector for over 30 years before retiring in 2015. It was only when his father died in 2006 that he rediscovered his grandfather's letters and diaries from the First World War which he had first read as a student and which he assumed had subsequently been lost. He had always been intrigued by them and, since his father's death, has spent much of his spare time trying to find out more about his grandfather, who died before he was born, and visiting the battlefields where he fought. John is now working on a second book about his grandfather's life after the war.

BEST LOVE TO ALL

Best love to all
your ever loving son
Eric.

2nd Lieutenant Eric Rigby-Jones, The Liverpool Rifles. (Author)

BEST LOVE TO ALL

The Letters and Diaries of Captain Eric Rigby-Jones,
MC and Bar and His Experiences as a
Young Officer with the Liverpool Pals on
the Western Front in 1917 and 1918

John Rigby-Jones

Helion & Company Ltd

Helion & Company Limited
26 Willow Road
Solihull
West Midlands
B91 1UE
England
Tel. 0121 705 3393
Fax 0121 711 4075
Email: info@helion.co.uk
Website: www.helion.co.uk
Twitter: @helionbooks
Visit our blog http://blog.helion.co.uk/

Published by Helion & Company 2017
Designed and typeset by Farr out Publications, Wokingham, Berkshire
Cover designed by Paul Hewitt, Battlefield Design (www.battlefield-design.co.uk)
Printed by Short Run Press, Exeter, Devon

ISBN 978-1-911512-05-9

British Library Cataloguing-in-Publication Data.
A catalogue record for this book is available from the British Library.

For details of other military history titles published by Helion & Company Limited contact the
above address, or visit our website: http://www.helion.co.uk.

We always welcome receiving book proposals from prospective authors.

Contents

List of illustrations

List of maps

Acknowledgements

I am profoundly grateful to all those publishers, organizations and individuals who have given me permission to reproduce text extracts in this book. These provide a different perspective on my grandfather's own experiences and I am sure it is a much better book for their inclusion. There is a short bibliography at the end of the book which lists all those publications from which I have taken extracts as well as those that I, as a novice student of the First World War, have found particularly useful, relevant, or inspiring.

I would like to make special mention of some sources of information. The National Archives at Kew, with its helpful staff and magnificent setting, is always a special place to visit to examine original documents and I would like to congratulate it on its organization and its efforts to make all the war diaries of the First World War available online; I have found Wikipedia an invaluable resource both to check facts and to find out information quickly – I just wish it had been available when I was a student; and there are a number of exceptionally good websites on the First World War, many of which are clearly a labour of love – I have included a selection of those that I have found the most useful in the bibliography.

The images used in this book include family photographs and documents collected by my grandfather and father as well as photographs that I have taken on my visits to the battlefields. I am particularly grateful to the following institutions for their permission to reproduce images, the copyright and other rights in which are, and shall remain, the property of those institutions – the Imperial War Museum, the Australian War Memorial, and the National Portrait Gallery, London. I would also like to thank the following organizations which have also given permission for the reproduction of photographs – Oxford University Press, Mary Evans Picture Library, and Liverpool Echo/Trinity Mirror PLC (the last for photographs that originally appeared in Brigadier-General F C Stanley's *The History of the 89th Brigade 1914 – 1918*).

The map of the battleground south of Arras is based on a map that I found on Paul Reed's website, Old Front Line Battlefields of WW1 (http://battlefields1418.50megs.com/). I am grateful to Paul for his permission to use it.

There are a number of people that I would like to thank in particular and without whom I might never have been able to complete this book: my father, Peter, for his extraordinary efforts to collect and preserve family photographs and documents and to research our family tree, which he largely drew in his inimitable architect's hand before the days of personal computers and the internet; my aunt Ann, Eric's daughter, for providing a invaluable and first hand link to the past; my oldest friend, Eric Stenton, for reading an early version of my manuscript with a critical eye and making many suggestions for its improvement; Tony Wainwright, Keith Page and everyone connected with the Liverpool Pals Memorial Fund – it was a privilege to be invited to the unveiling of the memorial to the Pals at Lime Street Station by His Royal Highness Prince Edward, Earl of Wessex, on the centenary of their formation on 31 August 2014; David Dixon, a former President of the Rossallian Club who is undoubtedly one of the proudest Old Rossallians, for his hospitality and for allowing my wife and me to attend the unveiling of the plaque to the Old Rossallians who died in the First World War at St George's Memorial Church in Ypres on 24 October 2007; Charles

Dutton, the grandson of General Gough and keen guardian of his reputation, for his gracious encouragement after I had contacted him out of the blue and for allowing me to use extracts from his grandfather's book, *The Fifth Army*; and Richard Daglish who provided valuable information on the Reverend Rowland Gill.

Above all others I must thank my darling wife, Frances, for all her love and support and for being my long-suffering companion on my trips to France and Belgium. I am sure that she never realized at the beginning how long it would take for me to get this book out of my system.

1

21 March 1918

When, however, I search the pages of my diary, which is concerned with the personal leadership of platoons, companies, and the battalion itself, for the particular qualities which give to a few dominion over their fellows I can discern only the simplest virtues. Yet these men with their gift of leadership were in the last war the cement strengthening the hastily built edifice of a national army.

Lord Moran, *The Anatomy of Courage*[1]

Having arrived in January 1918 on the Amiens front from Ypres we spent some time in the La Fère sector which we had taken over from the French. In the middle of February we moved north to the St Quentin sector where we spent our time in intensive training and in the laborious construction of a maze of defences reaching miles behind the front line trenches. Trenches were dug so wide as to make the passage of tanks impossible and so extensive that the enemy, in order to destroy the whole, would require, according to a high artillery officer to whom I spoke, a bombardment of at least three weeks.

From 1 to 9 March I spent my time in completing the fortifications of a redoubt on the St Quentin-Amiens road at L'Épine de Dallon which I occupied with my company. The garrison of this little fort was one and a half companies and our armament was 16 Lewis guns, 16 Vickers guns, four 2-inch Stokes mortars, two 6-inch Stokes mortars, gas projectors, and a small tank. It was surrounded by a maze of wire and held food and water to last two days: in addition each man carried an extra day's iron ration. I spent much time and thought on making this place defensible from all sides and in all circumstances that I could imagine. Consequently it was a source of great satisfaction to me to know that when 'The Day' arrived it held out until the enemy had passed miles beyond it – a veritable thorn in his side.

During my rounds one night I slipped and cut my temple on a piece of corrugated iron which, in spite of careful attention, became septic. I managed to carry on until the battalion was relieved but was then obliged to go for treatment to a rest station in Ham. My face being healed I left this rest station on 14 March. Although I was still run down from its effects I rejoined my battalion in the support area at the village of Vaux. While in this area we practiced day and night – after our return from eight hours digging a day – the manner in which we were to get into action in case of alarm. This we brought to such a stage of perfection that whatever the hour the battalion was able to be on the move with baggage packed within a few minutes of the receipt of a message.

---

1   Lord Moran, *The Anatomy of Courage,* London, Constable, 1945, p. 197 (with permission of Little, Brown Book Group Ltd). Charles Wilson, who was ennobled as Lord Moran in 1943 for his services as Winston Churchill's personal physician during the Second World War, served as a doctor on the Western Front during the First World War. From 1917 he was based at a hospital in Boulogne where his study of 1,500 mustard gas casualties was later published in the Quarterly Journal of Medicine in 1920. It is possible that my grandfather may have been one of the men that he studied. *The Anatomy of Courage* is his account of his experiences in the Great War and his analysis of the psychological effects of that war on officers and men. I have my grandfather's copy which he bought when it was first published in 1945.

On Sunday, 17 March, the 89th Brigade became the Corps Reserve Brigade and the battalion moved back further to the village of Villers-St Christophe. The next day was very wet and I spent most of it trudging across the fields to find a suitable place for a rifle range. On Tuesday there was a wonderful change in the weather, it being very sunny and warm. Our gloomy spirits of the previous day disappeared and we began to wonder if there was any truth that the enemy was about to make his colossal attack. I sent two or three of my officers into Ham to have a change of surroundings.

The following day, Wednesday, everyone was more certain of the approaching attack. The staff now had definite news of it and all men on leave were recalled. During the day the anxiety became greater for every man in the brigade. Brigadiers spent the whole afternoon wearing gas respirators to become quite accustomed to wearing them for a prolonged period. There were nine officers in D Company apart from myself and that evening we had a very excellent dinner forgetting for the time all our surroundings. The gramophone was employed continuously. During the evening we almost persuaded ourselves that there was no such thing as an attack impending. We turned in just before midnight and were talking in our Nissan hut about Blighty and other such topics.

At midnight there commenced a terrific bombardment on the north of our front. We turned out to look at it in the distance and, although I was aware that a raid was due to take place, I was convinced that the bombardment signified something more. I ordered my officers to get into their battle clothes, to pack their kits, and get to sleep. I myself went round my company to see that all my men were sleeping in their boots with their rifles and equipment handy. I told them that there was a raid on but went to see my sergeant-major and told him to expect a 'stand to' at dawn. I inspected my field kitchen to see that all was in order and then turned in myself and slept soundly until 6.00am when the first shell arrived in the village. I turned out the officers and servants, told the latter to pack up, and sent the former round to their men while I waited for orders.

At 6.07am I received the order to move. Although my company was out and on the road five minutes earlier than required we unfortunately had to wait for the others who were all late. Meanwhile I reported to Colonel Watson at battalion headquarters. On my way there I had a near escape from a heavy shell falling on the road which I am afraid I took for a bad omen. I reported my company ready and obtained my secret code book from the adjutant as well as a good tot of whisky to warm one up and give one a little Dutch courage.

I had a wait there of about twenty minutes. The people of the house, Madame and her children (her husband being a soldier), were very upset. She knew not how she was going to save her house and furniture and, although she did not want to leave, yet she was determined never again to be under the rule of the Boche. I remember her talking excitedly to the colonel and praying to him not to let the Boche advance. He promised that we should all do our best and that the Boche would probably not get to this village. Yet we all knew that, if this was the great attack, how small were our chances of stopping it at once. I was doing my best to comfort a little girl of about ten who was weeping with her arms thrown around my neck. When the time came it was difficult to tear myself away from these poor ones.

Then started our last march forward for many a long day. As we bent along these roads starting some eight miles behind the battle front every cross-road, every dump, and every railway siding was receiving its share of Germany's hate. A more wonderful distribution of artillery I never saw. As we approached the line the shelling became more severe and we were obliged to divide into artillery formation. At last we reached our position of readiness at Beauvois. Although we were merely there until called for we distributed ourselves out in defence of the village and during the day the heavy shelling compelled us to dig in. I held the front of the village with my company but had no information as to the progress of the battle. To be prepared for the worst, namely a break-through by the enemy, I carefully chose my positions and sent out patrols. On several occasions I thought that the enemy were closing up on us when a number of artillery men ran past carrying their breech blocks; they, however, returned later.

During the night I received orders to move and take two companies, my own and C company, to Attilly where I should report to another brigade headquarters. We set off about midnight on a very weary march as it was very cold and rain was coming down in torrents. I reported at the rendezvous and went to interview the brigadier to whose brigade I was now temporarily attached. He told me how the Boche had already swamped our front area and had broken our battle line which was nearly two miles in the rear. At present he was established in the valley north of Holnon Wood and was expected to push rapidly and strongly forward up this valley before dawn.

My orders were to place my men in a position in the valley where we would be well-concealed and, when we saw the Boche advancing, to go and meet him in the open. It was realised that it was impossible to hold the enemy in check with so few numbers but it was thought that the sacrifice of two companies in this manner would check him sufficiently to allow reserves to come up. Never before had I received such an order and it came as a blow. I had been in tight corners and had always before had a sporting chance but this I soon realised was nothing short of suicide. It took me quite a few minutes to collect my thoughts and recover my full senses before I left the deep dug-out in which were the headquarters.

When I reached my company again I moved immediately, not telling even my second-in-command the exact nature of our job but giving him and the others the dispositions I intended to make. At last we reached the north-west corner of Holnon Wood on the south side of the valley. I positioned the men at the edge of the wood and in some ditches avoiding a sunken road which I felt sure would be badly shelled. Then Captain Henry, a great friend of mine who was the commander of C Company, arrived on the scene and, as he was my senior, I handed over the situation to him. We decided however to remain together and run the two companies as one.

At 9.00am the enemy opened a terrific bombardment and we realised that the time of our nasty business was not far ahead. We talked things over and came to the conclusion that we were in for certain death and, shaking hands, wished one another as much luck as possible. Shortly afterwards the enemy came forward and through the dense fog we could just distinguish his storm troops. Henry and I were with a platoon some 50 yards behind our foremost line and we commenced to fire at the Boche advancing.

At that moment a runner came up waving a paper. I rushed across to him and read the message – 'Withdraw at once and proceed as fast as possible to Fluquières for a counter attack via Germaine'. Thanks to the fog we managed somehow or other to get out of our position and to escape round the edge of the wood, going for a while parallel to the advancing enemy. We were only just away in time for, as we came along, parties of Germans came out of the wood. Henry led the way through Attilly which was now a mass of bursting shells and flying debris while I brought up the rear. Gradually as we retreated the shelling became less and we marched across the fields towards our new positions some eight miles way.

Our route lay about 1,000 yards to the rear of the reserve and last line of fully organised trenches. The Germans were now concentrating on them with all their heavy guns. The villages of Vaux and Étreillers were a mass of flames. It was now nearly 10.00am and the sun was scorching. On and on we plodded very weary. We stopped for half an hour near Germaine and then pushed on. Towards 11.00am I saw Aviation Wood ahead which I knew was our new position. I pointed it out to the men. They pulled themselves together and marched well until we got within 200 yards of it. Then they commenced to fall out, many of them foaming at the mouth. Quite a few of those who fell had to be left behind as they were too weak to get up.

We stopped in the ravine in front of Aviation Wood and the colonel, who had now joined us, went forward to get in touch with the troops in front and see what we were required for. As we were too few to make a counter-attack on the village with any hope of retaking it, it was decided to hold our present line. Accordingly we dug in behind the ravine on the training area of our own brigades. We had a glorious position and, as we knew every inch of the ground, we were prepared to hang on to it against almost any attack. We carried up ammunition and bombs and deepened the existing trenches. Then, just as we saw that the advancing Germans were almost within range, we received orders to withdraw to Ham.

ชื่อ

I never knew my grandfather. He died in 1952, three years before I was born. He was only 54. Although he achieved a lot in his life my father always said that he never fully recovered in body or spirit from his experiences on the Western Front. I was in my early 20s, and so not much older than he was when he wrote them, when I first found and read his diaries and letters home. However it was not until my father died in 2006 that I rediscovered them in the old cigar box in which they had always been kept. They still smelt of tobacco after almost 90 years. Until then I had known my grandfather only from family stories and from an unsmiling photograph in middle age when he was a captain of industry. I wanted to find out more about where he was and what he did in the war.

This, then, is the story of Captain Eric Rigby-Jones, MC and Bar of the King's Liverpool Regiment, and of his experiences as a young officer on the Western Front in 1917 and 1918. It is the story of a single man but it is one that is shared by countless other officers and men whose names and deeds are now forgotten.

2

Liverpool and Orsmkirk

Eric's family and early life

A good name is rather to be chosen than great riches, and loving favour rather than silver and gold.

Proverbs 22.1[1]

My grandfather was born into a comfortable and successful Liverpool merchant family whose fortunes had grown in the 19th century at the same pace as the city's. The Jones family, as they then were, originally hailed from Denbigh in North Wales where they had worked for several generations as flax dressers, extracting and treating the fibre from harvested flax to use in the making of rope and linen. Like many in North Wales the family had gravitated towards Liverpool at the end of the 18th century with the coming of the industrial revolution. Eric's grandfather, John Jones, was born there in 1846 and, after serving a year's apprenticeship in another firm, joined his father's flax dressing business in the city centre – in Cheapside, opposite the Bridewell prison – when he was 14.

John showed early promise and, when he was 16, his father was happy to leave him in charge of the business while he and his wife went on a sight-seeing holiday to London. Two years later, in 1862, he was left in charge again when his father took himself off with his wife and two youngest children for an extended stay at the spa in Buxton to try to cure his rheumatism. John was left not only to look after his other siblings but also to supervise the firm's move to new premises around the corner in Dale Street.[2] Although he and his father exchanged regular letters on this and all other aspects of running the business it was John who was left with the responsibility for settling the lease on the old premises and for equipping and staffing the new. It was a short but significant move. Dale Street was one of Liverpool's main commercial thoroughfares and home to some of its largest businesses

---

1   This quotation has been used regularly at Rigby-Jones family funerals and was printed on the order of service for Eric's funeral in 1952.

2   Originally built in 1819, this terrace in Dale Street received a Grade II listing in 2008 as 'an unusual survival of the shop house, a building type that is nationally rare, especially outside of London, and shows the development of new forms of retail premises in late Georgian England ... The terrace has group value with other nearby listed buildings in the Dale Street/Cheapside area, such as the Bridewell and Municipal Offices. Together these buildings epitomise the changes in the physical fabric of the city during the C18 and C19, and represent the city's changing wealth and development as an international port city': (© Historic England 2016. The National Heritage List Text Entries contained in this material were obtained on 5 February 2016. The most publicly available up to date National Heritage List Text Entries can be obtained from 'http://www.historicengland.org.uk/listing/the-list/').

Left unoccupied since the 1990s, plans were approved for the terrace's restoration and redevelopment in 2013. However it subsequently had to be demolished as unsafe in 2015.

H and J Jones' premises in Dale Street, Liverpool prior to their demolition. (Author, 2012)

and most impressive buildings. More importantly the Jones' new premises were directly opposite the entrance to the city's magnificent new Municipal Buildings, which were then under construction but would be completed in two years' time.

John's energy and ability to attract new customers ensured that the business expanded rapidly in its new premises. His father quickly made him his full partner. However when John pressed for his elder brother, Henry, to be allowed to join the business as well – he was at the time working for a maternal uncle in a firm of general merchants – his father refused, claiming that the business would not be large enough to support two families when they both married. The brothers persisted and eventually persuaded their father, who was by then 63 and increasingly suffering from ill health, to retire to West Derby with a small pension from the business. He died four years later. And so John and Henry entered business together as H and J Jones: the business would continue under that name until John's eldest son, Harry, retired and sold it in 1945 at the age of 72, by which time his own son, Eric, had established and made a great success of his own company, Irish Ropes, in Ireland.

The young brothers – John, 21, and Henry, 24 – quickly built H and J Jones into a substantial venture. They secured their futures only three years later when, at the beginning of 1870, they acquired and then mechanised Tilsley's rope factory in Ormkirk, 10 miles to the north-east of Liverpool. Rope-making was an important industry in the town and, although it was not documented until 1679, its history probably went back to the middle ages. By the middle of the 19th century there were eight rope works in the town as well as at least three rope walks, the long sheds where the raw fibres had historically been laid out and twisted into rope by hand. At the time of the brothers' acquisition Tilsley's was the largest of them and had been in business for over 100 years. It had, according to Harry Rigby-Jones' later brief history of H and J Jones, 'a very old export connection on which the company's present widespread export trade was founded', and a ready market in the West Indies for its largely hand-spun rope and twine. John and Henry had now acquired interests in every stage in the manufacture of rope and twine, a base in one of the busiest and fastest-growing trading ports in the world, a factory with good railway links to the port (the Liverpool to Ormskirk railway having been opened in 1849), and an established export market which they could develop further. By the end of the century H and J Jones controlled nearly all rope production in Ormskirk, employing more people and producing more goods than at

John Rigby-Jones standing beside H and J Jones' factory
and ropewalk in Ormskirk, c 1924. (Author)

any time previously.

Liverpool was a boom town in the 19th century; and rope was vital to its development as a maritime economy. As one of the corners of the triangular slave trade between Great Britain, Africa, and the Americas the city's importance as a port had become by 1800 second only to London. Its population had grown in the previous century from 5,000 to almost 80,000: in the following century it would grow again, almost tenfold, to 750,000. The first half of the 19th century was a time of turbulence and adaptation when, first, slave trading was banned in the British Empire in 1807 and then slavery itself in 1833. However new markets had begun to open up in the Far East and the Americas. Then, in the second half of the century, Liverpool would become in the age of steam the main conduit for the import of raw materials from the Atlantic rim to the great manufacturing enterprises in the north-west of England. It was a trade in which cotton played a crucial part. By 1914 raw cotton accounted for 30% of Liverpool's imports and manufactured cotton goods for over 40% of its exports. Liverpool's global pre-eminence as a commercial port went unchallenged after the 1860s when the activities of America's merchant fleet were disrupted by the Civil War. Then, in the great migration of the second half of the century, when 5.5 million Europeans crossed the Atlantic in search of new opportunities, 85% of them would sail from Liverpool, making it the world's busiest passenger port as well.

At the top of the city's maritime hierarchy were the major shipping companies, many of which were still family-owned at the end of the 19th century. Below them the economy was still largely in the hands of a myriad of small family businesses and partnerships. The city offered exciting opportunities for ambitious and determined entrepreneurs like John and Henry who were prepared to work hard and take risks. As in all "tiger" economies some were successful while others failed.

John and Henry both made good marriages within a year of acquiring Tilsley's rope works. Sadly Henry's wife, Elizabeth, died shortly after their wedding and, although he quickly re-married, his second wife produced three daughters before a son was born in 1880. Henry himself died only 18 years later at the age of 55; and his son would never join the business. John was more fortunate in his marriage to Lilly Lloyd, who came from a family of prominent Welsh Methodists who lived in the same street as him, where her father, Richard, had been instrumental in the building of the Grove Street Chapel. Richard held an important civic position as Liverpool's official port gauger. A teetotaller, he was responsible for calculating and certifying the quantities in the barrels of imported wines, spirits, and oils that passed through the port and for applying the necessary tariffs and duties.

Although never as large as the city's Irish community the Liverpool Welsh accounted for 10% of the city's population and formed a powerful, affluent, and self-conscious minority. Many of them thought of Liverpool as the 'de facto' capital of North Wales. John Jones found himself after his marriage to Lilly as a member of a close-knit and influential family of Liverpool businessmen, ministers, authors, and academics that was united by its Methodist religion and liberal persuasion. One of his father-in-law's sisters, Sarah, was married to Thomas Snape, a Liverpool alderman who had established a substantial soda ash business in Widnes: after its success sale and merger with a number of other companies to form the United Alkali Company, which in turn would become one of the original parts of ICI, he stood for parliament and was elected Liberal MP for Heywood in 1892. Another sister, Mary, was married to the Reverend Andrew Crombie, the editor of The Methodist Monthly: its Christmas edition in 1896 would include a profile of Richard Lloyd and a long article on the history of the Free Methodist Movement in Liverpool. And Richard's son, Dr Richard John Lloyd, would somehow find a way to combine a life of scholarship with his full-time commitments in the family port gauging business. He briefly held the Chair of English Literature at University College, Aberystwyth and from 1898 was honorary reader in phonetics at Liverpool University. Author in 1899 of *Northern English*, an important and pioneering study of Northern dialects which is considered a classic by some phonetics scholars, and an early advocate of Esperanto, he died in tragic circumstances while attending an Esperanto conference in Geneva in 1906. He went out for a walk one afternoon and was never seen alive again. His body was fished out of the Rhine a fortnight later. His son-in-law, Thomas Jones, who found him a difficult man, commented later that it was an appropriate end for a man who had spent too much of his life thinking too hard.[3]

Then, five years after John and Lilly's marriage, her younger sister, Essie, married Silas Hocking. A Methodist minister turned best-selling author, his uplifting stories with strong religious overtones concerned themselves with innocent love and the triumph of good over evil. Although written off now as 'pulp Methodism' they held a massive appeal for the Victorian reader: his books may be forgotten today but Silas is assured a place in history as the first author in the world to sell a million books in his lifetime. The success of his

---

3   T. Jones, *Welsh Broth,* p.75.

50 novels earned him a Spy portrait in Vanity Fair as one of the 'Men of the Day' and a move to London, where Sir Edwin Lutyens designed a house for him and he stood twice, unsuccessfully, as a Liberal candidate for parliament.

The atmosphere within the Lloyd family would almost certainly be considered now unhealthily oppressive and close. On the death of his first wife Richard Lloyd married her recently-widowed younger sister; and John and Lilly's daughter, Elsie, would marry her grandfather's nephew. Thomas Jones certainly thought so. He claimed later that his only contribution to the happiness of the Lloyd family was to have rescued his wife from the clutches of a father who was overly ambitious for her academic success. John, however, seems to have had no trouble fitting in. He was already a keen Methodist – in his youth he had played the organ in church and later led Bible classes and taught in Sunday school – and he would remain one for the rest of his life. His obituary in the *Ormskirk Advertiser* in 1926 would say that he was 'a typical Christian gentleman and had spent much of his life in the interests of the Wesleyan Church, in which he held every office that a layman could occupy, except that of local preacher. He was one of the oldest members of the Liverpool District Synod and was twice elected to Conference.'

It may well have been his new found status and connections rather than his success in business that prompted him to change his name from Jones to Rigby-Jones in 1881. An unidentified newspaper cutting in a family album from 1925, when H and J Jones chose to celebrate the centenary of their original family business in Liverpool, suggests that the decision was a result of there being too many John Joneses in Liverpool, some of whom were slow in settling their debts. Such an association would not have been welcome to a man who would be a director of the Liverpool Guardian Trade Protection Society for 30 years and its president on three occasions. And yet neither John's brother, Henry, nor their business saw fit to change their names at the same time. John had chosen the name Rigby out of respect to Lilly's mother, Sarah Jane Rigby, who had died two years earlier, and without any apparent concerns as a teetotaller that Rigby's, one of Liverpool's oldest and most famous public houses, was no distance away in Dale Street. Eight-year old Harry, the first of their eight children, changed his name at the same time but his two younger brothers, Arthur and Walter, had already been given Rigby as a middle name.

After a two-year apprenticeship with Brocklebanks, one of Liverpool's leading family shipping companies, Harry joined H and J Jones shortly before his 16th birthday in 1887. He would not stay long as he quickly fell out with John and Henry's youngest brother, Bobby, who had by then also joined the business. Bobby was only 16 years older than Harry and almost certainly felt threatened by his arrival. Harry later wrote that it had been thought best that he leave as he had been made the scapegoat for his uncle's dissatisfaction. He told his disappointed parents that his heart was now set on becoming a farmer. His father however persuaded him to take a job in a friend's business in Manchester in which he had recently invested; and it was while working there that Harry met and married Alice Holland in 1896. Her father's family had been farmers in Staffordshire for many generations and her mother's family, the Shorters, owned a number of pottery businesses in nearby Stoke-on-Trent.[4]

---

4   Alice's uncle, Arthur Shorter, established the Shorter Pottery in Stoke-on-Trent in 1878 and later took over the Wilkinson Pottery in Burslem after the death of his brother-in-law, AJ Wilkinson, in 1891. Arthur's son, Colley Shorter, who joined his father's business as a 16-year old in 1898, is now best known as the man who 'discovered' Clarice Cliff. She is recognised as one of the most important British pottery designers of the 20th century, creating her Bizarre range for the company in the late 1920's. Colley, whose wife suffered from

Family photograph taken shortly after Eric's birth in 1897. Back row: John (grandfather), Alice (mother), Harry (father), Lilly (grandmother). Front row: Helen Lloyd (Richard's second wife), Eric, Richard Lloyd (great grandfather). (Author)

Harry and Alice's first child, Eric, was born in Manchester on 20 September 1897. They moved to Ormskirk the following year when, on the death of his brother, John turned again in desperation to his son for help in running the family business. They agreed that Harry would take over the running of the rope works from his uncle while his father, who also moved to Ormkirk and took over Claremont, his brother's house beside the factory, continued to run the business in Liverpool. Henry and John had by then finally fallen out with their youngest brother. Only three months before Harry and Alice's wedding a notice was placed in the *London Gazette* to advise H and J Jones' customers that Bobby was no longer a partner. Bobby retaliated by setting himself up in competition only a few doors away in Dale Street. Although the family never spoke of him again, he would remain a thorn in their flesh for years to come: he was still in Dale Street in 1922 when he fell out with another business partner.

Harry and Alice's second child, christened Alice Holland after her mother but known to the family as Judy, was born in Ormskirk in 1899. A second son, Jack, was born four years later, shortly after the family had moved to a new and larger house beside Ruff Wood on the eastern edge of the town. The Ruff would be their home for the next 40 years and the focus of family life for three generations. Alice's character and ideas were firmly stamped on its design; and the details were still fresh in her memory when she wrote to my father, Eric's oldest son, almost 60 years later.

poor health, had a long affair with Clarice, who was 17 years his junior, before eventually marrying her in secret in 1940, a year after his wife's death. His family disapproved strongly when they were told a year later.

The Ruff, Harry and Alice's house in Ormskirk. (Author)

You will note that there is a black and white check over the front door: that is the Old Bard's Check which has rough and smooth squares meaning the rough and smooth of life. I had a similar ring made for Grandpa when we were married but unfortunately he lost it blackberrying at The Ruff a week or two before we left as I also did my seal ring in the garden digging up potatoes.

In planning the house I arranged for the stairs to be near the kitchen door so that, if meals had to be carried upstairs, the journey was easy and they would not get cold; but the silly fool of a man there now has had them turned about so that you now go round by the front door and there is no boot cupboard. You will note also the roof of the dining and drawing room windows is carried across so that the garden seat was under cover. Photos of the family are in a bottle in the foundations. Needless to say I saw to it that there were big low oak window seats and that the cloakroom had a row of low hooks for children, and that they could reach every door handle and the scullery sink to wash their hands, and enjoy doing what grown-ups could do. I am quite sure that the men and women of the future will bless the impressions of their early years if given their opportunities.

We had to ask permission of Lord Derby for the big trees to be removed from next door's back drive as they overshadowed the house. So he sent his agent to look and, when he came, he said 'I think the house is very beautiful and you shall certainly have the trees down'. Another interesting thing about the house is that the oak panelling in the dining room was grown at Carnforth and the hall and drawing room mantels at Lathom Park. A table and three book cases, as well as Jack's grave cross, were from an old beam from Aughton's old windmill.

Jack, Eric, and Judy. (Author)

Alice was a talented craftswoman. Over the coming years she carved many pieces of oak furniture for the family home. Her saddest task however was to carve a wooden cross for her son, Jack, who died in 1910 at the age of seven. For her it was a way of coming to terms with her loss and she regularly visited his grave in nearby Westhead churchyard to treat it with linseed oil. It is still there today after more than a 100 years. She also built Jack's Garden below the window at the Ruff and planted it with lily of the valley, his favourite flower. Jack's death left The Ruff feeling very empty as Harry and Alice had packed 13-year old Eric off to boarding school for the first time only a month earlier. However Alice now found herself pregnant again at the age of 39. Seven months after Jack's death she gave birth to a third son, Guy.

By all accounts Eric's childhood was a happy one. Harry and Alice were devout and devoted parents. Like Harry's father and grandfather they were both teetotallers. Alcohol was kept at The Ruff only for medicinal use; Cantrell and Cochrane's lorry called each week only to deliver bottles of non-alcoholic Ciderette. As well as raising their own children (and, later, their grandchildren), they always found more to do than their time and energy allowed. Harry was a county magistrate, a trustee of the Ormskirk Savings Bank, and a member of the Liverpool Rotary Club, of which he would become president in 1921. A convert to his wife's Anglican church, he sat on the parish council and a number of diocesan committees as well as standing in as an organist when required. Alice was involved with her husband in running the local Sunday schools and would be secretary of the Mothers' Union for almost 30 years. In 1922 they were presented with a silver rose-bowl by the Ormskirk

Rural Deanery Sunday School Association to mark their long service and to celebrate their silver wedding. Dr Chavasse, the Bishop of Liverpool, was asked to make the presentation and to add his own thanks in a speech that was reported in the *Ormskirk Advertiser*.[5]

> He could only say that the longer he (the Bishop) lived in this diocese the more he learned to appreciate and be grateful for the services that they were both rendering to the service of Christ, to the deanery, and to the diocese. They could not have conferred a higher proof of their appreciation than by returning Mr Rigby-Jones as one of the church's representatives to the National Assembly. He could assure them that when he (the Bishop) saw his name amongst the elected members he thanked God. In every good work as far as he knew, connected with the Church of England in this part of the diocese, they found them in the front ... What they had done for the Mothers' Union they had done for almost all other diocesan societies in this deanery.

Harry would reciprocate the following year by speaking at the Rotary Club lunch held to mark the bishop's retirement.

There is little information now on H and J Jones' progress in the years leading up to the First World War. Without any evidence to the contrary it is almost certain that the company, with John as chairman and Harry as managing director, continued to flourish in the first years of the new century as Liverpool reached the peak of its commercial prosperity. It was a time when the buildings that have come to dominate the city's skyline and symbolise its success were commenced or completed. The 'Three Graces' on the waterfront – the Mersey Docks and Harbour Building, the Royal Liver Building, and the Cunard Building – were all completed in the seven years leading up to the outbreak of war; and the foundation stone of the new Anglican cathedral, the largest in the United Kingdom, was laid in 1904 under the auspices of Dr Chavasse, who had been appointed the diocese's second bishop only four years before.

The family's growing affluence enabled Eric to receive a private and more formal education than either his father or grandfather. After spending some time at Ormskirk's grammar school he was sent away to boarding school at Rossall in 1910 on the day after his 13th birthday. He was one of the youngest new boys in his year and, although there are few details of his time there, it is clear that the school made a lasting impression both on him and on the six members of the family who followed him there over three generations.

Founded in 1844 as a boarding school for the sons of clergymen and gentlemen in the north of England, Rossall lay on a bleak and windy stretch of low shore on the Fylde peninsula between Blackpool and Fleetwood. Its exposed position, where the sea often threatened and sometimes flooded the school's grounds and buildings, quickly earned it a reputation as a tough school which gave its pupils an enduring mental hardness. Sport was considered an essential element of a public school education. Like many other schools Rossall invented its own game, Ross hockey, which was played on the beach with special sticks when the weather made the rugby pitches unplayable. Although there is nothing to say how Eric fared on the playing field, he served in the Officer Training Corps – Rossall was the first school to establish one in 1860 – and was successful in the classroom. He won prizes of leather-bound books embossed with the school crest each year that he was there;

---

5   The rose-bowl is still in the family and is passed down through each generation whenever a silver wedding is celebrated. It is currently in the possession of Eric's grandson, Robert.

and in his last year he won not only his form's examination prize but also, as was perhaps appropriate for someone who left school early for a career in the family business, the school short-hand and book-keeping prize.

Eric was still 16 when he left the school at the end of the summer term in 1914 on Tuesday, 28 July. On the same day Austria-Hungary declared war on Serbia; and the Tsar, as the defender of Slav nationhood, retaliated by ordering first a partial and then, the next day, a full mobilisation of the Russian Army. Although the likelihood of war between the major European powers had been growing for many years the fuse that finally ignited the conflict had been lit only a month earlier when the Austrian Archduke Franz Ferdinand and his wife were assassinated on a visit to the Serbian capital of Sarajevo. At the time their deaths did not make the headlines in all the capitals of Europe. Few foresaw that this relatively minor flash-point would escalate so quickly into the bloodiest war that the world had ever seen.

Events gathered momentum as the posturing of the great powers made any climb-down impossible without an unacceptable loss of face before finally accelerating in the week after Eric left school. On Saturday, 1 August, Germany retaliated to the Tsar's threat to her ally, Austria-Hungary, by declaring war on Russia. Russia's ally, France, responded by ordering a general mobilisation. The next day Germany occupied Luxembourg and issued an ultimatum to the government of neutral Belgium to allow passage to German forces marching on France. When Belgium refused Germany declared war on France. On Tuesday, 4 August 1914 the people of Great Britain returned to work after a warm summer bank holiday to be told that Germany had invaded Belgium early that morning. Later the same day Great Britain, with the full force of her Empire behind her, responded to the violation of her ally's neutrality by declaring war on Germany. The great states of Europe were now at war. Within two weeks a British Expeditionary Force would land in France.

At first there was no reason for the war to interfere with Eric's plans. Not only was he too young to join up – recruits had to be 18 and could not be sent overseas until they were 19 – but it was also widely believed that the war would be over by Christmas. While others rushed to the recruiting stations, keen not to miss any chance of excitement, Eric started his apprenticeship with the rope makers, Jackson McConnan and Temple, at their offices in Goree Piazzas on the Liverpool waterfront.

A year later, when trench warfare had already brought a desperate stalemate to the Western Front and it was clear that the war would be both long and bloody, Eric knew that it was time to put his career on hold and fight for his country. He was still six weeks short of his 18th birthday when, on 6 August 1915, he received his commission as a 2nd Lieutenant in the 6th Battalion of the King's Liverpool Regiment. The 6th Battalion, more usually known as the Liverpool Rifles, was, like the Liverpool Irish (the 8th Battalion) and the Liverpool Scottish (the 10th Battalion), one of the regiment's six volunteer battalions. Although they were all units in the same regiment and together formed part of the country's volunteer army, which had been re-organised as the Territorial Force in 1908, each fiercely preserved its own history and identity. While the regiment had as its badge the White Horse of Hanover, which King George I had granted it, the badge of the Liverpool Irish had a harp surrounded by shamrock, the Liverpool Scottish the White Horse mounted on a saltire and thistles, and the Liverpool Rifles a bugle strung from the red rose of Lancashire. The bugle, which was the traditional symbol of all rifle and light infantry regiments, honoured the Rifles' origins as the country's first volunteer rifle corps in 1859, more than twenty years before it was integrated into the King's Liverpool Regiment.

While the city's large and relatively poor Irish population contributed to the reputation of the Liverpool Irish for drunkenness and lack of discipline the Liverpool Scottish and the Liverpool Rifles were careful to preserve their exclusivity and middle-class respectability. Young men joined the Rifles or the Scottish before the war in the same way that they joined their local amateur dramatic societies and tennis clubs: it was part of their social milieu. Admission to the Rifles was dependent on one's education, sporting ability, and occupation and was denied to anyone lower than a clerk on the social scale. These criteria continued to be applied for some time even after the outbreak of war when recruits included the sons of directors of the Royal Insurance Company and the White Star Shipping Line. Eric would find himself serving alongside friends from the Goffey and Brocklebank shipping families.

Similarly strict criteria applied in the Liverpool Scottish – in their case Scottish ancestry, a non-manual job, and the payment of a ten-shilling annual subscription. They were also allowed to wear the kilts and Glengarry caps more commonly associated with a Scottish regiment. Liverpool Scottish officers who served in the war would include the later Hollywood star, Basil Rathbone, whose family were non-conformist merchants and ship owners, and Noel Chavasse, one of the Bishop of Liverpool's four sons and the only man to be awarded the Victoria Cross twice during the war.

The exclusivity and social cohesion of these battalions resulted in there being a more relaxed discipline and less discrimination between officers and men than was usual in the regular army. One private in the Rifles was even reported to have offered the use of his estate as a training ground; and many able men preferred to remain as privates in these units rather than be transferred elsewhere as officers. By contrast, when the poet Robert Graves joined a regular battalion of the Royal Welch Fusiliers in 1914, he found not only that he had to be proposed by two other officers and to possess sufficient private income to allow him to hunt, play polo, and generally uphold the social standing of the regiment but also that 'warts', as junior officers like himself were called, were ignored in the mess by their fellow officers for their first six months.

The Territorial Force's primary purpose was to provide home defence. Territorials could only serve overseas if they signed the Imperial and General Service Obligation. Eric did so on the day that he received his commission when he was attached to the Rifles' newly established third-line unit, the 3/6th Battalion. As a reserve unit its role was to assume the home defence duties of the first- and second-line battalions when they went overseas and to provide a steady stream of trained officers and men to replace their casualties. Nearly all of the original pre-war battalion, the 1/6th, had signed up for overseas service at the outbreak of war and had been in France since February 1915; the first reserve battalion, the 2/6th, formed a month after the outbreak of war, was now based at Aldershot and would eventually leave for France in February 1917; and the 3/6th Battalion, to which Eric would be attached for a year until his age made him eligible for overseas service, was based first at Weeton camp near Blackpool and then, from early 1916, at Park Hall camp near Oswestry. It was joined there by the regiment's five other third-line Territorial battalions where it was amalgamated with the 3/5th Battalion as one of the units in the West Lancashire Reserve Brigade.

The only record now of Eric's time at Oswestry is a letter written by his commanding officer to his father at the end of 1916 when winter had finally brought an end to the horrors of the battle of the Somme. With Eric now eligible for overseas service his commanding officer's letter was a reply to his father's letter in which he had thanked him for all he had done for his son.

Eric (on left) standing in front of troops parading at Rhyl, North
Wales sometime before going to France. (Author)

It is difficult to say what a great pleasure your letter has given me. It is only clouded by
my feeling that you have far too good an opinion of me for you have put me on so high
a pinnacle that I fear a sudden fall. You should really have reversed the order of things
for it is I who should be, and I hope I am, grateful for all your son did for us off as well
as on parade. I owe a great debt to him. Knowing how modest he is I am wondering if
you know the work he did in the battalion. Certainly you would not hear from him
its extent.

     When I went to the division he took over the whole of the battalion musketry. In
addition to that he was given the thankless and worrying task of re-organising the mess,
then of winding it up, and finally of re-organising the new mess on the amalgamation
of the two battalions. After that he organised a new company. Everything he took up
he carried out with complete success. Slackness and inefficiency were abhorrent to him
and individually he is held in the highest esteem and affection by all for his ability and
the happy manner in which he carried out his duties and not least for his pleasant and
cheerful society. When it is remembered that your son is only 19 years old his record is
one of which anyone might be proud. That he will be as successful in France as he was
here there can be no doubt. For myself I ask nothing better than to be again associated
with him, this time in the big show itself, so that our friendship may be still furthered.

Although Eric had turned 19 in September his posting did not come through until the
end of the year. It meant that he was able to spend a final ten days' leave at The Ruff over the
New Year before leaving for France on 8 January 1917.

3

Somewhere in France

January – March 1917

I never realised in England the significance of the phrase 'somewhere in France' but I understand it now. I think 'nowhere on earth' would make it more plain.

Eric's letter home five days after his arrival in France

E ric's train stopped briefly at Gobowen station to pick up 15 more officers from Park Hall camp who had been selected for their first overseas posting. After a night in London they left for Folkestone early the following morning and, under an escort of four destroyers, reached Calais by noon. It was almost certainly Eric's first time on foreign soil and his impressions of Calais were of a small and rather dirty town. His orders were to proceed immediately to the British Expeditionary Force's main muster point at Étaples. Getting there would be his first experience of the railways in wartime France.

> Our train was due to leave at 6.00pm. After three hours waiting in a hailstorm, which afterwards turned to rain, the train arrived and, wet through as we were, we were glad to get into a windowless carriage. At 10.00pm the train left. Ten of us were in a carriage for eight but, as we were told that the journey would only last three and a half hours, we felt quite comfortable. They did not say how long the hours were in France! Thirteen and three quarter hours later we reached our destination – not quite 50 miles away.

Eric and his fellow officers then had to spend two bitterly cold days in a tented camp while they received basic instruction at the notorious Bull Ring training ground. They were issued with essential kit such as steel helmets, iron rations, and field-dressings and tested their respirators in the poison gas chamber. While there Eric wrote the first of his 250 letters home over the next two years and started the rough notes from which he would later work up a diary of his first nine months at the front. He was also told to his intense disappointment that, although he was considerably senior to some of the other officers in the draft, he was to be transferred from the Rifles to the Liverpool Pals. Apparently there had been some uncertainty over whether he was to have been included in this draft and his name had only been added at the last moment at the bottom of the list. As a result he was the last to be selected for duties. There was little he could do about it. By signing the Imperial and General Service Obligation he had consented unconditionally to such a transfer.

On the morning of 12 January Eric set out on another cold and slow train journey to his new battalion. This time the 50-mile journey to the railhead at Doullens took 24 hours. At Doullens he was met by a guide who escorted him on foot to Halloy, a village 15 miles behind the front line where the Liverpool Pals had been based since the end of the Somme. They were just beginning a month of rest and training.

It was a march of about eight miles but very pleasant on that dry, frosty morning through the quaint little village of Lucheux, which lies in a valley and is surrounded by dense woods in which wild boar are found. Halloy itself is not the sort of village one sees in England, with its paved streets, rows of houses, well-kept gardens and post office but rather a mass of houses thrown down with narrow winding streets. The houses are very badly kept and one sees barns and stables without a roof. I am billeted with 11 other officers in one large room in an old farmhouse so there is not an inch of spare floor space at night. Two large and badly-fitting windows look out upon the dirtiest of dirty farmyards in which half a dozen cows spend their time.

Although Eric could hear the guns for the first time he assured his parents that he was safe. As soon as he arrived he applied for a transfer back to the Rifles: it would mean a difficult interview with the Pals' commanding officer, Brigadier Stanley. Anyone living in Liverpool or Lancashire would have found it difficult to avoid the Stanley family, whose family had been ennobled as Earls of Derby after the battle of Bosworth Field in 1485. The Earls were the county's largest landowners. Their home and 21,000-acre estate at Knowsley stretched almost all the way from Liverpool to Ormskirk. They also owned large estates in the north of the county and in Cheshire, a substantial portfolio of commercial and residential property in Liverpool, and extensive farmland around Ormskirk, where they had close historical ties. Lathom House to the east of the town had been the family seat until its destruction in the Civil War and for many years the Derby Chapel in Ormskirk Church was the earls' final resting place.

Nor did the family choose to stand aside from public and political life. The 14th Earl served three terms as Prime Minister between 1852 and 1868; his eldest son, the 15th Earl, served twice as Foreign Secretary; and his second son, the 16th Earl, gave his name both to Liverpool's Stanley Park and to ice hockey's Stanley Cup during his time as Governor General of Canada. Sir Edward George Villiers Stanley had become the 17th Earl on the death of his father in 1908. By then he had already spent 14 years as a Conservative MP for a Bolton constituency, during which time he had also served in the Grenadier Guards in the Boer War, latterly as private secretary to the commander-in-chief. On his return he held a number of government appointments, including a position in the Cabinet as Postmaster General from 1903 to 1905. He also followed in his father's footsteps as Lord Mayor of Liverpool, Chancellor of Liverpool University, and President of Rossall School. Only four weeks before Eric's arrival in France he had been appointed Secretary of State for War, a post that he would hold until April 1918 when he was appointed British ambassador to France. A keen race-goer, his horses won many classic races including the Derby, which took its name from the 12th Earl. It was hardly an understatement then that, when Randolph Churchill was asked to write his official biography in 1959, he called it *Lord Derby, 'King of Lancashire'*.

Four of the Earl's brothers had also fought in the Boer War while a fifth rose to the rank of admiral in the Royal Navy. Two of them also followed him into politics. Sir George Frederick Stanley was MP for Preston from 1910 to 1922, and served as his brother's private secretary when he was at the War Office. Sir Arthur Stanley, who would later chair the British Red Cross and found the Royal College of Nursing, was elected MP for Ormskirk in 1898 in an unopposed by-election and went on to represent the town for 20 years, winning four general elections in two of which he was again unopposed. Eric's parents were unlikely to have voted for him. Harry, who had inherited his father's liberal politics, was at one time

Brigadier-General the Right Honourable Ferdinand Charles Stanley. (From Brigadier-General F C Stanley, *The History of the 89th Brigade 1914 – 1918*)

chairman of the Ormskirk Liberal Association.

Lord Derby, who had already earned a reputation as England's best recruiting sergeant, was appointed Director-General of Recruiting in 1915. That year, as chairman of the West Lancashire Association of the Territorial Force, he also signed and approved Eric's application for a commission. By then he had already played a significant role in the creation of the Pals battalions. Indeed he is credited with having coined the term 'Pals' and was proud that Liverpool was the first city to give its name to such a battalion.

Great Britain had faced a manpower crisis in 1914. Her strength as an island nation and imperial power was based upon the Royal Navy. Unlike most of the other European powers she did not have a large conscript army and so had no ready source of trained reserves at the outbreak of war apart from the volunteers of the Territorial Force. The government moved quickly to address the problem. On the day after war was declared Lord Kitchener of Khartoum, the country's greatest living military hero, was appointed Secretary of State for War and given the task of recruiting 500,000 volunteers. Unconvinced by the temperament, skills, and role of the Territorial Force, he chose instead to recruit new 'service' battalions to supplement the existing regiments of the small regular army. Some of these would be 'Pals' battalions. Alongside the recruitment campaign that featured his famous poster, 'Your Country Needs You', he was keen to encourage friends and colleagues from the same town or place of work to join up together to fight as officers and men in the same battalion. It would create, he thought, an immediate *esprit de corps*.

Lord Derby took up the challenge. In an open letter to the Liverpool papers on the last Thursday of August 1914, three weeks after the declaration of war, he called for the

Edward George Villiers Stanley, 17th Earl of Derby, c 1921.
(© National Portrait Gallery, London, x67462)

creation of a battalion of 1,000 volunteers from the city's commercial offices. He asked all who were interested to present themselves after work the next day at the Territorial drill hall in St Anne Street. The response was so great that the small hall was unable to cope and recruitment had to be abandoned – but not before Lord Derby had taken the opportunity to address the crowd. 'This should be a battalion of Pals', he told the volunteers, 'a battalion in which friends from the same office will fight shoulder to shoulder for the honour of Britain and the credit of Liverpool'. He asked that they return after the weekend, this time to the city's magnificent St George's Hall where separate desks would be set up for each employer. Two battalions, or 2,000 men, were recruited within two hours of the hall's opening on Monday morning. It was only the administrative burden which delayed the formation of a third battalion for another week. By the end of the year a fourth battalion had been raised, bringing the Liverpool Pals up to the strength of a full brigade. As the 17th to 20th battalions of the King's Liverpool Regiment they would serve together as the 89th Infantry Brigade.

Although four other service battalions were recruited at the same time from Liverpool's blue-collar workers the Liverpool Pals were always marked out for special treatment. It earned them the unwanted nickname of 'Derby's Lapdogs'. The earl, who persuaded the king to allow the Pals to use his family's crest of the Eagle and Child, formally presented each of the original recruits with a solid silver cap badge which he had commissioned at his own expense. He also persuaded Lord Kitchener that the Pals should be commanded by his younger brother, Ferdinand Stanley, who had fought in the Boer War and was a captain in the Grenadier Guards in the reserve of officers. Stanley's rank would advance as rapidly as

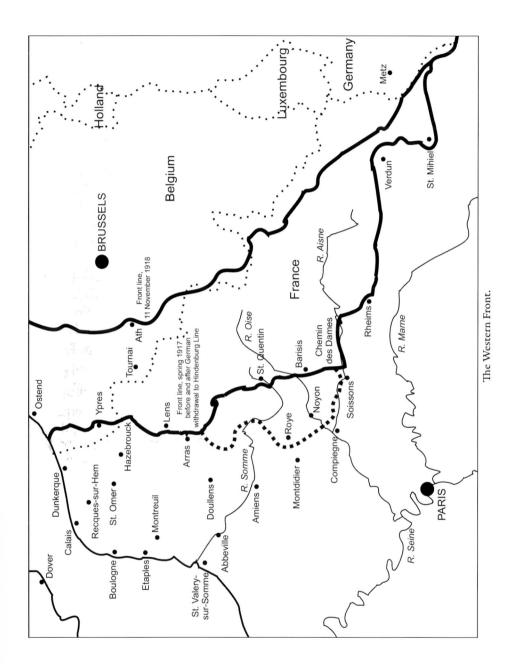

The Western Front.

the number of men under his command – from captain to major to lieutenant-colonel, and then, before the end of the year, to brigadier-general.

Recruitment however was only the first step in the lengthy process of turning the volunteers into a fighting force. The Pals had to be housed, clothed, equipped, and trained at local expense before the War Office was prepared take them over. Lord Derby provided huts at Knowsley for their accommodation where they also practiced digging trenches, thereby providing the earl, according to his critics, with a free landscaping service for which he later agreed to make a contribution to the Pals' comfort fund. The biggest problem however was the desperate shortage of uniforms and equipment. The Pals were not issued with modern Lee Enfield rifles until May 1915 and were only taken over by the War Office at the end of August, a year after their formation. Even then they did not leave for France until November. The regiment's four blue-collar service battalions had already left between May and September. Although a crowd of over 100,000 had turned out in March 1915 to see the Pals' final inspection in Liverpool by Lord Kitchener before they moved to Grantham for divisional training it was not unknown for them to be taunted on the streets of their home city when in uniform and to be presented with white feathers by young ladies as a mark of cowardice. Like so many other Pals' battalions they would prove their mettle on the Somme the following year.

The allied generals had met in Chantilly at the end of 1915 to finalise their plans for the coming year. General Douglas Haig, who would shortly take over from Sir John French as British Commander-in-Chief on the Western Front, argued for an offensive in British-held Flanders. However, with Great Britain the junior partner in the alliance, he was over-ruled in favour of a joint offensive on the river Somme at the point where the French and British armies met. Britain's new and inexperienced volunteer army, which had started to pour across the Channel in the second half of 1915, would be needed for the offensive; and, in order to stiffen them up and inject some fighting experience, a general re-organisation was ordered. Since April 1915 the four battalions of the Liverpool Pals had together made up the 89th Brigade which, alongside the equally inexperienced 90th and 91st brigades of the Manchester and Oldham Pals, formed the 30th Division. Now the 91st Brigade was replaced by the regular army's 21st Brigade; and, within the 89th Brigade itself, the Pals' 18th Battalion was swapped with the 2nd Battalion of the Bedfordshire Regiment from the 21st Brigade.

However the launch of the Germans' offensive against the French fortress at Verdun in February 1916 put paid to the allies' plans and limited the part that the French Army would be able to play. As a result the Somme became largely a British battle, and one whose aims now included relieving the pressure on the French further east. Although it was successful in that respect the first day of the Somme on 1 July 1916 would be one of the blackest days in British military history. Over 19,000 British soldiers were killed in a single day. Another 38,000 were either wounded, or missing, or taken prisoner. Kitchener's new service battalions were decimated. The close ties of home and workplace that had created their *esprit de corps* now left whole streets and communities in many northern cities in grief and despair.

At first Liverpool largely escaped this tragedy. The 89th Brigade which, in its first major action, had been given a position of honour on the British right wing beside the celebrated French Corps de Fer, had some of the greatest success that day. The three Pals' battalions quickly achieved all their objectives when they attacked and took the village of Montauban with the loss of only two officers and 41 men. The 18th Battalion, fighting with the 21st

Brigade on their left flank, was less fortunate. Seven officers and 165 men were killed when they came up against withering machine-gun fire, perhaps from a single German gun.

The 89th Brigade's good fortune held for less than a month. At the end of July they were ordered to attack Guillemont, two miles east of Montauban, across a mile of undulating open country without cover. The Pals had already been bombarded with gas the night before when they moved up to their jumping-off points under cover of darkness. Now they too were mown down by German machine-guns. Twenty-one officers and 439 men were killed: Brigadier Stanley reckoned that another 1,000 were casualties. He had made it known before the attack that he was unhappy with the plans: now, writing in his diary, he struggled to find the right words.

> Our poor brigade has suffered terribly, and it will take many a long day before we recover, if we are ever quite the same. We knew that we were in for a bad time and that very many people in Liverpool would be sad; that, unfortunately, has come only too true, and it makes one very miserable.[1]

The brigade was withdrawn from the line to rest and re-organise. It would not go back into action until October. By the end of their first year in France almost 1,400 Liverpool Pals, a third of their original strength of 4,000, had been killed. Perhaps twice as many, using average casualty rates, had been wounded. There cannot have been many who had come through unscathed. The four months of the Somme offensive accounted for 85% of those killed: the Pals' three blackest days – 1 July, 30 July, and 12 October – alone accounted for over 800 of them. When 19-year old 2nd Lieutenant Eric Rigby-Jones joined the 20th Battalion of the King's Liverpool Regiment on 13 January 1917 as a replacement for one of the 55 Pals' officers who had lost their lives on the Somme it was very different in composition and outlook from that which had confidently disembarked at Boulogne a year earlier.

Eric's indignation over his transfer to the Pals was tempered neither by the depleted and demoralised state of his new battalion nor by the prospect of an interview with Brigadier Stanley. Three days after his arrival at Halloy he spoke again to his company commander to insist that his application for a transfer be sent forward. The following day he saw Brigadier Stanley before writing home to his parents.

> It is very cold here today. There was a heavy fall of snow last night and it has continued during the day. This morning, as there was too much snow to drill, we had an inter-company snow-fight. I ended up with a black eye – the officers were marked down from the first – still the men got warm, which is the main thing.
>
> I have just had half-an-hour's interview with the brigadier with reference to my transfer. I think I put my case before him alright but he told me that it was impossible to get it through. He was very nice, quite chatty in fact, but I don't think he believes that he persuaded me that the Pals are better than the Liverpool Rifles. However I must try and settle down to my fate although it is very hard, especially as I have been with the 6th for so long. Of course my previous service counts for nothing here and I have to start again whereas I should have retained my position in the 6th. All I can do now is to hope for peace. I have lost all interest in this war. I am feeling very fed up.

---

1   Brigadier-General F C Stanley, *The History of the 89th Brigade 1914 – 1918*, p. 155.

There was little else he could do. As promised, Brigadier Stanley put his name forward a few weeks later for an assistant staff captaincy at brigade headquarters but Eric's short time in France meant that nothing came of it. He would remain with the Pals for the rest of his time on the Western Front. He now had to knuckle down. After his posting to D Company he gave his parents his new address and asked them to send him the Pals' cap badge and buttons for his uniform.

It was not the first such request that Eric made of his parents. While still at Étaples he had asked them to send him some large waterproof gloves, 'lined and with gauntlets if possible'. Indeed anyone who reads his letters now is struck by their frequent resemblance to shopping lists. The army censor, and Eric's own reticence, may have limited what he could write home about the real horrors of the war but the contents of the parcels that he requested and received in his first few weeks in France give an intimate insight into what often made life at the front bearable.

20 January: I have received the battery but not as yet the other things. I hope I am not troubling you too much in the way of sending things out to me but I shall have to have my prismatic compass. We are supposed to have one although I shall not place much reliance on it owing to the close proximity of so much steel. If you could also get me an inexpensive map measurer marked in the French scale and also English, the latter not essential, I should be very glad. There is a shop nearly opposite Exchange Station where they sell surveying instruments and who will probably have the right thing.

28 January: I have remained in bed to-day, the only item of interest during the day being the arrival of a parcel and some letters from home. The parcel contained some eggs. Most of them were broken and the whole mass was frozen solid – but not beyond hope, or so says the cook.

31 January: I have received your parcel of biscuits which in the language of 'Tommy' are now 'napoo' [no more, from the French 'il n'y a plus'] but which were enjoyed by all.

1 February: The men are provided with leather jerkins but the officers cannot get these. Some have leather waistcoats and some fur jackets. I think the former are better and more healthy. If you could get me something like that I should be glad as I am none too warm.

3 February: We go into the trenches for four days to-morrow and then 12 days rest – and real rest this time. Events seem to be moving fast now and you can expect more soon. In fact many think the end is near. Could you send me a couple of dish-clothes in your next parcel for use in the mess and also some Gillette blades?

9 February: There is no need to fear that any of your parcels will reach me in a 'dripping' condition: the trouble is getting anything to drip here. I could do with two more pairs of socks – long ones – anytime now and also a new battery. As it takes nearly a fortnight for me to get your return letter perhaps it would be as well if you sent me a refill every month as I use the torch a great deal. There are numerous kinds of electric lamps out here but none to beat mine with the result that everybody wants to borrow it.

PS I am now using the laces which you sent me in my trench boots. Could you send me another pair soon? Leather this time please. String is no good!!

15 February: I received your parcels of cake, sweets and writing materials last night. Your parcels seem to arrive just when I want them. We arrived in last night from a night digging party at 9.00pm. The rest were in bed and there was nothing ready for us to eat so we enjoyed the cake immensely. The men of course have their meals ready for them but we have to fix up our own things and consequently we have a job to get our meals sometimes. I am very sorry to have to trouble you so much for things but I cannot get them here.

18 February: I am glad I have my rubber gum boots. Other people are wearing sodden leather ones. As soon as I get in off a march, I put these on: they are quite loose and rest one's feet.

21 February: I cannot find time to read all the papers you send me so, if you reduced it to the [Ormskirk] Advertiser and one other each week, none would be wasted.

25 February: I received mother's parcel of biscuits, socks, and eggs on Friday. Unfortunately the parcel had been broken and was repacked at the base. The biscuits were excellent but the socks were a trifle 'eggy': at least it will help me to put them on.

1 March: This morning I received 12 [Liverpool] Daily Posts. An occasional magazine would go down well. Could you send me a small French dictionary or phrase book? When I send my washing to these French people I send an inventory and I am occasionally stuck for a word. I can usually manage ordinary conversation but on one occasion I was badly beaten. We were a little distance behind the line and the French people were still there. One of our officers was billeted in a house with an artillery officer and I went to see him. I had just come in and had my pack on and evidently the lady of the house had been troubled with officers trying to find a billet and she had no room. She thought, as soon as she saw me, that I was one of these and she started straight away to tell me what she thought of me and carried on as fast she could. I could not get a word in edgeways and, as she had not come to the end in 10 minutes, I turned and fled lest she should bring her family to join in the row.

26 March: Please don't send me a body protector. There is only one man in the battalion who wears one and he is a Quartermaster Sergeant. On the one occasion that he came under shell fire he took off his coat, body shield, and steel helmet and ran for it.

Eric's stream of parcels, from family and friends as well his parents, would come to include shirts and detached collars, lighter underwear for the summer, pyjamas, balaclava helmets, gas masks, Oxo cubes, jelly, chicken, tinned tongue, honey, writing pads, pencils, soap, and his mother's home-made sachets of 'flowers of sulphur' to see off lice. Like countless other parents Harry and Alice quickly found themselves at the centre of an informal but effective system of support for their son. Eric picked up the rules of the officer's mess and passed them on to them. Food parcels, which were always a welcome surprise and often

Eric's parents, Alice and Harry. (Author)

seemed to arrive just at the right time, were for sharing with the mess rather than private consumption. If an officer was away his parcels were opened, the food taken out and eaten, and the other items held by the mess president until his return. Although letters that could not be delivered were returned to sender parcels were sent on to the military hospitals and so never wasted.

Eric's letters also make clear some of the differences between officers and men. Even volunteer officers were expected to provide their own clothing and equipment except for items of standard issue, to organise their own laundry, and to find their own food. An officer's life had many attractions – better pay and billets, the use of a horse, an officers' mess with servants and batmen, and more opportunities for time away from the front on leave or training courses – but junior officers also suffered a higher casualty rate than any other group on the Western Front. They spent almost as much time in the front line as their men; they shared the same, if not greater, risks, as they led from the front and could be picked out by German snipers; and, at the end of a march or tour of duty, their first responsibility was to look after their men, and to ensure that they were healthy and properly housed and fed, before they considered their own needs and settled down to write reports and censor the men's letters.

In addition to the informal networks provided by their families whole industries grew up to cater for the needs of officers. Fortnum and Mason sent out food hampers, as they had since the Crimean War, and clothing stores like Cordings and Burberry competed to supply their uniforms. Gamages of Holborn, who advertised themselves as the 'Headquarters of Military Outfitting', offered a complete officers' kit for France for under £30. It contained

The Optimists, the 89th Brigade's concert party. (From Brigadier-
General F C Stanley, *The History of the 89th Brigade 1914 – 1918*)

everything from a cap, jacket, and cord breeches through marching boots and a British Warm
greatcoat to basic utensils such as a sleeping bag, water bottle, sewing kit and cutlery; and,
to carry it all, a holdall, haversack, and valise on which the officer's name and regiment was
painted. This basic inventory could then be supplemented with a range of field service kits
that included camp beds and chairs, waterproof sheets, and canvas baths and washstands.
Eric paid a similar price in Liverpool for his uniform and equipment. At £30 it was not
cheap: for a private on the King's shilling, or up to two shillings a day when allowances were
included, it represented almost a year's pay. At least Eric had been able to build up his kit
during his year at Oswestry. Smart young officers arriving at the front like novice campers
with a full range of spotless impedimenta must have been a source of great amusement to
the muddy, lice-ridden Tommy.

As 'Derby's lapdogs' the Pals were probably looked after better than most. The 89th
Brigade had its own concert troupe, the Optimists, who were in great demand. The profits
from their concerts contributed to the Pals' Comforts Fund which the wives of Lord Derby
and Brigadier Stanley had established when they left for France. Over the next two and a half
years the fund provided the men with many of the same items that officers had to request
from their families. Brigadier Stanley later provided a comprehensive list in his history of
the brigade which included 29,000 pairs of socks, 4,000 towels and bars of soap, 6,400 pairs
of gloves, 11,000 'tommy' cookers, 30,000 pounds of candles, 2,900 toothbrushes, 2,200
tins of foot powder, 50,000 cigarettes, 800 pipes, 52,000 newspapers and magazines (the
equivalent of over 50 a day), 4,900 pairs of bootlaces, and 2,000 mouth-organs and whistles.
The brigade even acquired a mobile laundry from the Liverpool Merchants' Mobile Hospital
and, when this proved impossible to move from camp to camp, a deputation was sent to
Paris to find a replacement.

Eric settled in quickly. George Brighouse, his company commander, was a family friend from Ormskirk although he was away on a course when Eric arrived and would not return to the battalion; two of his fellow officers had been to Rossall; and, after only a few days, he could tell his parents that he had found himself among friends.[2]

> There are quite a lot of officers in this division who have been in the ranks in the 6th so I am not a stranger. It is quite strange to find yourself continually called by name in a place like this after spending a week without recognising more than a few of the people around you. There are also a lot of men from the old battalion and I have been able to remember most of their names. Nothing cheers them up more than to stop them in the village and have a chat with them, especially if one can remember their names and a little bit about them. I was very amused, as I often am, when I was censoring a letter today. The man concerned was writing to a friend in the 6th and telling him all about me: I don't think he realised that I would be censoring his letter.

Eric also drew brief pen portraits of his fellow officers. The company's acting commanding officer was Lieutenant Charlie Moore, 'a clever Irishman but very young and a little childish at times'; Harkness was 'a very sane Scotchman who is a solicitor in Glasgow and is continually quoting Rabbie Burns and legal phrases: he also drinks a little whisky occasionally – medicinally'; and Walker 'an insurance sub-manager with a strong Manchester accent who is always ready to tell you how successful an equestrian he is – historians have however only recorded one ride'. Eric already knew West who 'got seven days leave to get married but had to come back here on the fourth day – he can't forget this and does not love the War Office'; and Pierce was 'very talkative and will walk a mile to avoid a bit of work: however he does good work chopping a bit of wood when he can get it and keeps our little stove going'. All in all, Eric reported, 'we get on very well together although we are always grumbling about something or other'.

Billets were the luck of the draw and, when Eric arrived at Halloy, the 12 officers of C and D companies ate and slept together in one large room in an old farmhouse. Eric's arrival only made it more crowded. The following day the officers of D Company decided to decamp to a Nissen hut which they found in an adjacent camp occupied by Indian troops. There they shared a table, two sofas, and a small stove; and in the cold weather they preferred its wooden floor to the damp flagstones of the farmhouse. Eric soon found that others had more luck. When out walking one day he ran across another old friend from Ormskirk, Frank Dallimore, who was a medical officer in the 2nd Battalion of the Yorkshire Regiment, which was stationed in the next village. When Frank invited him to dinner in his mess the

---

2   Eric would come across many Old Rossallians on the Western Front where the casualty count for public school-educated junior officers was disproportionately high. 1,600 Old Rossallians fought in the war: 297 were killed, 300 were wounded, and 300 were awarded medals that included two Victoria Crosses, 154 Military Crosses, and two Military Medals. When Rossall celebrated its delayed centenary in 1947 after the end of the Second World War, Eric attended along with his brother, Guy, and his two sons, Peter and Michael, all of whom had followed him to the school. (Three more members of the family – Guy's two sons, Tim and Nick, and Michael's son, Robert – would go there later). Sir Thomas Beecham, one of the school's most illustrious old boys, conducted a concert by the Blackpool Philharmonic Orchestra but the high point of the celebrations was the brief appearance of the school's president, the 82-year old Earl of Derby. Although he was too old and infirm to leave his car he was formally welcomed by the chairman of the school's governors, driven round the main quadrangle to the cheers of the boys, and then driven home to Knowsley.

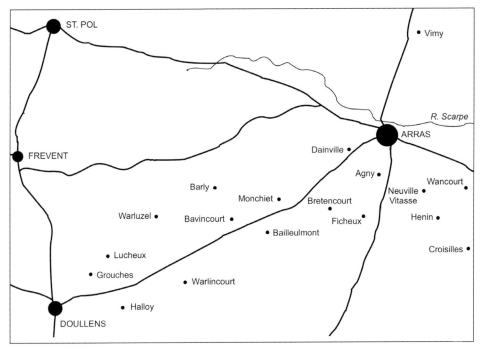

The area between Doullens and Arras.

following evening Eric found him in a fine old chateau where, he told his parents, he 'has a bedroom with electric light, a huge fire, and a likewise huge bed with those rare things here, clean sheets'. To cap off an enjoyable evening he was challenged by a sentry on his way back to his Nissen hut and, after being out in the cold air, found himself unable to speak. 'I did not want to return in an ambulance and did not know whether to put up my hands or go down on my knees. The sentry however was a sympathetic fellow suffering himself from a cold and allowed me to proceed with a whole skin.'

It is wrong to assume that the British Tommy spent all his time in the trenches. Units were rotated regularly and spent a greater part of their time 'at rest' or training behind the lines: and, even when a battalion took its turn in the trenches, only two companies usually manned the front line with the third in support in case of attack and the fourth further behind in reserve. In winter, when both sides were on the defensive, the trenches were held as lightly as possible. However life behind the lines was anything but restful. The men were either given further training, from elementary drill to rehearsals for the next offensive, or were requisitioned for working parties where they often had to march considerable distances and then work through the night to avoid enemy observation.

Eric's first job, four days after his arrival, was to escort a working party of 50 men four miles to Grouches for a hut-building detail and then bring back in the dark the party that they had relieved. That winter was already one of the coldest on record with six inches of snow on the ground. The journey took Eric four hours each way. The following week the whole battalion had to help dig a second track for the railway line from the rail-head at Doullens to the front line at Arras. The ground was frozen solid and the work, of widening the cuttings in the chalky landscape and carrying the debris down the line to enlarge the embankments, back-breaking. A man often had little more than a spadeful of excavated earth to show for his labour after working at the chalk with a pick. After two days Eric went down with a cold accompanied by neuralgia and a bad cough. The medical officer confined him to bed. 'The weather is still bad', he told his parents; 'the water has trickled through the hut and the wall by my bed is covered with a quarter of an inch of ice. Still it is nice to lie in bed and look at it.'

If anything it was getting colder. Many of the men were sent to the sick bay with trench foot or frost bite. When Eric tried to write home at the end of January he found that the ink in his fountain pen had frozen and that, by the time that he had unfrozen it, his fingers were almost too numb to write.

The weather here is the coldest I have ever experienced. We had 20 degrees of frost last night and, to make things worse, we cannot get fuel. It is very difficult to get water. My orderly brought me a little in a bucket this morning when I got up and by the time I had shaved it was covered with ice. My sponge has been frozen hard for a day or two and in the morning, if you drop a towel, you hear it crack. There is a frozen bottle of pickles and a jug of water on the table in front of me. These defied all our efforts with candles at lunch time.

Eric was fascinated by the Indian soldiers in the camp beside them.

They must be having a very bad time. It is amusing to watch them cooking their food. They receive their meat ration alive and go through much ceremony in the killing and cutting up of the animal; after this, it is cooked in their own special way. Often, as we leave our camp in the morning, we see the Indians who have died overnight from the cold being carried from their huts.

When the weather was too bad for training or working parties the men were kept busy with snowball fights between companies or inter-battalion cross-country runs and singing competitions. The Optimists put on a show each evening until the barn in which they performed burnt down 10 days after Eric's arrival, destroying all their props as well as their recently-purchased and much-prized piano. It was enough of a tragedy to be mentioned in the histories of both the brigade and the regiment. Eric however was able to add some details.

Shortly after 11.00pm last night I was awakened by the light of a fire outside. Turning out we found the barn used as a theatre to be on fire. The alarm had been given and we had three hard hours' work preventing it from spreading. We soon discovered that there was little hope of putting out the flames which were leaping up the wooden and straw plaster walls and consuming the thatched roof. At last it was got under control and only a small fire remained and the battalion was dismissed with the exception of a few men told off to see the whole thing out. These men were pouring on water from one side where there was a well but their efforts had little effect. Going round to the other side they found the Indians putting on all the wood which had been pulled away from the building and thoroughly enjoying a good warming such as they had not had for many weeks. When we went out this morning we found them still sitting round the

Indian labourers and butchers at work near Arras in October
1917. (© Imperial War Museum, Q6120)

smouldering debris, occasionally stirring it to kindle a flame and putting on what little
wood was left.

Eric's first experience of the trenches came three weeks after his arrival when, at the
beginning of February, the 30th Division relieved the 14th Division in the front line at
Agny, a village two miles south of Arras. Large troop movements such as this required
careful co-ordination. It would take the Pals three days to reach Agny; and food, billets, and
latrines had to be provided along the way. Leaving Halloy on the morning of 4 February it
took three and a half hours to march the 10 miles to Warluzel, their halt for the first night.

Here we struck a very good billet in the house of the mayor of the village. He is merely
one of the farmers in the village but he looks after us very well. In our mess room we
have a piano and a huge fireplace which Monsieur le Maire continually replenishes
with logs. We succeeded in purchasing a fowl in the village for supper this evening. The
servants brought us each a microscopic portion which they assured us finished the bird
entirely. We were left wondering whether the bird we bought was really all feathers or
not. However, we have decided to have it brought in whole next time and we will carve
it up ourselves.

The following day they marched a further seven miles to Monchiet.

Here the whole battalion is in a Nissen hut camp and, since fuel is hard to find, we go cold. As soon as we arrive the companies are shown to their quarters by the Company Quartermaster Sergeant who has cycled ahead with the Quartermaster to fix up accommodation. A return is rendered to headquarters showing the number of men arriving and those, if any, who have fallen out from the line of march. There are usually one or two slight trench-foot cases in the winter. Then the dinner, cooked on the march and usually consisting of stew on these occasions, is served out to the men after inspection by an officer. After this we find our own hut, get some food, and send for our kits which are carried on the transport and then dumped at the Quartermaster's stores. If there is time before it gets absolutely dark we then explore the village while the mess president goes in search of butter, eggs, etc – if there are any to be found.

Agny was finally reached the next day.

We left Monchiet this morning and marched by companies with an interval of 200 yards between each as we have now reached the zone which can easily be observed by the enemy, either from positions on the ground or from aeroplanes flying behind his lines. We passed through Dainville, a village on the outskirts of Arras which is badly knocked about and especially the church, of which only part of the tower walls is standing, and then proceeded to the main Arras-Doullens road and the railway running parallel to it. This part receives continual attention from the enemy guns and is under direct observation. A dummy railway engine made of wood and canvas has suffered badly to the satisfaction, no doubt, of the Boche gunners.

Here we entered a communication trench which, after a little over two and a half miles, brought us to Agny. The village is practically a complete ruin save for one or two little houses. We passed down the main street past the church, of which part of one wall alone stands, its one big bell lying amid the ruins, and past the crucifix to a sunken road. D Company is the reserve company and we live with C Company, the support company, in dug-outs along the side of this road. We have as our mess a little shack which is constructed of branches, sandbags, and a few doors from the village and is at the top of the entrance to the dug-out. We live and sleep in here and do not use the dug-out although it may prove useful some time. As soon as we get in we inspect the men's quarters which are much the same as our own except that their dug-outs are bigger and they live down in them. Also we have a look at our men's feet so that any blisters can be treated before anything more serious develops. Each platoon officer looks after his own men. My platoon is number 13, the lucky platoon.

Their shared quarters were so cramped that the officers of D Company decided to move back the following morning to more comfortable billets in the village. Although there was no glass left in the windows they at least had the luxury of a good fire and wire netting beds. In the afternoon Eric went up to the front line for the first time to find his bearings and to acquaint himself with their position in case of attack. After tea he wrote to his parents: although he could not tell them where he was – his letters were headed only 'BEF, France' – he at least tried to give them some clues.

Now that we are a little more settled I have more opportunity of writing. I am now sitting in front of a huge log fire in the only room left in a little house. We are in reserve in a village about 600 yards behind the line. We are two miles from a large town which has been badly shelled. Perhaps you may have heard what it is: if so you will know where I am. We have just had tea which consisted of tea made with the tablets you sent me and the box of biscuits that Grandma sent me – so you can see that your parcels are not altogether superfluous! I have just walked along the whole front and taken my first look over no man's land. We can't see the enemy trenches as they are over the crest of a slope. All is very peaceful and quiet. In fact it must be as quiet as any part of the line and, but for a few shells of ours flying over, one might almost forget the war. I am getting quite accustomed to the life here and in fact I am quite enjoying myself. It is a holiday compared to the work at Oswestry and, although it entails a little personal inconvenience, I much prefer it. Well, I will say goodnight now. Perhaps I shall be able to write to-morrow: don't however rely on getting letters regularly.

While in reserve D Company was responsible not only for the defence of the village but also for making barbed wire concertinas, supplying whatever working parties the Royal Engineers required, and taking rations and ammunition up to the trenches each night. Even in reserve they were not safe. The enemy kept up continuous machine-gun fire on the village cross-roads each night to disrupt them; and during Eric's next tour one of the houses in the village received a direct hit from a shell, which killed 11 and wounded 20 pioneers from the South Lancashire Regiment. Officers and men slept in their battle-dress with their equipment and box respirators to hand. With no chance of a bath before being relieved Eric used his mess tin to boil water for washing his feet.

Although it was still bitterly cold it would soon be the start of another campaign season. After five days at the front half of the Pals' officers were sent to the divisional school 10 miles behind the line to find out what was planned for them. Eric was one of those left behind and, when D Company finally took its turn in the trenches for the last two days of their tour, he found himself unexpectedly in command. It was, he thought, 'a bit thick for my first time'.

As soon as we got up I went to the company headquarters which was a dug-out where the communication trench from Grouse Street to Gravel Street passed under the railway. Here I signed a receipt for the trench stores which I was taking over and which included ammunition, bombs, wire, stakes, gas rattles, strombos horn [an air horn used to warn of gas attacks], spades, picks, sandbags, rations, and water in petrol tins besides other odd things too numerous to mention, such as a wind-vane and maps. This is returned to the out-going company commander who gives me a copy of the list. He also hands over an up-to-date map drawn by himself, showing present dispositions, and the log book in which each company commander notes everything that happens such as artillery and machine-gun activity, any change in the position of the enemy's machine-guns, snipers and sentry posts, an account of the wire put up by us and the enemy, all work done in making or improving trenches, and any suspected enemy mining – in fact everything of daily occurrence with his suggestions. In addition there is in the headquarters an aeroplane photograph of the ground in front. All these documents have either to be taken away or destroyed by the company commander in case of attack.

Meanwhile the platoons are being led by guides to their positions and, as soon as the platoon relief is complete, their commander reports in writing to company headquarters. When all platoons have reported their relief complete the other company commander departs, having pointed out that the rain comes in through the roof and that the dug-out is on the point of collapse and that he is going on leave to-morrow. 'Anyhow, I hope you have a good tour – cheery-ho!'

The first thing then is to report the relief complete to battalion headquarters by code over the telephone and then to go round the sector to see that all is in order. The men who are not actually on duty stand down and all the officers except the officer on duty return to headquarters. In this case there were only the two of us so we took shifts of four hours each. As we were so few in numbers we were unable to do much work at night but we put up about 50 yards of wire. I managed to get half an hour's sleep after breakfast but the fact that one was entirely responsible for the part of the line held by the company did not encourage sleep.

The Pals were relieved the following evening for six days rest. On their march back to Monchiet Eric experienced for the first time the luck that would stay with him throughout his time at the front when an enemy shell scored a direct hit on his dug-out only half an hour after he had left it, killing one officer and severely wounding another.

Back at camp Eric had little opportunity to catch up on his lost sleep as the work of the working parties intensified. Although the snow had melted and the ground was no longer frozen the thaw brought with it mud up to a foot deep. The battalion was kept busy digging cable trenches, loading and unloading timber, and moving ammunition dumps – a dangerous job when, as was often the case, it was done under enemy shelling or aerial observation. A 6-inch shell was as much as a man could carry. A 15-inch shell could only be rolled, and three of them were a full load for a three-ton lorry. Eric and his men had to march seven miles to the railhead to start their work. Once there they stayed for 24 hours with the men working in shifts of four hours on and four hours off. Often their duty was extended for another 24 hours. Eric survived on flasks of hot milk made with the tablets sent by his parents. Having now experienced both the trenches and 'rest' he was unsure which he preferred. He had originally told his parents that rest was better – 'there is plenty of work to be done but we do get a bed of sorts'. Now, after a week of working parties, he was keen to get back to the trenches 'because there at least you know what work you have to do and are treated with a little more respect by the higher command'.

The battalion moved back into the front line in the last week of February. With the build-up to the new season now well under way officers had to leave most of their kit behind. They were restricted to 35 pounds each, comprising 'a pack and perhaps a haversack in which we put all that we require such as a good supply of socks, iron rations, and perhaps a blanket'. The trenches had been badly knocked about in their absence and were collapsing with the thaw. Repairing them took up most of their spare time. However it was potentially a wasted effort as rumours were already circulating that the Germans were planning a withdrawal to a stronger defensive line. The priority now was to send out patrols each night to find out how strongly the enemy line was held and, if possible, to take prisoners for interrogation.

Eric led out patrols for the next three nights. It was, as he told his parents, dangerous but exciting work.

I have been over no mans' land each night to see if their line is occupied. We crawl out when it is absolutely dark and stay out for about three hours and then come back. I am rather fond of these patrols and feel quite at home as long as I have a compass.

On the first night he took with him a lance corporal and six men but was unable to get far. The following night they managed to work their way forward between two German saps to reach the enemy's front-line before being spotted by a sentry and making a lucky escape. On the third night Eric took only two men with him and worked his way up the railway line until he reached an enemy machine-gun post and strongly-held sap. The Germans were clearly on their guard. No man's land was suddenly ablaze with flares and search lights. Eric had great difficulty getting back to his own lines. At least he was able to report that there was no sign of an imminent enemy withdrawal.

Eric's company was relieved the following morning and went back into reserve in Agny for four days. It was then due to go back to the trenches for another four days before being finally relieved for six days rest behind the lines. Eric was already short of sleep. He was dirty and desperately looking forward to a bath: he had not taken his clothes off for a week. It would be some time before he had one.

Shortly after the company returned to the trenches on Sunday, 4 March, Eric witnessed his first German trench raid. An enemy raiding party managed to work its way down an old sap on his right, where the 17th Battalion was stationed, shoot the sentry on look-out in the trench, and then clear off again without being seen. It was an unfortunate incident. From then on two sentries were stationed at the end of the sap with orders to send up a flare if the enemy tried it again. Eric was still on duty three nights later when they did.

This time the Boche came as before but, when the two men in the sap tried to fire their pistol, it would not fire. These two men were taken prisoner and also a complete Lewis Gun team with their gun. Apparently a sergeant had shown the men how to load the pistol but had not told them that they had to cock the trigger before it would fire, assuming that they would know this. The whole affair is most disgraceful and the battalion is in for trouble.

Although no blame would be attached to the officers concerned the loss of the Lewis gun meant that the incident had to be fully written up by the 17th Battalion's commanding officer and then reported all the way up through brigade and divisional command before being sent finally to Third Army HQ by the commander of VII Corps, Lieutenant-General Sir Thomas D'Oyly Snow.

Meanwhile Eric's patrols became progressively more difficult. Gas alerts forced them to wear respirators, the combination of a full moon and heavy snow made them conspicuous, and no man's land often seemed as crowded as Piccadilly Circus. When one of Eric's men was hit on their first night out they had trouble getting him back. On the second night they passed within a few yards of a large German patrol but somehow managed to avoid being seen. And, when Eric returned after the third night's patrol at 4.00am, he found that the two bunks in his dug-out were already occupied, leaving him to make himself as comfortable as possible on an ammunition box and three petrol tins. Exhausted, he fell asleep immediately.

However he had no chance to rest. Almost immediately he was called to the telephone and told to report at once to battalion headquarters where his orders were to arrange billets for the battalion in Arras after their relief later that day. After walking three miles to the town he spent the rest of the day making the necessary arrangements before returning to escort the battalion back and make sure that they were properly provided with food and blankets. It was midnight by the time he got to bed again. He was looking forward to his first night in a proper bed for almost a fortnight. Once again he was woken almost immediately. He was told by a runner that he was again wanted at headquarters. On arrival the adjutant told him that he had been selected for a course at Le Touquet and was to leave from the railhead at Warlincourt the following day.

Barely able to stay awake, Eric borrowed the adjutant's horse and set off for a two and a half hour ride on 'a gloriously frosty and moonlit night' to the transport lines at Monchiet. Here he spent the rest of the night on a chair in front of a little stove in the quartermaster's office. He was still covered with the mud of no man's land and had no clean clothes with him. He managed to wash in the morning and after lunch was taken in the mess cart to the railhead where he had to wait four hours in a snowstorm for a train to take him the eight miles to Doullens. He had to make do with a cattle truck but was grateful to be given some tea and bully beef and biscuits. It was 9.00pm by the time he reached Doullens where he was to change trains for Abbeville. The 25-mile journey to Abbeville took another 12 hours and, after a two-hour wait there, he finally reached Étaples at 2.00pm on Saturday, 10 March. After a quick meal he then had only a quick carriage ride to Le Touquet where he was finally able to enjoy a vapour bath and a change of clothes. By then he had been constantly on the move for three days since leaving the trenches after three nights of patrols. That evening he wrote to his parents to apologise for his lack of letters.

> I'm afraid that I have already broken my resolution to send you at least a field postcard each day but you will understand why when I have related my doings during the last three days. The place where I am now is on the coast and nearer London than the firing line. It resembles Bournemouth but is considered superior: there are plenty of hotels and hydros as well as golf links. It is very mild and beautiful country with the trees all green: in fact one of the pleasantest spots I have ever been. We are under canvas with an excellent mess hut and the cars run quite close to the camp so we can get to the town in a few minutes. I shall be here for a week.

The purpose of the course, at GHQ's Lewis Gun School, was to provide company commanders with an understanding of the tactical use of Lewis guns. However, like many courses, it was anything but strenuous: for the participants it was as much a period of rest as one of instruction: some officers made a career of trying to go on as many as they could. For the first time that year the weather was gloriously sunny. Eric was able to catch up with friends and to make day-trips to Paris-Plage and Boulogne before returning each evening for concerts organised by the Duchess of Westminster. As he told his parents, 'the contrast between this place and the one I have just left is so great that I can scarcely believe my own eyes'. For the conscientious junior officer one can only wonder whether such glimpses of peace and normality were sufficient compensation for the dangers, squalor, and horror of life at the front or whether they just made a return to the trenches even more difficult.

Eric left Le Touquet on Sunday, 18 March. On his way back he treated himself to a night at the best hotel in Doullens. He was looking forward to meeting the battalion's new commanding officer, Lieutenant-Colonel JWHT Douglas, who had taken over a fortnight

Johnny Douglas in 1924. (© National Portrait Gallery, London, x122886)

earlier while Eric was still in the trenches. Johnny Douglas, or 'Johnny Won't Hit Today' as the Australians called him, was a sporting hero. As well as playing soccer for England as an amateur he had won the middleweight boxing gold medal at the London Olympics in 1908 and had led the England cricket team to an Ashes victory in Australia in 1911/12, when he captained the side on his debut after Pelham 'Plum' Warner had been taken ill. In 1915 he was one of Wisden's five Cricketers of the Year; and he would go on to captain Essex for 17 years and to play 23 test matches, 19 of them as captain. But, although exceptionally fit and tenacious, he was not always a crowd-pleaser, his reputation as a slow and stolid batsman being considered no match for his natural ability as a swing bowler.

Douglas had originally joined the Bedfordshire Regiment as a 2nd lieutenant at the outbreak of war. However, after promotion and with the 2nd Bedfords now part of the 89th Brigade, he was first given temporary command of the Pals' 20th Battalion in November 1916 when their own commanding officer, Lieutenant-Colonel Cobham, had to stand in for Brigadier Stanley as brigade commander. Douglas left the Pals before the end of the year, first to get married on Christmas Day and then to take over command of a battalion of the North Staffordshire Regiment. However, when Cobham was himself promoted to the command of the 24th Brigade early in the new year, Brigadier Stanley was able to persuade him back to take his place. For so illustrious a Pal it is surprising that Douglas is hardly mentioned in any history of the battalion, brigade, or regiment. Maybe it was because, like Eric, he was seen as an outsider and never first and foremost a Pal; or maybe it was because he was kept safe and on the battle field, unlike on the cricket field, never led his men into action. For the time being Eric would have to wait to meet him. Douglas went on leave again only 10 days after his appointment and would not return until 28 March, by which time the battalion was well into the final preparations for its first major action of the year.

And so, after two months in France, Eric had experienced almost every aspect of daily life at the front, from the squalor of the trenches and the monotony of working parties to the camaraderie of the mess and the brief respite that courses offered. He had grown used to the constant noise of heavy artillery and had seen the devastation that it wreaked on French towns and villages; he had come to terms with how different life was in a foreign country; he had spent too much time on or waiting for trains; and he had got over the disappointment of his transfer to the Pals and found himself among friends. He had come to rely on the parcels and letters that his parents and family sent. He had learnt to go without sleep. He had never been so cold in his life. Now the calm before the storm was coming to an end. Eric would soon have his first experience of battle.

4

The Battle of Arras

April 1917

Nivelle was a new arrival at French Headquarters; he shot up like a rocket and fell like the stick.

Thomas Jones, Lloyd George[1]

As the battle of the Somme drew to a close the allied generals met again at Chantilly in November 1916 to decide their strategy for the following year. They faced some difficult choices. As 'westerners' they remained convinced that victory on the Western Front was the key to winning the war. However Germany now seemed content to fight a defensive war to retain the territory that she had already won; and recent experience had confirmed the disproportionate cost of an offensive strategy. It would be another year before advances in tank design and tactics gave the allies the means to overcome the enemy's impenetrable defensive armoury of barbed wire, concrete, machine-guns, and heavy artillery. Although Joffre and Haig, the French and British commanders in chief, agreed to renew their offensive on the Western Front in the spring of 1917 their decision was ambushed within a month by a series of major political and military upheavals.

In Britain the leadership of the Prime Minister, Herbert Asquith, had come under increasing scrutiny as the full horrors of the Somme became known to the electorate at home. It was already widely recognised that his Cabinet colleague, David Lloyd George, was the better man for the job. Even his opponents accepted that he had the drive and dynamism needed to win the war even though they were deeply suspicious of both the man and his methods. After seven years as Chancellor of the Exchequer Lloyd George had been appointed Minister of Munitions in 1915 and then, in June 1916, Secretary of State for War after Lord Kitchener had drowned in the North Sea while en route to Russia. That autumn he was a determined but deeply demoralised man. The continuing loss of life on the Western Front had become unacceptable both to him and, so he thought, to the electorate; and he saw no hope of a breakthrough there without further heavy casualties. At the end of the year he confided to a cabinet official – almost certainly his long-time confidant and later biographer, Thomas Jones – that he thought that the country was in danger of losing the war.

Lloyd George made his move for power on Friday, 1 December, when he sent a private memorandum to the Prime Minister in which he made a strong case that a smaller and more effective war cabinet was required if decisions were to be made quickly and the war won. He made it clear that he was minded to resign as Secretary of State for War if his recommendations were not accepted. While the overall thrust of his proposal was uncontentious his suggestion that the Prime Minister should not merely stand down as chairman of the war cabinet but

---

1   T. Jones, *Lloyd George,* p.110 by permission of Oxford University Press.

that he should not even have a seat at the table was never going to be accepted. Asquith rightly insisted that, as Prime Minister, he had to have supreme and effective control of war policy and not be relegated, as he put it, to the position of an irresponsible spectator of the war. Lloyd George however had made sure of his support before making his move and, after a weekend of secret meetings, threats of resignation, and judicious leaks to the press, Asquith conceded that his position as Prime Minister was no longer tenable. On Tuesday he offered his resignation to the King. Other candidates were briefly considered before Lloyd George was offered and accepted the premiership the next day. His coup had taken less than a week. According to Lord Derby's biographer, Randolph Churchill, 'he rose to power, not only because of his war-winning qualities and his native genius, but by elaborate intrigue and skilful manipulation of the Press which exerted at that time a political power far beyond anything which Fleet Street has enjoyed before or since'.[2] He had, he added, 'clambered up the greasy pole of power by every Welsh artifice of political and newspaper machination'.[3] In the government re-shuffle that followed Lord Derby, who had been Lloyd George's deputy in the War Office for the previous six months, was promoted to Secretary of State for War. It was, he told friends, the only position that he had ever really wanted although he would never have stooped so low as to ask for it himself.

As Prime Minister Lloyd George had a three-point plan for the effective prosecution of the war – the re-organisation of the cabinet into an effective decision-making executive; the unification of the allied military command on the Western Front; and, as a confirmed 'easterner', a fundamental re-direction of the war effort away from the stalemate of trench warfare in France and Flanders. The first he achieved immediately with the creation of a smaller war cabinet, which was supported for the first time by a professional secretariat under Sir Maurice Hankey which included Thomas Jones as a deputy cabinet secretary; the second took a year to achieve, and even then it was only in response to one of the greatest crises of the war; and the third he never achieved.

Thomas Jones was related to Eric by marriage, having married his father's cousin, Eirene, the daughter of the younger Richard Lloyd, the port gauger and academic, in Liverpool's Grove Street Chapel in 1902. Born in humble circumstances in South Wales in 1870, where his first job at the age of 14 was as a timekeeper and clerk in the local ironworks, TJ, as he would become known, went on to secure a first-class degree in economics from Glasgow University before being appointed the first professor of political economy at Queen's University, Belfast in 1909. He stayed for only a year before returning to Wales to take up a succession of positions in public administration. Lloyd George followed his progress and, from 1912 onwards, had been hearing good reports of him as the secretary to the Welsh National Insurance Commission. Although he had no particular role in mind for him when he summoned him to London in the autumn of 1916, he was sure that he could make use of his administrative skills, sound advice, and reputation for absolute confidentiality. He appointed him deputy cabinet secretary shortly after he became Prime Minister.

Although TJ was virtually unknown outside Wales and was viewed at first with the same suspicion as the Prime Minister, his critics quickly realised that he exerted considerably more influence than his role suggested. As a fellow Celt he had the ear of Lloyd George; and their conversations in Welsh, often in the presence of others, did nothing to dispel his reputation

---

2   R. Churchill, *Lord Derby, 'King of Lancashire'*, p. 220 by permission of Churchill Permissions at Curtis Brown Group Ltd.

3   R. Churchill, op. cit., p. 221.

The Cabinet secretariat in 1918: Thomas Jones is seated front left with Sir Maurice Hankey (later Lord Hankey) in front middle. (From Thomas Jones, *Whitehall Diary Volume 1, 1916 – 1925*. Image reproduced by permission of Oxford University Press)

as an 'eminence grise'. However he tried when he could to stand aside from party politics, preferring instead to work behind the scenes as a go-between and fixer. It meant that over his next fourteen years in Whitehall he worked closely with and was trusted by four consecutive Prime Ministers of every political hue – David Lloyd George, Andrew Bonar Law, Stanley Baldwin, and Ramsay McDonald. He would go on to play important roles in the 1920s in the resolution of the miners' and general strikes and in the government's final negotiations with Michael Collins and Arthur Griffiths over the creation of the Irish Free State. Made a Companion of Honour in 1929, his biography of Lloyd George was published in 1951 and three volumes of his Whitehall Diaries were published after his death. He is considered by many to have been the most important Welshman in British public life in the 20th century after Lloyd George himself and Aneurin Bevan.[4]

While Lloyd George trusted TJ he had little respect for his generals, almost all of whom came from a very different background, and he did not hesitate to challenge the soundness of their strategic thinking. He could make a strong case for the unification of the allied military command on the Western Front. It was, as he thought, not so much a case of one general being better than another but of one general being better than two: but, in saying this, he

---

4   Thomas' daughter, Eirene, later Baroness White of Rhymney, would also make her mark in public life, becoming the first accredited female parliamentary correspondent before being elected Labour MP for East Flintshire in 1950. In 1966 she became the first woman to hold a ministerial post at the Foreign Office when she was appointed Minister of State by Harold Wilson, himself a one time MP for Ormskirk. She was Chairman of the Labour Party in 1968, Chairman of the Fabian Society, and, having been made a Baroness in 1970 when she stood down as an MP, served as Deputy Speaker of the House of Lords for ten years to 1989.

also understood that, with France the senior partner in the alliance, any such generalissimo would almost certainly be French and that the British military hierarchy would vehemently oppose any such subordination. For them it would represent not just unwarranted political interference in military affairs but also the surrender of their country's independence. As soldiers they had sworn their allegiance to King and country and not to any 'here today and gone tomorrow' politician.

Unlike his generals Lloyd George remained, like many politicians, a convinced 'easterner' even after the failure of the British landings in Greece and Turkey in 1915 which had cost Winston Churchill his job as First Lord of the Admiralty. He was sure that, if the props that supported Germany's war machine were removed by victories over her weaker allies on the Italian front and in the Balkans and the Near East, then Germany herself would collapse. The generals on the other hand were agreed that Germany could only be beaten where she was strongest, even if this entailed the continuation of a war of attrition and a high casualty count; and any transfer of their troops elsewhere would jeopardise their ability to hold the enemy on the Western Front.

Lloyd George was given a heaven-sent opportunity to pursue his strategy when there was a re-organisation of the French high command only a week after he became Prime Minister. Aristide Briand, the French Prime Minister, was, like his British counterpart, a confirmed 'easterner' who encountered the same resistance from his generals. In a cabinet re-shuffle in December he used his appointment of General Lyautey as Minister of War as the opportunity to side-line his commander in chief. 64-year old General Joffre, who had been Chief of the French General Staff since 1911 and who would now be relegated to a desk job, resigned in protest and was replaced by Robert Nivelle. Although only five years younger than Joffre, Nivelle was the rising star in the French Army. It was still less than two months since he had taken the credit for the final repulse of the Germans at Verdun with his symbolic recapture of the fort of Douaumont.

The promotion of Nivelle, a man with big ideas and a talent for self-promotion, over the heads of his more senior colleagues was always likely to be either a resounding success or a dismal failure. Fluent in English through his English mother, he made an immediate impression on the equally maverick Lloyd George. They met for the first time in Paris early in 1917 when the British Prime Minister was returning from a conference of allied prime ministers in Rome at which he had argued unsuccessfully for the transfer of troops to the Italian front. Nivelle took the opportunity to outline his plans for a spectacular Spring Offensive that would, he claimed, destroy the German Army in two days: and, if by any chance it did not, then he was prepared to call an immediate halt and so prevent a repetition of the previous year's protracted slaughter on the Somme. What was more, the French Army would bear the brunt of the fighting in an assault on the Chemin de Dames ridge east of Soissons. All he asked of the British was a large-scale preliminary diversion at Arras, 80 miles to the north-west, to pin down the enemy and prevent them moving reinforcements to the main battle zone.

For Lloyd George it must have seemed like manna from heaven. He invited Nivelle to present his plans to the British war cabinet in London in the middle of January. Field Marshal Haig and Sir William Robertson, the Chief of the Imperial General Staff, were asked to attend the meeting and added their support to what was, after all, a French offensive and hence, in their view, a French decision. It was only at a subsequent Cabinet meeting at the end of February, which neither Robertson nor Lord Derby were invited to attend, that it was agreed that the British forces would be placed, albeit temporarily, under French command. Outmanoeuvred, the military triumvirate of Derby, Robertson, and Haig was lost for words. A helpless Robertson wrote to Haig when he heard the news, expressing his disbelief that so deceitful and dishonest a man could remain for long as prime minister. Lord Stamfordham, the king's private secretary and an Old Rossallian, wrote to Lord Derby a week later to say that, although things were now being done very differently from what they might have expected, there was nothing that they could do except register a protest and carry on.

Meanwhile there had also been changes in the German high command. At the end of August 1916 Erich von Falkenhayn, the architect of the failed Verdun offensive, had been replaced as Chief of the German General Staff by Paul von Hindenburg, the successful commander of the German armies on the Eastern Front. With his trusted lieutenant, Erich von Ludendorff, he quickly implemented a new strategy of making the German defences on the Western Front impregnable while they starved Great Britain into submission. They were probably correct in thinking that, if Britain was forced to surrender, then France would follow suit. While Germany herself was being slowly starved by the allies' sea blockade Britain's food and coal supplies were also running dangerously low. A new campaign of unrestricted submarine warfare against all shipping might bring her to her knees in only a few months.

Germany had tried the tactic before in each of the two previous years. On both occasions she had abandoned it in the face of protests from the neutral United States, and not least after the Lusitania was sunk by a U-boat off the coast of Ireland in May 1915 with the loss of over 100 American lives. By announcing its re-introduction at the end of January 1917 Hindenburg and Ludendorff were gambling that, even if the United States was finally pushed into a declaration of war, she would not have the time to put an army in the field before the war was lost. The American president, Woodrow Wilson, was in a weak position. He had reflected the overwhelming feelings of his electorate in opting for neutrality at the start of the war; and it was now less than three months since he had been re-elected in one of the closest presidential contests of all time. Although he broke off diplomatic relations with Germany at the beginning of February he would hold off declaring war for another two months.

Hindenburg and Ludendorff completed their plans in the third week of March when their land forces made a strategic withdrawal to the Siegfriedstellung, or Hindenburg Line. This new line, which ran from Soissons to Arras and was the first stage in the fortification of the whole German line on the Western Front, had been completed with astonishing speed and secrecy over the autumn and winter. Siegfried Sassoon described it as 'that triumph of Teutonic military engineering' when he saw it at first hand in April;[5] and it would remain an almost impregnable defensive wall until late in 1918 when its capture effectively signalled the end of the war. A comprehensive and carefully-sited system of defence up to five miles deep in places, it comprised a succession of impressive trench systems dug, where possible, on reverse slopes for protection. Enormous concrete underground bunkers, built to withstand even the heaviest of shells, were able to accommodate the main body of the German infantry in absolute safety. A series of thinly-held outposts in front of the trench system was designed to slow up any assault and, behind these, thick belts of barbed wire directed the enemy

---

5   S Sassoon, *Memoirs of an Infantry Officer,* p. 155 (copyright Siegfried Sassoon by kind permission of the Estate of George Sassoon).

Français souvenons-nous !

1528. La France reconquise (1917) — LASSIGNY (Oise)
Dans la Cour d'une Ferme, essais de Kullure !

Phot-Express · Visé Paris

'La France reconquise': an image of the German destruction of Lassigny, between Roye and Noyon, after their withdrawal to the Hindenburg Line. (From Eric's postcard collection)

into the line of fire of strategically-sited concrete machine-gun emplacements. In contrast the allies' offensive trenches were by their nature temporary and often poorly sited. In addition to being stronger and more easily defended the new German line was also 25 miles shorter. By cutting out the bulge in the existing line 13 divisions could be released for duties elsewhere.

Operation Alberich, the code name for the German withdrawal to the completed Hindenburg Line, was as meticulously planned and executed as the construction of the line itself. 35 divisions were withdrawn in secret in three days. At the same time the territory that was given up was systematically devastated under a scorched earth policy that left it a desert full of wretchedness according to one contemporary German newspaper. Every farm and village was razed to the ground and every tree and bush cut down: wells were poisoned and roads and railways blown up. The official French report claimed later that women and young girls were carried off and the civilian population enslaved. All manner of bombs and booby traps were left for the unsuspecting British soldier. 'There was no souvenir hunting on this occasion', Brigadier Stanley remembered grimly; 'it was far too dangerous an amusement.'[6]

The allies tried to make what political capital they could from the withdrawal. The French produced postcards of the devastated towns and villages which they over-printed with the slogan, "La France reconquise (1917)". Everard Wyrall claimed in his history of the King's Liverpool Regiment that it could not be described 'in any other terms than that of a movement of defeat'.[7] The troops on the ground however quickly came to appreciate it as an outstanding defensive manoeuvre. When Eric arrived back from his course at Le Touquet on 19 March he found that the Germans had already withdrawn two days earlier and that

---

6   Brigadier-General F C Stanley, *The History of the 89th Brigade 1914 – 1918*, p. 191.
7   E Wyrall, *The History of the King's Regiment (Liverpool), 1914 – 1919, Volume II*, p. 385.

the Pals had pushed up after them from Agny to Mercatel. The following morning, when he went up to arrange guides for their relief, he was able to wander over what had been until recently no man's land.

> Yesterday I wandered about the old German lines. They had been wonderfully made and contained huge concrete emplacements and palatial dug-outs but our artillery had smashed it all up so that you could hardly recognise it as trenches. Coming back I had a good look over the ground which I had previously patrolled. Among other things that I found I had crawled over were the skeletons of 25 Frenchmen in a line along a road. They had evidently been caught by a machine-gun in the early days of the war. Their rifles were all rusted up but their ammunition was still quite good.

By the evening of Thursday, 22 March, the battalion was again at rest in Monchiet. They had comfortable billets and hoped to be out of the line for some time. Eric was lucky to share a bedroom in a private house with two other officers where their friendly French landlady was happy to take care of their laundry. Her husband was away with the French Army and her son, a medical student whose room they were using, had already been killed. Eric sympathised with her:

> I wish some of the conscientious objectors and other people of that ilk could see the sights we see out here and, if some of the people who are doing nothing could see the condition of the French people driven from their homes, they would realise the condition of things a little better.

He and his men were otherwise in good spirits. 'It is marvellous how the men keep their spirits up', he told his parents, 'men who have been out here for two years in every show and without any leave. Everybody becomes a fatalist. Still we are always merry.' On Sunday, after communion and church parade, he found it 'glorious to have the day to oneself with nothing to worry about'. Others were not coping so well. Only the day before Eric had run into 'young' Parker from the 18th Battalion, 'the one who tried to remove a detonator from a grenade with a pin and so blew off several fingers of his left hand. I think he is to be tried by court martial tomorrow for intentionally maiming himself so as to render himself unfit for service. I hope he gets off, as I think he will, although he must have known that in doing what he did he was bound to have an accident.' Parker did indeed get off and had tea with Eric the following day to celebrate.

The following week, to prepare for the British 'diversion' at Arras, the Pals moved back a further five miles to Bavincourt. Here they first dug and then rehearsed on the 'picture ground', a practice system of shallow trenches which replicated the German lines. Eric was also appointed the battalion's Lewis gun officer in addition to his other duties as mess president and second in command of D Company. As such he was not only responsible for maintaining their 10 Lewis guns and training the gun teams but had also to attend Colonel Douglas' battalion conference each evening along with the battalion's second in command, the adjutant, the four company commanders, and the signals officer. There he found out what was expected of them.

Nivelle's plans had been upset by the German withdrawal along the whole front between the two prongs of his offensive at Arras and Chemin des Dames. In particular the enemy had already given up the ground immediately south of Arras that the British were to have attacked. It forced not only a last-minute adjustment to their battle orders but also a wider re-assessment of their tactics and their chances of success against the formidable new German defences: but, even without these hitches, delays in French preparations meant that Nivelle had already had to postpone his original deadline of the end of March.

The Pals completed their training on Thursday, 5 April. 'Today was our last practice', Eric wrote in his diary, 'and I think everyone knows their job and feels confident. I hope our first show of the season will be a success'. The following day was Good Friday. After a final French postponement the attack had been set for Easter Monday. Eric inspected his Lewis guns for a final time before they were packed away and, after attending a Good Friday service, the men spent the rest of the day relaxing and playing football. They began their move forward the following morning, first to Bretencourt and then under cover of darkness to their jumping-off points just west of Hénin where they dug in as best they could for the rest of the night. They were now within range of the enemy's observation balloons and artillery and their casualties began to mount under heavy shellfire. Eric woke in the middle of the night to find that his greatcoat and tunic had been set on fire by a piece of burning debris. The last-minute postponement meant that they had to sit out another day. All movement was kept to a minimum and on a sunny Easter Day, while his men were asleep on the grass beside him, Eric wrote a final letter home before the battle. He wished his parents a happy Easter and hoped that they were enjoying their short break with Alice's brother and family at Edingale.[8] He assured them that they had been in his thoughts all day: 'it seems a long while since I saw you all last but I have always got your photos with me'.

What Eric could not have known was that Nivelle's plans were now close to collapse. When Haig met him on Maundy Thursday to review the situation he had been left with no option but to accept a final day's delay. The French Army, which was to launch its assault on the Chemin des Dames ridge a week after the British diversion, had still not completed its preparations even though Haig's preliminary bombardment at Arras had already begun. Nivelle moved on to Compiègne the following day for a more difficult meeting with President Poincaré and the new French Prime Minister and Minister of War. General Lyautey, whom Briand had appointed as Minister of War in December, had always been deeply sceptical of Nivelle and his plan. His resignation on 14 March triggered the fall of Briand's government two days later. The new French Prime Minister, 75-year old Alexandre Ribot, and his Minister of War, Paul Painlevé, had been in post for only three weeks when they met Nivelle on Good Friday. He now had to tell them that the enemy had discovered the time and place of the French attack. French security had been horrendously lax and, in a trench raid two days earlier, the Germans had captured a French NCO who had with him a complete copy of the plans. Although Nivelle offered to resign his new political masters felt that they had no option but to leave the final decision to him. He chose to carry on.

8   Alice's youngest brother, 27-year old Jos Holland, had moved with his mother and other sisters to Edingale in Staffordshire sometime after the death of their father in 1893. Although Jos was a delicate child – he suffered badly from asthma and bronchitis and twice had pneumonia – he went on to run Edingale House Farm until his retirement at the age of 94 in 1984. Known to all as the Master of Edingale – even his wife addressed him as Master – he would become one of the world's most distinguished breeders and judges of shire horses and was awarded an MBE for his services to shire horses in 1983. For many years a trip to see his horses at Edingale was a popular Sunday outing for families from Birmingham and the Midlands. Over 4,000 people attended the final auction of his horses in April 1984 where the buyers included Queen Elizabeth II, who bought Edingale Lady in White.

Ribot and Painlevé's baptism of fire coincided with developments in Russia and the United States that would have a major impact on the conduct of the war the following year. The Russian Army had already mutinied that spring; and the demonstrations and strikes in St Petersburg that followed had led to the resignation of the Tsar's cabinet. The already shaky Eastern Front was now close to collapse. The feeble and out-of-touch Tsar, Nicholas II, who had taken the extraordinary decision to assume personal command of the army in the autumn of 1915, abdicated on 13 March. The German government did what it could to foment the crisis. On Easter Monday, as the British offensive began at Arras, it allowed Lenin and a group of his fellow revolutionaries to pass through Germany in a sealed train on their way back to Russia from Switzerland. But, as one major ally edged towards the exit, another entered the fray. On Good Friday the United States of America finally declared war on Germany. However, as Hindenburg had predicted, it would be a year before she was in a position to play any significant role on the Western Front.

The British offensive at Arras fell largely on the shoulders of her First and Third armies with Gough's Fifth Army joining the battle two days later at Bullecourt. At 5.30am on Easter Monday, 9 April 1917, Horne's First Army launched its assault on Vimy Ridge, the high ground six miles to the north of the city which was known as the 'shield of Arras'. By the end of the day almost all the ridge was in their hands, and it would remain so for the rest of the war. To the east of Arras six divisions of Allenby's Third Army were able to advance three and a half miles along the River Scarpe in what was described in the Official History as the longest advance in a day since trench warfare had set in. Following on from this to the south of Arras Allenby's four remaining divisions had the task of capturing the Hindenberg line in a staggered attack, the aim of which was to get control of its northern end and then 'roll it up' southwards. The 14th and 56th divisions were to start the attack at 7.30am; General 'Jimmy' Shea's 30th Division, which included the Liverpool Pals' four battalions in the 21st and 89th Brigades, would follow up on their right in the early afternoon; and the 21st Division, furthest south, would finally join in at 4.15pm. The success of the later assaults would depend entirely on the cumulative success of those that had gone before. If these failed then the units to the south would be annihilated when they came up against an unbroken Hindenburg Line. In his subsequent report on the battle Shea summarised the task facing his division as 'a long advance over an exposed tract of land on a wide front against a trench system which might or might not be stoutly defended, but which was certainly strongly wired and which we were unable properly to reconnoitre. The first task was obviously to cut the wire.'[9] Unfortunately the artillery had been unable to do this.

Overall the first day, except in the south, was a considerable British success; but it was one on which they failed to capitalise. By the end of the day the infantry were exhausted, cold, and hungry; the cavalry had been held too far back to exploit the infantry's success by breaking through the enemy lines and spreading out over the open country behind; and the artillery could not be brought forward fast enough to cover any further infantry advance. The Germans struggled desperately through the night to plug the holes in their defences. They had to call on their final reserves, often stationed many miles behind the front and comprising only boy soldiers. It would take them up to 12 hours to reach their front lines; and in many instances they reported passing no other German troops on the way. For the British it was a missed opportunity. After an interlude of bright spring weather heavy snow

---

9   Report on Operations, 8–12 April 1917, 30th Division War Diary, The National Archives, WO 95/2311/4.

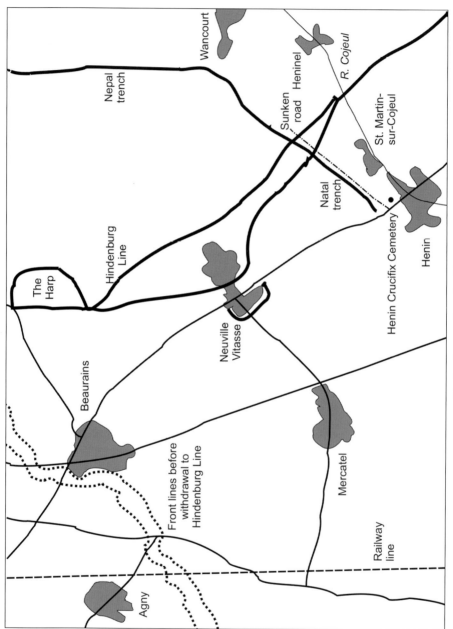

The battleground south of Arras.

over the next three days prevented any consolidation of their success.

Although the majestic Canadian memorial on Vimy Ridge now dominates the local skyline, Arras has until recently been the forgotten British battle of the war. It has never had the same resonance in the British psyche as the Somme or Passchendaele where the mighty memorials at Thiepval, Tyne Cot, and the Menin Gate overwhelm the visitor with their physical testimony to the sheer scale of the sacrifice. And yet, although the battle of Arras was shorter, its daily casualty rate was higher than both those offensives and indeed every other British battle of the war. And the battlefield south of Arras, where the Liverpool Pals were among those brought up short by the Hindenburg Line, is the forgotten sector of the forgotten battle. For Eric Rigby-Jones it was his first experience of battle. He wrote a detailed account of it in his diary to ensure that he would never forget.

The 89th Brigade's orders were to attack the Hindenburg Line by advancing along both banks of the Cojeul river from Hénin through Héninel and then on to the higher ground south-east of Wancourt. The Pals' 20th and 19th battalions, each in two waves of two companies, would lead the attack north and south of the river respectively, with the 2nd Bedfords in support and the 17th Battalion held back in reserve. The 2nd Bedfords had already taken the village of St Martin–sur-Cojeul between Hénin and Héninel in the early hours of the morning. The 20th Battalion's northern boundary was marked by Natal trench, an old German sap which ran alongside a sunken road and extended south-west into no man's land. To their left the 21st Brigade first had to complete the unenviable task of eliminating the strongly-held enemy outpost at Neuville Mill in front of the village of Neuville-Vitasse.

Easter Monday, 9 April
To-day is 'Der Jag'. The attack is commencing further north at daybreak but we are not due to advance until after 3.00pm, by which time Neuville-Vitasse and 'The Harp' should have fallen.

Soon after daybreak the enemy's shelling practically ceased and everything was very quiet in our vicinity while up north the din of the battle already in progress was hourly growing closer. At about noon the army corps on our left advanced. We had a glorious view of their lines of attack going forward in perfect order while our shrapnel was bursting over the Hindenburg Line and our heavies fell on Wancourt, Héninel and around. The attackers advanced across a shallow valley and over the ridge and down again on to their objective: but beyond the far ridge we could not see. As far as we could see everything was proceeding splendidly, the enemy shelling not being exceptionally heavy on this side of the ridge. We all felt certain that their objective was taken, namely to take the line north of Natal Trench and to occupy this trench. Our job was to take the part south of Natal Trench and, as I had the extreme left of the division, I was to join up with our troops already in Natal Trench.

As the minutes went by the artillery activity increased though as yet our way lay more or less clear. At 3.07pm to the minute every man was up and moving. The 20th Battalion's attack was made with C and D companies in front in two lines each of two waves while A and B companies formed the third and fourth lines. My platoon was in the leading line with my bombers and riflemen in front and the Lewis gunners and rifle grenadiers with myself about 20 yards behind. This was the formation that had been laid down by headquarters. Making our way through the ruins of Hénin we somewhat

The 'easy slope of nearly a mile just beyond the top of which lay our objective'. On the left is the sunken road up which the 20th Battalion advanced from Hénin to the Hindenburg Line: on the right is the church in St Martin-sur-Cojeul. (Author, 2013)

lost our formation but, emerging on to the level grass-covered plain, we soon regained it and could see in front an easy slope of nearly a mile just beyond the top of which lay our objective. On the skyline on the ridge beyond Wancourt Tower stood out very plain and from this the Boche gunners were no doubt watching their opportunity. Hardly had we gone 20 yards when he put down a heavy barrage of 5.9s. In a moment the air was thick with dust and splinters were buzzing and sighing past like a swarm of bees. We managed to keep our lines but they were rapidly thinned. After about a quarter of a mile we seemed to have got through the worst but had lost nearly half the company while the companies in the rear were still getting a bad time. Things were still fairly unhealthy for us. One shell dropped between myself and my runner, Merritt, who was walking about two yards to my right.[10] I was blown into the sunken road on the bank of which we were walking and, when I managed to crawl up again, I found that the poor fellow was badly hit but, strange to say, quite comfortable and happy. I was unable to wait with him but, after making him comfortable, I left him with a stretcher-bearer and ran after my platoon, now a few yards in front of me. As I ran a hare, slightly wounded, came rushing in fright towards me, leaping over all obstacles.

We were now nearly on top of the slope and we paused for a few minutes on a road that ran across our line of advance. I then saw a few men a little way up the road to the left. Going along, I found they were wounded from the people who had attacked on our left. Eager for news I asked a sergeant-major how things had gone. He told me that their attack had failed and that nearly all had been killed and that they were lying in heaps on the other side of the crest. Meanwhile our men were gradually being reduced and, as I got back, I ran along to Captain Gooch, the officer commanding D Company, to tell him what I had learnt. He sent me another platoon to support me on the left and by this time the line was moving forward again. Reaching the top we saw on our left

10   Eric's runner was almost certainly Private A Merrills of the 20th Battalion who died of his wounds two days later.

Barbed wire defences in front of the Hindenburg Line near
Héninel, 3 May 1917. (© Imperial War Museum, Q5286)

men lying dead in heaps, some of them several feet high. In front, down the slope, we saw the long-expected Hindenburg Line showing not a sign of having been bombarded and with its rows upon rows of wire still intact. Instantly a dozen machine guns in front of us opened up, knocking men down like ninepins. We only did about 50 yards of this when the signal was given to lie down as it was impossible to advance further until the artillery had done its work – or at least some of it. At once the men commenced to dig themselves in for cover while scouts crawled forward. Messages were sent back to recall the creeping barrage, now playing merrily on Héninel.

At dusk Lancaster, the officer commanding B Company, who as the senior company commander had assumed command, decided to attack again. Colonel Douglas meanwhile remained in his dug-out at Hénin from which he apparently expected to be able to control the advance by telephone. We attacked and met with the same rebuff, losing still more men, so it was decided to dig in for the night. The Boche gunners had by this time registered on our line so we knew that at day-break we should have our breakfast egg served with plenty of shell. We therefore withdrew some 200 yards and dug in with all the energy we still had. By morning we had quite a useful trench. We had also patrolled the ground in front well during the night. We had now to wait for orders for a properly organised attack with artillery support.

The tank, 'Iron Duke', passing through Arras on its way to the front, 10 April 1917. (© Imperial War Museum, Q6418)

Tuesday, 10 April

Early this morning we were quite cheered to see the enemy heavily shelling our position of yesterday, assuming that, it being the most forward trench, it was occupied. About 11.00am a tank approached us from behind: we had expected some assistance from them yesterday but saw nothing of them. This one came grinding up the hill and then stopped on the skyline about 100 yards from me, apparently pausing to make sure the Boche could get its position exactly. We made our way over to it and, as we approached crawling on hands and knees to avoid the machine-gun bullets, a very smart officer jumped out. He explained how awfully sorry he was to be late but he had had some trouble with his engines and so had spent the night at Neuville-Vitasse. He seemed glad that we had not got on very far as he would now be in time to join in the 'fun'. While he was telling us this Betts, another of the platoon commanders, was endeavouring to show him that it was not a healthy spot to linger. He took no notice but a minute later got a shot through the fleshy part of his arm – quite a nice blighty! – and was carried away groaning. Presently a corporal appeared at the door of the tank and seemed quite delighted to hear that his officer had been slightly wounded since he would now be in command. We managed at last to get him to understand the situation and sent him off to cruise along the German trench to flatten it a little and to look for a good spot for us to get through. Before he had started off the Boche had commenced to shell the place and several fell very close to the tank. At last it reached the Hindenburg Line where it promptly stopped and expired.

During the morning we attacked again, still without artillery support, and again met with no success. The weather had by now quickly changed. Yesterday the heat was unbearable: today it is snowing. At dusk we again made a further attempt on the flanks while the Boche counter-attacked on the right after a heavy bombardment.

Wednesday, 11 April
Last night, after becoming very cold, it began to snow and today we are sitting in our narrow trench cold and wet through and with an inch or two of snow on the ground. When we started out it had been hot and so we did not bring great-coats but just mackintosh sheets or coats. During the day, which has been much quieter, the flank of the Boche was finally turned and he retired in the evening very hurriedly, fresh troops following up and we ourselves being kept in reserve.

The first reports of a German withdrawal had come through at noon on the third day when progress was finally made to the north of the Pals. By then Captain Lancaster had made another five attempts to reach the enemy's trenches but each time had been driven back by heavy machine gun and rifle fire. He had eventually given up when, according to the battalion diary, he 'saw the impossibility of the task and the uselessness of throwing his men against the enemy's wire which was very thick and very deep'.[11] By 4.45pm however it was reported that the northern end of Natal trench had been taken and that the Hindenburg Line was clear of the enemy down to the Cojeul river; and by 9.00pm British troops had completed their 'bombing down' and were now in full occupation of it. Finally, once sentries had been posted, the 20th Battalion was at rest, 'all cheery though tired' according to the battalion diary.[12]

Thursday, 12 April
We were occupied all morning in collecting up the bodies of those who have been about here – a very gruesome task. How many there were I do not know but we ourselves must have carried in a hundred or two. Later on we were relieved and marched back to Ficheux. Unshaven and covered in mud, we were a queer looking crew and it was a few moments before our commanding officer, whom I passed on the way, recognised me since I had last been reported missing by someone. On our arrival at Ficheux we bivouacked in a field and, although it was still cold and the ground wet, we were glad of some sleep.

Although the 20th Battalion had failed to achieve its objectives Brigadier Stanley made it clear when he submitted his report of the battle that:

The infantry were faced with an impossible situation as regards a frontal attack owing to the uncut wire and machine guns. From a careful inspection of the ground I have satisfied myself that it was impossible for the 20th Battalion to have advanced any

---

11   20th Battalion King's Liverpool Regiment War Diary, 11 April 1917, The National Archives, WO 95/2335/4.
12   Ibid.

further up the road ... According to the map it would appear to be sunken the whole way but this is not so and when some distance from the German wire it can be swept by machine guns from the high ground.[13]

The poet, Siegfried Sassoon, was horrified by what he saw when his battalion of the Royal Welch Fusiliers relieved the Manchester Regiment in St Martin-sur-Cojeul that afternoon. 'As we entered it', he wrote in his fictionalised Memoirs of an Infantry Officer, 'I noticed an English soldier lying by the road with a horribly smashed head; soon such sights would be too frequent to attract attention, but this first one was perceptibly unpleasant.'[14] The following afternoon he walked up the ridge to the Hindenburg Line.

> Higher up the hill the open ground was dotted with British dead. It was an unexpectedly tidy scene since most of them had been killed by machine-gun fire. Stretcher bearers had been identifying the bodies and had arranged them in happy warrior attitudes, hands crossed and heads pillowed on haversacks. Often the contents of a man's haversack were scattered around him. There were letters lying about: the pathos of those last letters from home was obvious enough.[15]

For Sassoon the carnage was a final straw in his growing revulsion with the war and the unimaginable sufferings of the troops that he had seen and experienced for himself. Wounded shortly afterwards and sent back to England, he wrote his famous letter of protest to his commanding officer that was read out in the House of Commons on 30 July. While he accepted that he had acted in wilful breach of military discipline, by the time the letter was read out, so members of parliament were informed by the Under-Secretary of State for War, he had already been diagnosed by an army medical board as suffering from a nervous breakdown and therefore not responsible for his actions. To avoid a court martial his friend and fellow poet, Robert Graves, who also served in the Royal Welch Fusiliers, had helped secure his admission the week before to Craiglockart psychiatric hospital for treatment for neurasthenia or shell shock.

Today the Hénin Crucifix Cemetery, which lies opposite the calvary on the road north from Hénin to Neuville-Vitasse, is one of the smaller but more poignant reminders of those terrible first few days of April. Only 61 soldiers are buried there. Two are unidentified; 24 are from the Yorkshire and Manchester regiments that captured the village on 2 April; and of the remaining 35, all of whom died on the first three days of the Battle of Arras, all but two are Liverpool Pals. The 20th Battalion alone accounts for 24 of them. They lie together in a single line at the foot of the long slope up to the ridge where they lost their lives. In all 140 Pals were killed on the first day of the battle with another 109 losing their lives before the end of the month.

The 20th Battalion withdrew further the following day to Bailleulmont, nine miles behind the lines. Here at last they could wash and change their clothes and Eric had time to write home and to start to come to terms with what he had just been through. His thoughts swung wildly from the most practical of considerations – he had lost a lot of his clothing

---

13   Report on Operations, 8–12 April 1917, 89th Infantry Brigade War Diary, The National Archives, WO 95/2332/1.
14   S Sassoon, op. cit., p. 147.
15   S Sassoon, op. cit., p. 149.

Hénin Crucifix Cemetery. (Author, 2013)

and equipment and needed it to be replaced as quickly as possible – to the relief and sheer exhilaration of survival. Back in February he had assured his parents after his first tour in the trenches that 'I don't know what you want me to tell you. I certainly don't conceal anything from you. When I am fed up I think I let you know it'. His letters had become more circumspect as the battle approached. At the beginning of March he told his aunt Lu, one of his mother's younger sisters, that 'it is very difficult to find news that will pass a censor but there is plenty which would not, so please excuse this short letter'. Then, just a week before the battle, he had knowingly misled his parents when he assured them that 'mother's anxiety about my returning from the line is unnecessary. It is nearly a month since I was in a front line trench and it is likely to be another month before I see one again'. By Good Friday he told them only that 'we shall be moving about for the next few days from village to village so don't expect too many letters'. A week later, when he had survived his first battle, he no longer felt so constrained by the censor or concern for his family's feelings.

> I wrote my last letter on Easter morning in a little trench from which we were waiting to attack. We went over on Monday and have now returned to-day, Friday, to rest. I cannot tell you of the things that happened in those few days nor would I if I could. I try not to think about it but it keeps coming back and I thank God for a safe return. We have lost so many that we are bound to be out for some time now – in fact we are in corps reserve. On Wednesday I was reported missing but I do not know whether the report has gone forward or not. If however it does reach the papers during the next few weeks please remember it is a mistake.
>
> I have had several marvellous escapes. I had two pieces of shrapnel through my haversack which I carried on my back: this destroyed my soap box, towel, knife, fork, spoon, etc. I had some of my things buried so I am in need of a few things. I will give you a list later. Part of my trench coat is burnt away so I need a new coat. Personally I have not had a scratch though I was covered with mud yesterday. I received your parcel this morning containing cake, biscuits, chocolate, etc. and also parcels from Claremont

and Edingale.[16] As Mess President I am going out presently to buy in foodstuffs. We are going to have a good feed to-night. We have been living on bully and biscuits. Sometimes our rations could not be got up so one had to keep alive and sane with cigarettes and rum: but for these I should never have got through. I tell you of what happens to me because I know you will not worry about it. The only thing that really ever troubles me out here is that you may be worrying about me.

As my trench coat is done for I must have some sort of waterproof. I have still got the fleece lining so I think the best thing would be a trench coat made from hurricane smock. I have asked the opinion of several and they advise me to get this. Could you get me one sent out as soon as possible? I also require a collapsible knife, fork, and spoon, a towel, and three pairs of socks: the rest I can get out here. I could have got plenty of souvenirs but they are a burden in one's kit and I think it is a waste of time and trouble. I enclose a postcard which a Boche left in a shell-hole. I have received your four letters of 2, 3, 7, and 10 April: that I should get one in three days is remarkable. Thank you for the notes. Your Easter prayers for me have been answered. I had a feeling that I would come through alright.

Well, I will stop now and tell you more later. We are now in billets and quite comfortable. I think you may be very optimistic about the war now. The situation out here is that we can take anything we want and the comparison between our losses and German is absurd.

Well, love to all – your loving son, Eric.

Two days later, when the battalion had withdrawn to Bavincourt, Eric wrote again with a more comprehensive shopping list.

I have just been chopping some wood to keep our fire going before settling down to write letters. We left our last place yesterday having spent only one night there and are now in a very small village some nine miles further back. There are only three officers left in the company as several have gone to England with trench fever. We have our mess in an old farmhouse kitchen: the ceiling and big fireplace are of old oak and there is a huge chimney in which we can all sit and read in the evenings. Today we are keeping as Easter Day and we had a service and communion this morning.

I have plenty of work to do in overhauling the guns and ammunition and training new teams. The weather, I am glad to say, is gradually improving but we still get plenty of rain at times. I should like the waterproof out as soon as possible as I am on the rocks at present. Your parcels are always very nice but you asked me in one letter if there was anything I should like specially. I will mention one or two things: honey – we get tired of ration jam, and honey can be opened and packed again; chocolate biscuits – plain; butterscotch (Callard and Bowser) – this is packed in compact packets and so is easy to carry in the haversack; and a Tommy's cooker – not the ordinary kind but one comprising a small pan: I think Boots have them. I have lost my waterproof gloves. I left them with one or two other things in a bit of a trench and, when I returned half an hour later, there was no trench and likewise no gloves. I have therefore only got the pair you sent out recently which are rather light. Could you get another pair of strong

---

16   Eric's grandfather, John Rigby-Jones, had taken over his brother's house, Claremont, which was beside the rope works in Ormskirk, when he assumed control of the business after Henry Jones' death.

gloves of any kind you think serviceable: the waterproof gloves were rather big for me. Also could you send me a pair of puttees: mine are torn to bits. There are one or two pairs in my bedroom at home: could you send the best pair? I have plenty of Aytons tea, sugar, and milk for the present. I could do with some handkerchiefs: a cheap kind is best as they are so easily lost. Will you let me know what these things cost? I am afraid I am troubling you rather a lot but don't go out of your way if you can help it.

I must stop now as I have several letters to write to people whose sons etc. have been killed. It is a painful task. These I must do at once so I may not have time to write to Grandma. Will you explain to her that I got her parcel and will write later.

By the time that he wrote to his aunt Lu a week later to thank her for the parcel from Edingale Eric had been admitted to a field hospital with a temperature and a chill on the kidneys. She must have heard of his special request for honey. Almost 50 years later she wrote to my father to tell him that she had regularly sent his father honey that was made by two young men in her village. One of them had been killed in the war but the other was still alive and making honey in Tamworth. She had, she said, just been reminded about him by an article in her local paper in which he claimed that his honey was the reason why he had lived so long without ever having been ill.

Although at first the doctors described Eric's condition as NYD – 'not yet diagnosed' or, as he suggested, 'not yet dead' – it turned out to be another case of trench fever. The main symptoms were an influenza-like fever, severe headaches, and pains in the eyes and legs. Almost a third of all troops on the Western Front succumbed to it but it would not be until the following year that the excreta of body lice were identified as its cause. It usually took a month, but often much longer, to recover; and even then it was likely to return.

It was from the field hospital that Eric also wrote to his 17-year old sister, Judy. She had just left school and started at Liverpool's college of domestic science in Colquitt Street. Although Eric wrote only a few letters home to her specifically they have a sibling intimacy that is perhaps missing from those that he wrote to his parents.

I have just been picturing to myself a certain young lady sitting with an air of supreme importance in the corner seat of an electric train and reading no doubt the parliamentary columns of the morning paper, considering the franchise question, and criticising the Food Controller's latest rulings with regard to the inserting of currants in cakes. Occasionally she raises her dignified brow from the paper to reassure herself in the mirror at the end of the compartment that her hair is still as it should be. I do not know whether this is or is not the case but I hope you are enjoying the change in work.

As for myself I am still in bed but feeling very much better for the rest. I shall get up tomorrow and get back to the battalion as soon as possible. (Please excuse the exceptionally bad writing but I am lying down and it is not the ideal posture for writing). There are eight of us in the hut which forms the officers' hospital. We are quite comfortable under the circumstances and get very good food although I personally have been on what they call a 'light diet'! The village we are in is larger than most and is the one which we were in prior to our 'going over'. It must now be some 20 to 30 miles behind the line. In fact Sir Douglas Haig is coming here to make it his headquarters.

I should like you to have seen me when we came back last week. I was simply one mass of mud: my face was quite covered with it. Of course the officers who go over in

Eric's sister, Judy. (Author)

Eric's aunt, Lucy Holland. (Author)

the front wave of an attack are dressed like the men in every respect. It is very funny to see some officers in Tommy's clothes for the first time. They get pulled up by every sergeant that passes them and told to make themselves respectable: the poor sergeant is often hard to convince of the mistake. I have rather a good set of Tommy's clothes which happen to fit me and I have been mistaken for a sergeant-major several times by my own commanding officer. Well, as I was saying, I came out of the line in these togs, mud up to the eyes, and carrying slung round me in all sorts of ways the following: rifle, bayonet, field gloves, spade, tin hat, gas helmet, revolver, 1½-inch signal gun, compass, water bottle, haversack, entrenching tool, box respirator, bag of bombs, wire cutters, etc. I give you the list so that you may try and imagine what it looks like. To imagine what it feels like spend five days in the following manner:

Dig a small hole in a clay field and fill it with water. Sit in this and let the snow fall to a depth of four inches and freeze for four days and nights and then a day of scorching sun to dry the mud on you. You will then feel like nothing on earth. Add explosions of a violent nature and other minor horrors of war to taste.

Well they are bringing my dinner – a plate of soup – so I will stop now, your loving brother, Eric.

PS My frugal meal over I remember that I have not told you that I received Father's letter of 13 April and also the parcel containing cake, Oxo, socks, laces, etc. These were brought on to me by an orderly. I shall get no more letters now until I rejoin the battalion. I hope to get out shortly. My temperature was 100 when I came in on Wednesday – it is now 97. Well goodbye for to-day, Eric.

Hospital gave Eric the time to become more stoical about his recent experiences. 'It was hard luck on us to strike a bad spot at first', he told his parents on 22 April. 'Our division is one of the top divisions and was given what was afterwards pronounced an impossible task.' He would be able to tell them more about it when he got home, he said, but in the end it had only been a small check in a large and wholly successful attack. His trench fever meant that he missed the dinner for the 100 or so officers in the 89th Brigade that Brigadier Stanley held in the chateau where he was billeted. In spite of the grand surroundings each officer had to bring his own mug, plate, and cutlery, which had to be washed between courses. 'I wanted to do something for all the officers who had done so well during this time', Stanley recalled. 'It really was rather a masterpiece, and those who were there will not forget it for many a long day … I don't suppose that any other brigade has done such a thing out in France.[17]

Eric had been in hospital for five days when the 20th Battalion was ordered back into the line on 23 April for the Second Battle of the Scarpe, a largely unsuccessful attempt to build on the successes of a fortnight before: and he would still be there six days later when the battalion was finally relieved for an extended period of rest and re-organisation behind the lines at Rougefay to the north-west of Doullens. He had been moved two days earlier to the 7th Corps Rest Station to convalesce. Instead of the huts of the field hospital he now found himself in the magnificent Chateau de Barly where he had a beautiful room, lived on a diet of hot milk, played billiards, and was eventually allowed to go out for walks in the grounds. The house, he told his parents, was about 200 years old and in the usual French style with a mass of windows and doors and outside walls that were three feet thick. Although

Chateau de Barly. (Author, 2013)

it had a fine appearance from the outside it was marred, he thought, by 'a most appallingly ugly and dingy roof'; and the grounds, although very fine, were dilapidated due to lack of attention. The beauty of the surrounding pine woods and the occasional sound of a train in the distance reminded him of the Ruff. 'These trivial things mean a lot to one out here', he said. His only regret was that his letters from home were no longer being forwarded to him.

Eric was eventually discharged from Barly on 5 May after 17 days in hospital. For his batman, James Tatlock, who stayed with him throughout, it had been a welcome holiday. Although they anticipated the usual transport difficulties getting back to the battalion they managed to hitch a lift in a lorry – 'here was luck in its undiluted state!' – which dropped them off only two miles from Rougefay. Eric's letters, and the parcels containing his new clothes and equipment, were waiting for him. He soon discovered that a lot had happened while he had been away.

5

The Ypres Salient

May – June 1917

Gentlemen, we may not make history tomorrow but we shall certainly change the geography.

General Plumer addressing his staff before the Battle of Messines, June 1917

On Monday, 16 April, a week after the British diversion at Arras, the French delivered their own attack further east along the 40-mile ridge at Chemin des Dames. Far from being the speedy and spectacular success that Nivelle had promised Lloyd George at the start of the year, it immediately became apparent that it was a disaster on a scale to rival the Somme. On the first day alone the French sustained 40,000 casualties, or four times the number that Nivelle had predicted; and, by the end of the fifth day, the figure had reached 120,000.

This time Nivelle refused to resign when asked to do so. He even argued, when summoned to a meeting with senior ministers at the Élysée Palace on 25 April, that he had won the most brilliant of strategic victories. It would be the middle of May before he was finally removed. In the meantime the British were left to continue fighting at Arras to relieve the pressure on the French. The Battle of Arras did not officially end until the capture of Bullecourt, two days after Nivelle's removal. Success had come at a cost of 160,000 casualties. Brigadier Stanley reckoned that the fighting strength of the 30th Division had been reduced from 12,000 to 4,000 men.

The repercussions from Nivelle's failed offensive, and from the British failure to take the Hindenburg Line on the first day of the battle, left their scars on both Shea's 30th Division and Allenby's Third Army. Colonel Weber, the divisional staff officer who was responsible for liaison with army headquarters, was dismissed from his post at the end of April for reasons that were never disclosed. When General Shea went to his defence he too was dismissed by Allenby. Brigadier Stanley, who must have been well-placed to find out the facts from his brother, thought both men had been harshly treated but would not be drawn further. However, as the division's longest-serving senior officer, he took it upon himself to get formal confirmation from General Snow, the corps commander, that no blame had been attached either to the division or to any brigade within it. Then, at the beginning of June, General Allenby was relieved of his command of the Third Army. It would not be long however before he was given command of the Egyptian Expeditionary Force where he promptly re-employed Shea as one of his divisional commanders. By the end of the year they had advanced into Palestine and recovered Jerusalem from the Ottomans.

After the debacle at Chemin de Dames Lord Derby expected the French to go on the defensive for the rest of year while awaiting the arrival of the Americans in the spring. The decision was largely taken out of the hands of Nivelle's successor, General Pétain. If the

French government had seen enough of Nivelle, then the French Army had, like Sassoon, seen enough of the war. Compared to the British Tommy, the French poilu had a long list of complaints – poorer food and pay, longer stretches in the same trenches without rest or leave, and a general indifference on the part of his officers to his health and welfare. Fighting on his own soil, he was also more exposed to pacifist propaganda and political agitation. After the horrors of Verdun Chemin des Dames was the final straw.

The first signs of mutiny appeared on the second day of the offensive when 17 men abandoned their positions. Although it spread rapidly its true scale and extent remains unclear. The French generals managed to keep the details away from both their own politicians and their allies; and the Germans chose not to believe or act upon the stories that they picked up from prisoners taken in trench raids. Although the rate of desertion increased, the soldiers' protest was more often limited to a work to rule and a refusal to obey orders: while they were prepared to continue to defend their line they would not take part in any attack. Of the 112 divisions in the French Army 68, or 60%, are likely to have been affected to some extent. More than 23,000 men were convicted of mutiny by court-martial with 554 of them sentenced to death. However all but 49 of the sentences were commuted as Pétain chose to make an example only of the ringleaders. His over-riding priority was to restore his men's morale. Although he started to address their complaints immediately, he knew that it would be some time, and almost certainly not until the end of the year, before they could again be relied upon as a fighting force. In the meantime the British were left to take the fight to the enemy. It was down to Haig and his generals to review and carry through the allies' plans on the Western Front for the rest of 1917.

Britain was now facing an immediate and growing threat from the German U-boat. Shipping losses in the three months since Germany's re-introduction of unrestricted submarine warfare reached 862,000 tons, five times the level of the previous year. In April, the month before convoys were introduced, losses hit an all-time high of 449,000 tons. A quarter of all ships that left the British Isles that month never came back. Furthermore cautious optimism about Russia's ability to carry on the war on the Eastern Front under her new provisional government turned to disappointment when a final Russian offensive collapsed in the summer. As Eric told his parents at the beginning of June:

> It's up to everybody to put all they know into things now. I am quite convinced that we cannot risk another winter. I think we could manage alright but am certain that we are the only country that could. If Russia can only pull together and launch an offensive however small it should ease things on this front considerably. The Boche will get a good knocking before we have finished this summer. Well, we shall see.

Haig had always argued for a major offensive in Flanders where the once prosperous but now battered medieval city of Ypres formed the bulwark of the British sector. With the ports of Calais and Boulogne only 50 miles away, Germany knew that, if she could break through here, then she could not only roll up the allies' line from the top but also cut off Britain's supplies of troops and materiel from across the Channel. As a symbol of dogged and precarious resistance Ypres became for the British what Verdun had long been for the French. Like much of Belgium the city was at sea level. The coastal area to its north beyond the Yser canal had been flooded by the Belgians at the start of the war to prevent a German breakthrough; and the German Army was now dug in to the north, east, and south of the city on a saucer-like rim of ridges and low hills which it would be costly for the British to try to recover. The resulting bulge, or salient, meant that the British forces were, like goldfish in a bowl, constantly exposed to enemy observation and shelling from three sides.

Haig's staff had worked up plans for an Ypres offensive the year before. Resurrected at the beginning of 1917 to follow on from Nivelle's Spring Offensive, these plans now underwent final but significant revision. Haig recognised that, if he could break through to the Belgian coast 25 miles north of Ypres, he could destroy the German U-boat bases at Ostend, Zeebrugge, and Blankenberghe and so eliminate the threat to British shipping. It was a spectacularly ambitious plan based on previous offensive experience; and, even if it was successful, it was unlikely to be achieved without significant casualties and loss of life.

Haig started preparations immediately while waiting for the war cabinet to give their approval. After the delays and debacle of the Spring Offensive time was short. The weather in Flanders usually broke at the beginning of August. The clay soil of the farmland around Ypres had a water table of just 18 inches which, in peacetime, was held in check by an intricate network of drainage channels; and, when these were deluged by rain or destroyed by shelling, the whole area quickly turned into a quagmire. Unfortunately the weather had a habit of siding with the enemy. After one of the coldest winters on record the second half of 1917 would be one of the wettest.

Eric had re-joined the 20th Battalion in Rougefay on 5 May where the Pals were in comfortable billets in a quiet and beautiful village well behind the lines. With the return of warm spring weather they were looking forward to an extended period of recovery and re-organisation. Training had begun again, new recruits were arriving and being assimilated, and, as Lewis gun officer and second-in-command of D Company, Eric spent most of his time either with his gun teams or supervising musketry training. He was once more in fine spirits when he wrote to his parents at the end of his first week back.

I have received Father's letter of 4 May. You will by now know that I am out of hospital and that all chance of Blighty is past. We are having a very good time here: the weather is glorious and we get very good rations which makes a great deal of difference. On Friday we had a concert in the evening, last night we had some revolver shooting, and we often go for a ride in the evenings. We get plenty of recreation and of course the powers that be do not forget to keep us busy during the day. There is a probability of our remaining in this area for another month. By then the war will probably be over!

Seriously speaking, things are very black in Germany. Last night I read the translations of some 50 odd letters captured in the various theatres of war. These refer to both military and civil matters and in every one there is much the same sort of news: no bread, horseflesh and animal foods used for human consumption, children and old people succumbing to the trying conditions, munitions works exploding, people at Krupps and other factories on strike, epidemics of fever and other diseases, whole companies of men shot for cowardice, and trenches and other works absolutely shattered by our shell fire. One man says that all parcels received by the men are taken by the quartermaster and a note for their value given and that all one can do is to go away and eat the paper note. I could fill pages with their agonising tales and stories of riots, etc. Every letter finishes with a desire for peace no matter what the terms: in none did I see the faintest hope of victory. So we have every reason to be cheerful.

Let me know when you want me to send you a parcel of food!! Love to all, your ever loving son, Eric

Training intensified the following week after Nivelle's removal. The whole brigade practiced fighting in woods with live ammunition and trench mortars. Eric, who admitted that they made 'rather a mess of what was once a pleasant little valley', realised that they were 'evidently being prepared for some stiff open fighting but where we don't yet know'. Rumours began to circulate that they would soon be leaving for another sector some distance away. Then suddenly everyone seemed to be on the move and transport was in short supply. When the Pals left Rougefay on 20 May it was on foot and for an unknown destination. Colonel Douglas at least was confident that it would be somewhere pleasant.

The Pals' 60-mile march to the Belgian frontier took a week. It would always be remembered by those who took part as one of their most splendid achievements. They marched from eight to 16 miles a day with a day's rest in the middle and were inspected en route by Lord Derby who motored past with his brother as they were drawn up by the side of the road. After the shorter marches there was time to play football and swim in the streams near their camps. As an officer Eric had a horse to ride: it meant that he was not so tired by the day's march and could work each evening after their arrival in billets. He was fully fit once more and in temporary command of D Company as Captain Gooch had gone down with trench fever.

The countryside changed as they left behind the rural French landscape 'where one can travel for 50 miles and not strike a town as large as Ormskirk' and found themselves skirting round the coal mining district of Béthune. They were halfway through their journey by the time it dawned on Eric that 'although we still don't know where we are going our visions of a quiet spot are rapidly vanishing as we draw near the infamous Ypres salient'. Leave however had opened again and he was hopeful that it would only be another month or two before he was able to get home for the first time. At the Belgian border he was surprised to find a British policeman on duty alongside the French and Belgian sentries. The next day, while the men rested and played sports, the battalion's officers were introduced to their new corps commander, General Sir Claud Jacob. Theirs was the first division to arrive, he told them, to make up his reformed II Corps: they were now part of Gough's Fifth Army.

From the corps commander's remarks we gathered that we have something in front of us. He came to see the sports to-day and a few of us were introduced to him. He had a short talk with us, asked us where we came from and why and then, in a few remarks to the officers, he welcomed us and said something about our making history next month. We then went back to the mess for tea and unanimously decided that history-making was not exactly what we had hoped for up here.

They crossed into Belgium the following evening when a six-hour march took them through Poperinghe to a camp near Brandhoek where they bedded down for what was left of the night. They were now only four miles west of Ypres. At daybreak, before attending divine service and medical inspections, they saw for the first time the scale of the preparations already under way. It must have come as a shock. Beside them the wide seven-mile road from Ypres to Poperinghe, with a railway track running alongside it, was asphalted and well-maintained so that transport and ambulances could run smoothly; and the surrounding

The Grand Place and Cloth Hall in Ypres before the war. (From Eric's postcard collection)

The same view in July 1915. (From Eric's postcard collection)

countryside was swarming with troops and materiel. Every field had its camp, munition dump, or wagon line. The enemy's constant shelling only intensified at dusk. 'We took it at first for something unusual', Eric said, 'but find it is merely the ordinary wakening up for the night in these parts'.

They had little time to take it all in. At 9.00pm on Tuesday 29 May, less than 24 hours after their arrival in Belgium, they set off for Ypres for the first time under cover of darkness.

We got into a much battered train which each night made a perilous journey into the city. The engine was specially constructed so as to show no light and, owing to the bad track, was obliged to travel slowly. A few shells fell near us on the way but, when we got within a mile of Ypres, the track in front was being heavily shelled so we were obliged to get out. Then we marched by platoons at an interval through Ypres. I was detailed to bring up the rear of the battalion so my progress through the heavy shelling was naturally very slow, much to my dislike. We were obliged to skirt the railway station which appeared unhealthy and went past the prison to the centre of the city. The cathedral and its surroundings were being badly shelled as we passed and one place was ablaze, flaming pieces of timber falling across the street and making our passage difficult. At last we reached our quarters in the infantry barracks at about 1.00am.

Our quarters quite exceed our expectation. The infantry barracks is a very substantial building with a court-yard and a vaulted roof. An upper storey has been knocked down by shell-fire and has fallen on the vaulted roof, making it some five or six feet thick. The first floor has collapsed all round but a strong support of iron girders

The infantry barracks in Ypres taken from an observation balloon, 31 October 1917. (© Australian War Memorial, E01256)

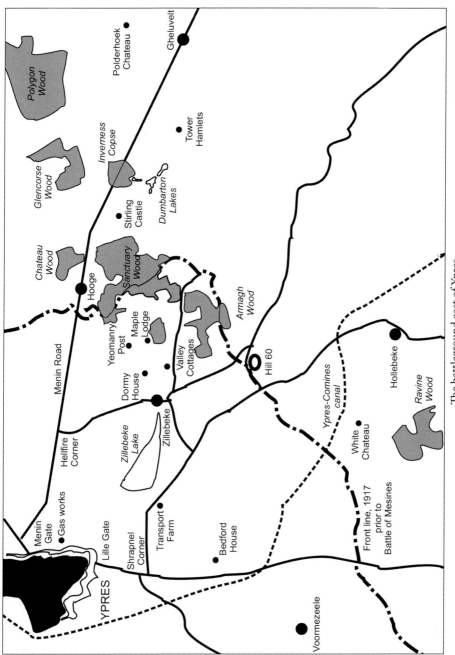

The battleground east of Ypres.

has been built to cover the rooms on the ground floor. The result is that a shell hitting the roof explodes before penetrating. If it made a hole the debris would fall on the girders and no damage would be done to the occupants below. Battalion headquarters selected some little rooms for themselves on the west side of the building, thinking that there would be more protection there but, as a matter of fact, they get all the splinters from the many shells which fall on that side. In addition, while we were there, a huge cornice over the main entrance fell down obliterating a motor lorry and a limber and two mules, and at the same time blocking up the entrance to their retreat.

On getting up on Wednesday morning after a good night's sleep in the bunks in our quarters, we found the Boche shelling the place. It took us a little time to accustom ourselves to the shells falling on the roof and exploding against the massive walls. Throughout the day we busied ourselves making things comfortable and as safe as possible. In the north-east corner where I was with my company we found that the outer wall was falling over so we filled some hundreds of sandbags and buttressed it up.

The following day the Pals settled down to their new nocturnal routine. 'No movement here is possible in daytime', Eric wrote. 'We sleep most of the day and work like bees all night'. The salient came alive as darkness fell. The landscape filled with animals, men, and wagons as working parties replenished artillery batteries and took rations and supplies up to the dumps behind the front line. Even on a moonless night flares, or Very lights, lit up the sky. The enemy's constant shelling from three directions was targeted on dumps and cross-roads. Gas alerts forced the working parties to wear respirators, making a difficult job next to impossible. The casualty rate was high: Eric was only surprised that it was not higher.

The 20th Battalion's first jobs included digging cable trenches south of Zillebeke Lake and carrying up duck-boards and revetting frames to improve the front-line trenches. Their working parties were from 20 to 100 men strong and their usual route took them out through the Menin Gate to the east of the city to the Royal Engineers' dump at the ruined gasworks, where they picked up their loads, and then on around the city's moat and medieval ramparts to the Lille Gate in the south. From there they skirted Zillebeke Lake, sometimes to the north but more often to the south past the cross-roads at Shrapnel Corner and on to Transport Farm, and made for the support trenches and forward dumps at Dormy House and Valley Cottages, which were themselves more than 1,000 yards behind the front line trenches. It was a long and dangerous journey which often had to be made more than once a night. Conscientious as always, Eric had familiarised himself with the routes in daylight on the afternoon of his arrival. Then, three hours after he had escorted his men back after their first working party, he went out again to take his first look at the trenches in their sector. For his own safety he had to be back before daybreak. He did not like what he saw: the clay soil and low water table meant that the trenches south of the Menin Road in Sanctuary Wood were shallow and had only the most meagre of breastworks.

Although Eric had reassured his parents that he would not be taking part in 'anything that happened', the following Monday, 4 June, was the start of an eventful three days for him.

We had an easier time last night for, when we reached the dump at Valley Cottages, the whole show was on fire and things were so lively that we were ordered to return to Ypres. This evening I have got a special job, taking up gas cylinders on a tramway which runs practically to the front line. The first stage is to get the trucks up to Zillebeke from the gas works. I have just been out to have a look at the track and find that it is in quite good condition.

I arrived at the gas works with 80 men shortly before dusk to find it being well strafed with shells of every calibre. I decided to wait until the strafe was over as I had already had several casualties in getting across the moat. After waiting 20 minutes the shelling had not decreased so I concluded that we were in for an all-night strafe and started out. We had got all our trucks ready when the Boche started putting over gas as well as high explosive. It is no use trying to work hard in gas helmets so we waited for another hour and then tried again, still in gas masks, but we did not get far as the line had been completely demolished in many places by the earlier shelling. We soon found the Royal Engineers and got them on to repairing the line. As they would not have it ready for some hours I sent my company back to barracks until they had completed their work. By dawn, however, there was still several hours' work to be done when I went back to report. My report was forwarded to Brigade and instructions came back a little later that the work was to be done by daylight – a pleasant job!

We started out again early in the morning to carry out our task. This time I took only 40 men since we would be under observation throughout. After arriving at the gas works we got out the trucks and arranged that two men should push each truck. I left Sergeant Ellis to send off one truck every four minutes, or longer if he thought fit, and started off myself with the first truck. Everything was perfectly quiet and the line, though a bit shaky, was quite intact. In due course we arrived at Zillebeke Lake and pushed along the lakeside to the village where the advanced dump was. As soon as we had arrived and pushed the trucks as much out of sight as possible I sent the two men back to report to the company in the barracks. I did not wish to have them waiting about with nothing to do. In due course the second, third, and fourth trucks arrived and had come pretty fast, thereby losing the interval I had intended them to keep. After this there was a delay and, looking down the track, I could not see the next truck in sight.

While I was waiting I became interested in some rising ground not far away on the right and, being unable to locate it, I brought out my map and spread it out on the ground. I was at the time behind the ruins of a house and was not in view of the Boche lines at Sanctuary Wood. Having studied the map for a while I decided that the rising ground was Hill 60 and that I must be in view of the Boche from the south as well as from the east. Realising that I had been rather foolish in bringing so conspicuous an object as a map I started to fold it up when four 5.9s landed round me on each side. Thinking that more would probably follow I dived like a rabbit into a concrete signal shelter a yard or two away. However no more came and, feeling more a fool than ever, I came out again and had another look for the next truck. Fully quarter of an hour had elapsed since the arrival of the last truck so I decided to walk along the lake to meet it. When I reached the corner of the lake I saw that the Lille Gate was being heavily shelled, thus preventing work for the moment. I got back to the gas works as quickly as possible by No.1 Sally Port and the ramparts. There I found that two trucks had been lost and the men wounded.

After a while the shelling lifted with the exception of an eight-inch battery, which continued to plant a shell with unfailing regularity every 60 seconds on the junction of the Lille Road and our track. Although the rails had by now been pretty well torn up round here we found that it was just possible to get across the gap carrying the truck in a minute. To do this we pushed a truck to within 50 yards of the road and got down and waited for the next shell. As soon as it had fallen we got up and rushed across the gap before lying flat again for the next one. In this way we got all except five trucks across and sent them up to the dump. For the remaining five there were only three of us left but eventually we got these past and spent a strenuous hour pushing them up to Zillebeke. Part of our trouble was for nothing for here we had another direct hit on a truck. After considerable trouble I found the officer in charge of the dump and handed over the trucks. He seemed very glad to get them at last as he had asked for them a week earlier. However they were in time and the remainder of the job was carried out by the special Royal Engineers during the night.

When I got back to the barracks at 5.00pm that evening I learnt that I was due out again with the whole company at dusk. This time our job turned out to be much easier. We had to carry three loads of sandbags from the gas works to Valley Cottages. It was quite a good night's work but then we had little or no shelling to put up with. We finished our work soon after 2.30am and by 2.45am were back again at the Lille Gate. I had come back in the rear of the company and, while they lost no time in getting back to the security of the barracks, I stayed for a while at the Lille Gate. It was a beautiful night, perfectly still except for a distant rumble of transport and an occasional shot from some excited sentry at an imaginary patrol. Orders had been issued for all working parties to be out of the salient by 3.00am so there was less than the usual movement. Soon after 3.00am I saw an immense burst of flame from the Messines ridge and the ground literally shook. In a few moments, which seemed like years, I heard the report and simultaneously thousands of guns barked out from all sides. The Battle of Messines had begun. Battery fire from some 6-inch howitzers just behind me brought me back to my senses and in less time than it takes to write this I was back in our billets in the barracks and in bed, though still fully dressed. It was some time before I got to sleep in all that din but I was very tired.

Haig knew that, for his break-out to the Belgian coast to succeed, he had first to secure his rear to the south of Ypres where the Germans held the Messines ridge. He gave the task to General Plumer who had been at Ypres for two years and whose Second Army was immediately to the south of Gough's Fifth. For Plumer, who was a careful and meticulous planner, the Battle of Messines would be a spectacular success and secure his reputation as one of the war's great generals.

The British had begun mining operations under the Messines ridge more than a year earlier. By the beginning of June 1917 there were 450 tons of high explosive packed into 20 tunnels under the German lines over a 10-mile front. Plumer's artillery bombardment in the two weeks prior to their detonation was impressive in its own right, with an average of 350 shells a minute being fired throughout the second week. But, although this would have softened up the German troops on the ridge, nothing could have prepared them for the shock and awe of the simultaneous explosion of the mines just after 3.00am on the morning of 7 June. 19 of the 20 mines went off successfully. The explosion was so loud that it was said to have been heard in London and not least by Lloyd George, who was working late in Downing Street. Those Germans who were not killed outright were shocked out of their senses. The 80,000 British and colonial infantry who followed up to secure the ridge were

Shell craters at Hill 60 after the Battle of Messines with Zillebeke Lake in
the background, 6 July 1917. (© Australian War Memorial, E01911)

able to advance three miles along a five-mile front. Messines was taken in two hours and
Wytschaete four hours later. Hindenburg later admitted that the effect on German morale
was devastating. His only surprise was that the British again failed to capitalise on their
success. There would now be almost eight weeks of inactivity before the start of the Third
Battle of Ypres.

Eric must have felt some satisfaction that the most northerly of Plumer's mines had
exploded under Hill 60 from where he had been spotted and almost killed by enemy shellfire
only the day before. What little was left of it was now in British hands. However he had no
time for further reflection. After a late breakfast he was told that his company had been
temporarily attached to the 17th Battalion and would be taking over the support trenches
north of Dormy House that evening.

Eric's first time in the trenches at Ypres, although short and uneventful, would stand
him in good stead for his first proper tour. He was able to see for himself the precariousness
of their position and to get used to the aircraft that crowded the sky from dawn to dusk.

At dawn the following morning we witnessed several lively encounters in the air over
the salient and had the satisfaction of seeing several enemy planes shot down, although
this was countered by a piece of ill-luck later in the day. During the early afternoon a
squadron of enemy scouts flew overhead and, after manoeuvring for a time, succeeded
in singling out one of our machines. He put up a good fight but they got him at every
turn and at last his machine burst into flames some 12,000 feet up. In falling the pilot
became released from his machine and shot like a stone to the ground. We knew that
he had no chance when we saw the mass of flames break out but little expected this. As
it was we saw him falling directly over us. In a few seconds – it seemed like hours – he

fell not quite on top of us but only ten paces behind our trench. The sound of his rushing through the air was just like the sound of a heavy slow-moving howitzer shell. The poor fellow was barely recognisable and would have died long before reaching the ground due to the speed of his fall from so great a height. Immediately after this we were severely strafed and our trench blown in several places. Thanks however to its depth we had no casualties.

D Company were relieved after only 30 hours in the trenches when the Pals were withdrawn for a period of rest behind the lines. Eric's luck again held when he led his men out.

At 2.00am our relieving company arrived and we filed out past Dormy House and down to Zillebeke. I took the north side of the lake as I had previously found it the safer in spite of there being no trench and then made for Shrapnel Corner. Soon after this we came upon the rest of the battalion and continued our march by platoons at about 50 yards interval. The route lay across country, avoiding all roads with their traffic, and was marked the whole way with white stakes which were easy to see in the moonlight. Gradually the din of the shelling became less violent and the shell holes less frequent and we came at last to fields and houses – only a few but still homes. The silence was very strange after the continuous din in the salient and, though dead tired, we were looking forward to the next few days with all the eagerness of schoolboys for the holidays. I was walking just to the rear of the last platoon of my company and there was only one platoon behind, O'Connor's, which had missed its own company. The head of the battalion halted and I was making up some of the distance that we had lost before doing likewise. Our route lay across a main road and, when I reached the road, I was about to blow my whistle for the halt but reflected that it would be better to go a further 50 yards to enable O'Connor's platoon to cross the road as well in case he should be cut off by a column on the road. Accordingly I waited until he reached the road and then blew a long blast for a halt. Hardly had I done this when a 15-inch shell came over and landed in the middle of O'Connor's platoon, killing several and wounding almost all. It was the only shell in the neighbourhood in a fortnight. This piece of bad luck made a bad finish to the whole tour.

At 5.30am we reached a small hutment camp at Brandhoek. After a meal we all turned in and slept until noon. At 1.30pm we were again on the road, this time in close formation, and marched on past the hop fields to Poperinghe, and then on to Hipshoek where we found comfortable billets awaiting us. I found that I had plenty of room for my whole company in a farm house with ample accommodation for officers and NCOs. It was after 5.00pm when we arrived so, as soon as possible, we got into our valises again and forgot that there ever was a war.

Eric had had little time to write home in the fortnight since his arrival in Belgium. Although he was now heading his letters 'Belgium' rather than 'France' he could not say exactly where he was. However he dropped enough hints for his parents to guess, describing the place as 'this city of the past which once upon a time was an extremely unpleasant spot'. He now scribbled them a quick note to let them know that he was alright and 'out of the line, or alleged line, after a very warm fortnight' and then settled down for ten days of rest.

The Pals were now too far behind the lines for working parties and fatigues. They spent their days instead on general training and sports. In the evening the officers often rode over to one of the local towns. 'Colonel Douglas has gone mad on sports, particularly football', Eric wrote in his diary, 'so we play every day'. Under the captaincy of the former amateur international, who marshalled the defence from centre half, the Pals, with an average height of five feet, managed a goalless draw against the six-foot giants from the Grenadier Guards. At a dinner after one divisional sports day Eric told his parents that, while Major Campbell Watson, the battalion's second-in-command, 'quite distinguished himself in a little after-dinner speech', Colonel Douglas 'was, as usual, like a fish out of water'. As he himself admitted he was not one for making speeches: he preferred to let his fists doing the talking in the boxing ring. Eric also ran into several of his friends from the Liverpool Rifles only to be disappointed that they held out little hope for his immediate return. Although he would come to admire Campbell Watson more than any other man under whom he served he was again unhappy with his lot. 'I am afraid that the officers in this battalion are not up to much', he had written home while on the march to Belgium, 'and nor is the battalion for that matter. There is no discipline here such as we have in the 6th and no esprit de corps which is so important. Well, I will stop this or I shall be wanting to get back to the 6th – to which I still belong properly.'

After almost two years in the army, and in spite of his being temporarily in command of D Company, 2nd Lieutenant Eric Rigby-Jones had still not received a promotion. His hopes of an acting captaincy were raised when Captain Gooch was finally invalided home at the beginning of June: and, although he was now with the Pals, he was also due a permanent promotion in the Rifles where he had heard that his contemporaries, Brocklebank and Goffey, were now lieutenants. However he did not want to raise any expectations. 'I don't expect I shall be able to keep the company', he told his parents. 'Seniority is worked in this battalion from the time one joins and not from the date of one's commission as it should be so I am seen as quite junior here although I am really senior to all the subalterns and acting captains. I hope to be able to keep it and, as I have had it in the line, I may have a chance.'

Hope turned to disappointment only a week later when Captain Bickersteth joined the battalion from England and was given command of D Company. The following day Lieutenants' Eric Beaumont and Charlie Moore, the battalion's only two lieutenants to fight on the first day of the battle of Arras, were both promoted to acting captain 'while commanding a company'. It was no consolation when Colonel Douglas thanked Eric for what he had done and told him that he was sorry that he had had to lose the company. In spite of his recent arrival, however, Bickersteth was expecting to stand in for Campbell Watson when the latter went home on leave and then to be appointed adjutant on his return. As a result, when the battalion went back into the trenches a few days later, Eric found himself once more in charge of D Company but without any proper or permanent recognition – 'in other words', he complained, 'all the work without the privileges. I seem to have commanded in the line for a long while now but someone usually turns up to command it when we are on rest. This is most unfortunate but I usually have my own way and the company sergeant-major and quarter-master are very loyal to me.'

It would be another three weeks before Eric was promoted to acting captain 'while commanding a company' although it was effective from 28 May, the date of the Pals' arrival in Belgium. The notice appeared in the *London Gazette* on 8 August alongside Gooch's relinquishment of his acting captaincy. Eric's permanent promotion to lieutenant came through at the beginning of July.

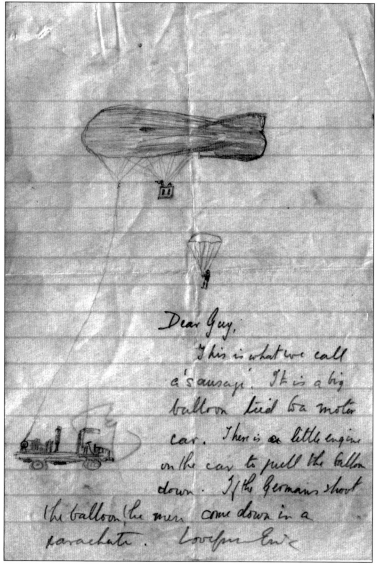

Eric's drawing of a barrage balloon for his six-year old brother, Guy. 'This is what we call a 'sausage'. It is a big balloon tied to a motor car. There is a little engine on the car to pull the balloon down. If the Germans shoot the balloon, the men come down in a parachute.' (Author)

After only four days at Hipshoek the Pals started back towards the salient. For the second half of their rest they would be based in a tented camp at Ouderdom, three miles south of Brandhoek, where riding lessons for those officers who could not ride provided the men with a source of free entertainment. Eric's second-in-command, Lieutenant Dawson, was the star of the show on a white mule. Although Eric enjoyed being under canvas in the hot weather the Pals' new camp was poorly sited in the middle of a triangle of railway lines and beside a "tank-o-drome", ammunition dump, anti-aircraft battery, mobile workshop, and main road. It was a frequent and easy target for enemy aircraft and artillery as Eric discovered when he was out practising with his revolver on the rifle range.

> The shells come with such tremendous velocity that one does not hear them coming until they have gone. The first one landed right under the solitary tent in the middle of our field and, of course, buried itself deep in the ground before exploding. Up went the tent like an umbrella caught in the wind and it came down about 20 yards away in an awful mess. We were just saying something about any poor fellow that might have been inside when the mass of tangled canvas moved and a man, disentangling himself, looked round in amazement and fled like a hare – a genuine case of shell-shock. While we were marvelling at such an extraordinary escape another shell fell on the other side of us. Reckoning that, if he bracketed the next shot, we should just about get it we moved away – and only just in time for the next moment the firing point of the rifle range absented itself. For an hour or more they played with us but fortunately did no more damage.

> The nearby anti-aircraft battery got its own back the next day.

> It was an exceptionally clear day, observation balloons were up all along the line, and the Boche made several attempts to get them down. At last he succeeded. Suddenly a plane dropped from the clouds and managed to bring down three balloons in succession. In each case the occupants were able to get clear in parachutes before the balloons burst into flame. Had he gone home after this the Boche might have returned with a very successful exploit to his credit but instead he turned and fired on the men slowly descending in parachutes. Our Archie friends were now hammering away fast and eventually they brought him down with a shot which set his plane on fire.

Three days later, on 26 June, the Pals started back to the front for their first proper tour in the trenches at Ypres.

6

Sanctuary Wood

June – July 1917

They win or die who wear the rose of Lancaster.
                    Motto of the territorial battalions of the King's Liverpool Regiment

The Pals were soaked to the skin by a violent thunderstorm when they moved forward under cover of darkness to Sanctuary Wood at the end of June. It was perhaps a warning of what was to come. They were expecting a lively time. 'For a while the guns prevented one from distinguishing the peals of thunder', Eric remembered, 'but the lightning was most vivid. It soon increased and all the guns ceased, leaving the field to the battle of the elements. For an hour the storm ranged, eclipsing anything I have previously seen. I myself saw no less than six thunderbolts strike the earth, one felling a tree within a hundred yards of our shelter.'

By 1917 Sanctuary Wood was a wood in name only. The few trees that remained were shattered stumps surrounded by mud and shell holes and, where they existed, the trenches were poor and shallow. No cooking could be done in them: rations were issued already cooked

The preserved trenches at Sanctuary Wood Museum Hill 62. (Author, 2013)

Looking back towards Ypres from the Canadian Hill 62 Memorial at the southern edge of Sanctuary Wood. Maple Copse is on the left, with Maple Lodge and then Dormy House behind it, and towards the right is Yeomanry Post. Beside each other in the middle of the background are the spires of Ypres' Cloth Hall and Cathedral. (Author, 2013)

along with a small supply of solidified alcohol for heating them up. It was D Company's turn in the front line. Their sector ran immediately north from what is now the Hill 62 museum, where there are some of the few remaining trenches in the salient. Although they were in support C Company was half a mile to their rear in Wellington Crescent, a trench that ran north from Maple Lodge; B Company was a further 400 yards behind in Ritz Street, which ran north from battalion headquarters at Dormy House; and A Company was held in reserve back at Zillebeke Lake. Brigade headquarters was west of the lake at Bedford House, more than two miles from the front. If D Company ran into any trouble, as Eric quickly realized, they would have no immediate help on which to call.

> Our new position consists of a strangling trench about 250 yards long. The trench is only some 18 inches deep as the ground is very swampy. In front is a low parapet of no thickness and in no place exceeding four feet in height, while in many places it does not exist at all. I am told that it is futile to attempt to build it up as the Boche persistently knocks it down immediately. There are no shelters except a few brushwood ones and the men have to spend the day lying in the mud at the bottom of the trench. Some six yards down the communication trench – there is only one – are two shelters of corrugated iron and mud, about eight feet by five and not quite four and a half feet high. One is occupied by the signallers and the other is company headquarters. On our left is a gap of 400 yards which is reckoned to be untenable although I fail to see how it differs from our position. At all events it is not occupied but defended by machine guns positioned some 400 yards to the rear. What a chance for an enterprising Boche patrol to get behind us! But I don't think he is likely to try. However we have to patrol this stretch and this job is made most uncomfortable by reason of our machine guns keeping up their harassing fire from behind. On our right is another gap, impassable by reason of the depth of water, and then about 150 yards away is the left post of the 17th Battalion near Observatory Ridge sector. In front of us we have little or no wire and the

racecourse [soldiers' slang for no man's land] is a mad jumble of smashed timber and iron and other wreckage where there are the remains of numerous trenches, including the once famous International trench, of which both sides held part alternately. Behind us there are no troops for nearly half a mile and a mile behind is battalion headquarters at Dormy House connected to us by a rotten communication trench. The nature of the ground is such that it is practically impossible for supporting troops to advance except by this trench; and this in any action would be a death trap from enfilade fire. And we are told to expect a raid by the Boche! Altogether it looks like something doing and some fun when it comes. All this would be passably tolerable were it not for the appalling stench of the partly decomposed bodies that fill the shell holes.

After a good tour of the line I returned to my palatial headquarters to write out the numerous necessary reports in time for a runner to take them to battalion HQ and return before dawn. Knowing that the Boche was likely to return the raid made by our predecessors we stood to in good time. What a cheery sight it was to look out on the waste in front of us in the cold grey light of dawn! Gradually we were able to discern the outline of the Boche trenches about 150 yards away in places and considerably higher than us. Before long we had another treat when a squadron of enemy planes – painted bright red all over, the mark of Baron von Richthofen's famous circus – flew over and patrolled our line at a height of barely 40 feet. Up and down they flew, firing their guns and pouring stuff into our wretched little trench. We tried having a shot at them and I got two guns, concealed as far as possible, to open up on them. I soon regretted this as we had casualties in both teams. We discovered later that this was to be a daily performance and found that it was best not to fire at them, except with a gun placed somewhere away from us and very carefully camouflaged. It is practically impossible to do any work during the day for, besides observation from the ground, the Boche has a balloon up quite close and right opposite us.

During the morning I decided to get a little sleep as I was rather tired after the first night's work but was then sent for by battalion headquarters. I found it a rather difficult job to get down the trench without showing myself and was on several occasions spotted and fired on. It took me the best part of an hour to get there and I was glad of some grub at the end of it. The commanding officer, Major Campbell Watson, who was standing in for Colonel Douglas while he was on leave, had his headquarters in the cellar of Dormy House in which there was plenty of room for all the usual personnel as well as some additional stretcher-bearers. I spent nearly an hour with him going over various maps and discussing the coming raids, ours and the Boche, and then returned to my company. It was close on 4.00pm when I arrived and I had to start at once to fix up the various fatigue parties and work for the night as well as patrols to explore the ground in front preparatory to our raid.

I was rather unfortunate in my officers at the time. Nickel was an exceedingly good fellow but well on in life – for the army, at any rate – being, I should imagine, over 40 [he was actually 34]: he was, of course, useless for a raid and not too good at patrolling. I also had a young jackanapes called Jones who was rather new to the game and not reliable. My only other officer, and the one on whom I had to rely, was Dawson who, though he did very well later, had not then learned to view matters in their proper importance. I decided to send both Dawson and Jones on the raid, hoping that the latter would profit from the experience. As company commander I was not allowed to go myself. Accordingly I sent Dawson out to patrol on the right of the sector whence I intended to make the raid and Nickel on the left, leaving Jones on duty in the trench while I saw, among other things, to the improving of the defences and wiring. After the period of an hour at sunset, when all men stand to their posts, work began and the place that seemed deserted during the day began at last to hum with activity – only there was no humming: the Boche doesn't like it and is apt to strafe.

Shortly after midnight Colonel Watson came up and I had to take him round the line: this occupied a precious hour. Soon the patrols came in and I had the difficult job of putting their reports into a coherent tale on paper and endeavouring to extract a good proportion of truth. These and other reports occupied me till dawn when, at stand to, we had the visit of the Red Devils again. I tried to snatch some sleep but had to go to HQ first thing in the morning since it is slow work arranging a raid by correspondence and the telephone was of course unsafe.

During the afternoon the Boche artillery was very active and in the middle of it he started dropping trench mortar bombs on the trenches. After a while I discovered that he was registering on the junction of the communication trench with the front line and on two or three other important points, hoping, I assumed, that it would not be noticed under cover of artillery activity. This aroused my suspicion of a raid later on and it led me to wonder at what time the raid would take place. It was obvious that, if a raid on a large scale were attempted, it would be very difficult to keep direction across that appalling no man's land. I reckoned the best time would be at dusk when advantage could be taken of the departing light to get forward and then trust to luck to get back: if so 11.00pm would seem a good time for the actual raid. We normally stood down at 10.30pm but I decided that we would remain at our positions until 11.15pm that night. I mentioned this to the adjutant and told him that I would send a message if anything further occurred to strengthen my supposition and suggested that he might have a word with the artillery. As a matter of fact at this time everything was rather critical in the salient and we had been told that the Boche would probably try to obtain our identification at all costs.

Now the rule is that the SOS signal must not be put up unless the enemy are actually seen advancing and since, in a position such as ours, we would be very awkwardly placed if an attempt was made in force and we had to wait some ten minutes for a barrage, I suggested that I might put up the signal before actually seeing the enemy. During the afternoon I was again called down to headquarters and I found that the CO, though not placing too much upon the mere registering of trench mortars, had nonetheless been to see the artillery and told them what I thought might happen. I returned at about 3.00pm and an hour later the Boche opened up suddenly on our position with a box barrage of 4.2s, thus cutting off our support, and also trench mortaring the junctions of our trenches and hampering our movements. This did not last very many minutes but I definitely decided that a raid was on and sent the message 'raid expected' some time later in code to battalion HQ. The artillery were warned and were on a careful look-out. The officers from C Company came up later, having being sent by the CO, and I arranged what they should do if anything happened. We stood to at 9.30pm as usual and remained on for the extra time. I went a complete round of the line with the sergeant major and inspected all rifles and Lewis guns, returning to the company headquarters shelter a few minutes before 11.00pm. I had my watch on the table and we were watching the hand complete the last minute before eleven and arguing among ourselves that, if nothing happened by then, we should probably be alright until dawn.

Exactly at the hour by my watch a most terrific bombardment opened on us. We were up on the firing step in a moment and saw that we were having a repeat performance of the four o'clock strafe but much increased and with the addition of a shrapnel barrage over the front line. I decided at once to break the rule and put up the SOS, which was a rifle grenade rocket which threw up three lights, red over green over yellow: these descended slowly in parachute. In less than a minute our artillery opened up, first one battery and then a whole crowd putting down a magnificent barrage on no man's land. A minute later the enemy shrapnel barrage lifted off our front line and joined the box barrage. Our barrage was therefore down only a minute before the Boche intended to enter our trenches.

We saw no raiders. Whether they intended coming or not I do not know but certainly they could not have come had they desired. The firing on both sides continued until 11.30pm when I sent word for our artillery to cease. At 11.45pm the Boche stopped too. I then sent Jones out with a patrol to search the racecourse for any enemy wounded but he soon returned and said that there were none to be seen. This rather disappointed me as I had hoped to obtain some identifications so I sent Nickel and Dawson out as well. Hardly was the strafe over before the CO himself was up: he had started out soon after it had begun since he could get no news, our phone being off. Together we went round the whole line and saw that a lot of work would have to be done before daylight to make it anything approaching safe. Also we had a good number of casualties, particularly among the platoon of C Company who came and manned the trench at company headquarters during the storm. After seeing these fellows safely away I wrote out a report of the whole occurrence. I sent in my report the following morning and got into a bad row with brigade headquarters for sending up the SOS without seeing the enemy advancing. Colonel Watson, though rather perturbed, takes my view.

Junior officers were clearly not expected to show any initiative or break the rules. Brigadier Stanley was, like Colonel Douglas, away on leave at the time. The brigade's temporary commanding officer, Brigadier Norman, visited the front line the following day and almost certainly hauled Eric over the coals. Two days later, however, the 30th Division's commanding officer, General Williams, sent the battalion a letter of congratulations in which he commended in particular the prompt action of the forward company commander. Eric was delighted to be vindicated. 'One up for Brigade', he wrote in his dairy. As he told his parents it was not the only time that he ruffled feathers.

I am afraid I am getting rather a name for myself with the powers that be. My methods are Territorial and not New Army. We are always getting notes round asking why such a thing was or was not done. I usually manage in my reply to clear myself and get in a nasty one in return so they are getting more cautious now. I got an awful strafing one day for refusing to allow staff officers from another brigade around my trenches. I quoted several orders and stated that I was in charge in my part of the line and would not allow anyone in the line without I was warned of their visit by our own people: they might or might not be what they said they were. I heard no more of it but was advised of their visit the next time. Incidents such as this are occurring daily and I am getting rid of a few practices which seem to have grown here. If I am sent home as incompetent shortly, don't be surprised. I shall be glad, however, to get back to a real battalion again some day.

Meanwhile Eric had his orders to carry out his own raid on the German trenches to discover the identity, strength, and disposition of the enemy's forces and to kill as many of them as possible. Five days after the German raid, on the night of Tuesday, 3 July, he sent out two raiding parties under Dawson and Jones. Both had to be abandoned not just because of the brightness of the moon but also, so Eric believed, because a raid earlier that night by the 17th Battalion on their right had alerted the enemy, who had then withdrawn from and shelled their own front line. Although both raiding parties returned safely Eric could not get a consistent or coherent account from either of them.

Not long afterwards a runner arrived with the news that the leader of the 17th Battalion's raiding party, Lieutenant Aidan Chavasse, was missing and believed wounded in front of the enemy wire. Aidan's brother Bernard, the battalion's medical officer, and his commanding officer, Captain Torrey, were among those already out looking for him. Eric took a few men out to join the search but, as he later said, 'it was impossible to search thoroughly and one could only listen for a cry'. Chavasse was found in a shell-hole later that night by 2nd Lieutenant Peters and Lance-Corporal Dixon. Peters, however, was killed when he went back for help to carry him in; and Dixon, who had remained behind to bandage his wounds, eventually had to go back himself. However, when he returned with a stretcher party, he was unable to find him again and was forced to retire at daybreak. Although further attempts were made later that day Chavasse was never found. It was thought at the time that the enemy had probably found him and taken him in.

25-year old Aidan Chavasse was the youngest of the four sons of the Bishop of Liverpool, all of whom were serving on the Western Front in the summer of 1917. At the outbreak of war he had thrown in his studies at Oxford to join the 11th Battalion of the King's Liverpool Regiment, a pioneer battalion whose job was to construct trenches, dug-outs, and the like. Keen to see more action he had only joined his brother Bernard in the 17th Battalion in April. His two other brothers, the twins Christopher and Noel, were seven years older than him. They had gone up to Oxford together where they both won athletics Blues before competing in the 400 metres at the London Olympics in 1908. While Christopher followed his father into the Church, joining the Army Chaplain's department at the outbreak of war, Noel trained as a doctor and had joined the Liverpool Scottish territorials in 1913 while working at the city's Royal Southern Hospital. By the summer of 1917 he had a distinguished war record in the Royal Army Medical Corps, having been awarded the Military Cross in June 1915 and then the Victoria Cross a year later at the Somme when, under heavy fire and in spite of being wounded himself, he brought in 20 badly-wounded men from no man's land.

As stalwarts of their local church Harry and Alice knew the bishop well and, like many of his congregation, were concerned for Aidan's safety. There had still been no news of him when they wrote to Eric two weeks later to ask him what he knew.

It is rather strange that you should mention the bishop's son. My company was holding the line just to the left of where he was; and the part of the Boche line where he was hit was not more than 150 yards from my bit of trench. Every night we were sending out fighting patrols to try to get prisoners and it was on one of these that Chavasse was hit. He did not return with his party and several attempts were made before dawn to get him in as he was lying in no man's land. The next night I attempted a small raid in front of my sector while they tried to get him in again but without success. I personally feel sure that he was taken in by the Boche as everywhere was searched in spite of the machine-gun fire that was put up by the Hun. It was at a rotten spot – in fact I think without a doubt that it was the worst half mile of line in the whole front – so you may be sure I had a somewhat busy time.

In time it became clear that Aidan had not been taken prisoner. His body was never found, and his name is now one of the 55,000 engraved on the Memorial to the Missing at Ypres' Menin Gate. Another 35,000 names are engraved on the walls of Tyne Cot cemetery near Passchendaele.

It is impossible now to comprehend the range and depth of emotions that the bishop and his family must have felt that summer. It was a war that affected all, regardless of their status, rank, or position in society. Only a month later, when the bishop had still received no definite news of Aidan, he was told of the death of a second son. At the start of Haig's offensive Noel Chavasse would stay at his aid post for two days without sleep or rest to tend to the wounded even though he had again been seriously wounded and was in intense pain. Wounded a second time when his aid post was struck by a shell early on the morning of 2 August, he died two days later at a casualty clearing station in Brandhoek. He was posthumously awarded a bar to his Victoria Cross, the only man to be so honoured in the First World War. Bernard was wounded in the leg in the same battle and was awarded the Military Cross: and, at the end of the month, Christopher was also awarded the Military Cross for his part in recovering the wounded at Bullecourt in July. King George V was among the many who sent letters of condolence to the bishop.

After a week in the front line Eric's company was moved back into reserve at Ritz Street; and, two nights later, the battalion was relieved for a fortnight's rest. Eric's luck again held on their march back to Ouderdom. He usually went round to the north of Zillebeke Lake because it was less shelled but this time, for a reason he could not explain, he decided to take his company out to the south. The 17th Battalion had a bad time when they took the northern route; and a number of men were again wounded when a solitary 12-inch shell fell on the platoon of another company when it made the mistake of falling out at a crossroads.

The following day the Pals boarded a train for St Omer and Watten. From there a three-hour march brought them at midnight to the small village of Recques-sur-Hem. They were now 35 miles from Ypres and only 14 from Calais. As Eric told his parents when he wrote home the next day it was another all too brief vision of pastoral heaven.

The country we are now in is by far the best I have had the luck to strike in France, chiefly because it is not in the least like France but England. One might imagine oneself on the borders of Wales or in the hilly, wooded parts of the south of England: beautifully developed valleys, surrounded by low hills, topped with woods of fir and bracken and here and there a bare top crowned with an old ruin. The houses are substantial and their occupants homely and offering welcome to all. The roads are good and overhung with tall trees. When one has spent about six months in the poorer parts of France and among its people, one is able to realize what a rich and a poor country are. The difference would have been incredible to me a year ago, and to get back to a state of real civilisation again means a great deal. I have a room in an estaminet and our mess is there also. A billiard table provides us with some recreation in the evenings although the cushions are not A1 and the surface is somewhat corrugated.

I am sorry to say I have lost the ring which Mother gave me in England and, when I tell you later where I lost it, you will not blame me for not trying to find it again. It must have slipped off as I was making my way through some thick undergrowth. I lost it once before but was able to find it again: it was rather loose-fitting. Still I don't require anything to remind me of you all as I am always thinking of you.

7

The Battle of Pilckem Ridge

31 July – 3 August 1917

Good God, did we really send men to fight in that?
Remark attributed to Haig's Chief of Staff, General Kiggell,
on a visit to the battlefield

On 19 June, a fortnight after the Battle of Messines, Haig presented the final plans for his Flanders offensive to the newly-formed Committee on War Policy in Downing Street. He had always been an unconvincing speaker; and this time his ambitious plans lacked the full support of his staff. The committee – which comprised Lloyd George, Lord Curzon, Lord Milner, and General Smuts – examined them critically. With the French unlikely to play any further part there was a growing belief that it might be better to sit out the rest of the year and wait for the Americans to arrive in the spring.

Lloyd George, although chastened by his earlier advocacy of Nivelle, was unconvinced by Haig's proposals. As an easterner he was still keen to transfer troops to the Italian front in order to take Austria out of the war. However German U-boats remained the greatest single threat to the country's survival; and it was still too early to be certain that the introduction of convoys in May would be a success. When the Prime Minister asked the First Sea Lord for his advice, Admiral Jellicoe was adamant that, unless the U-boat bases in Belgium were destroyed, Britain would be forced to surrender in 1918 due to the unsustainable level of her shipping losses. He refused to back down when challenged on this and, in doing so, probably did more than anyone to swing the argument in favour of Haig. That, however, did not prevent a high level of brinkmanship over the next few days and weeks. After the generals had left the meeting Lloyd George proposed that, while the committee should restate its misgivings, it should leave the final decision to Haig and Robertson – but on the clear understanding that, if the offensive did not go according to plan, it would be called off immediately. The committee confirmed its decision two days later but held back from giving the plan its formal political approval. Meanwhile Haig had no choice but to proceed at full speed with his preparations.

The committee had still to give its final approval four weeks later. On 19 July it asked for further clarification of the limits to be placed on the first phase of the offensive. To avoid a repeat of the Somme it was keen to ensure that any decision to call off the offensive could not be challenged. The committee's final approval would not be given until 25 July, the day on which Haig had originally planned to launch the offensive and three days after he had started the final stage of his preliminary bombardment. General Gough, whose Fifth Army would lead the offensive, then requested a last-minute postponement: his supplies were not yet in position and he had had to make some final adjustments to his plans after the last hope of any French support was withdrawn. Haig agreed to a delay first to 28 July and then finally to 31 July. It was not, he thought, the way to fight a war. Two days before the start of the offensive he vented his frustration in a personal letter to Lord Derby in which he poured scorn on the government's failure to back his plan wholeheartedly at what he thought was a critical moment and compared the mean-spirited and shabby treatment of himself with the naïve and unstinting support that had previously been given to Nivelle.[1]

The Liverpool Pals had started their own preparations for the offensive as soon as they arrived at Recques-sur-Hem. There was now only three weeks to go. At nearby Tournehem they again dug shallow practice trenches to replicate the German lines. Then, to the dismay of the local inhabitants and with General Gough in attendance, the whole division carried out a full dress-rehearsal of the attack using live ammunition with tank and artillery support. According to Eric, 'acre upon acre of corn ripe for cutting is being trampled down and ruined. It seems wrong but I suppose it must be.' At least the local farmers would be compensated for their loss. When the battalion finally left the village Eric was himself presented by an old lady with an invoice for 3.80 francs to replace a broken window in one of his officers' bedrooms. He was so surprised by her elaborate receipt, in which she addressed him as Monsieur le Colonel, that he sent it home as a souvenir.

When they were not training the Pals were kept busy with the usual sporting competitions and concerts. Eric swam in the village millpond and was invited to dinner both by the mayor of the village, an Englishman born in Calais, and by his friends in the Liverpool Rifles who were billeted in the adjacent village. 'They did not recognise me at first with my three stars and brass buttons', he told his parents 'but it was a treat to see some decent people again and to see some old faces. The difference between the officers and men of the two battalions is very marked. I wish I was back with them even if it was only in the ranks.' He was again piqued because, with Major Campbell Watson back from leave, Captain Bickersteth had resumed command of D Company shortly after their arrival in Recques. The problem was resolved by Eric being given command of C Company, a move that was made awkward because its acting commander was a lieutenant senior to him. Although his opinion of the Pals continued to swing with his moods he was sorry to lose what he thought he had made into a crack company.

> I sometimes wonder whether it is a good thing always to have a good company. When I was with D Company the divisional general wanted to see a company carry out a practice attack on new lines so, of course, our brigade was detailed to do it. Of course the brigade detailed this battalion and the battalion detailed D Company for the job. It was a great honour and all that but it meant more work and that's the worst of it. Still we managed to please the old lady and he went away thinking, I suppose, that he had done a good day's work.

He would miss his men. He told his former employer, Mr. Temple, when he wrote to thank him and his wife for their recent parcel of food and soap, that 'it is like starting again for by now I know the names of all the men in my old company and the family histories of most of them. However I am now used to taking on jobs that I don't at first like.' C Company, he thought, had rather fallen to bits since its commanding officer, Captain Geoffrey Sutton, had been sent home on sick leave in April. He had less than three weeks to bring it back up

1   Letter from Sir Douglas Haig to Lord Derby, 29 July 1917, in R. Churchill, *Lord Derby, 'King of Lancashire'*, p. 286.

to scratch before taking it into battle.

The Pals started back towards the salient on 19 July when almost 100 buses and sundry lorries took them as far as Steenvoorde. By the time they marched on to the Belgian border five days later the final phase of Haig's preliminary bombardment was already under way. In its last nine days 4,000,000 shells, weighing a total of more than 100,000 tons, would be fired from 3,000 guns at a rate of more than 300 shells a minute.

The Third Battle of Ypres, or Passchendaele, as Haig's offensive has become known, was a series of battles that began with the Battle of Pilckem Ridge on 31 July and ended more than three months later with the capture of the evocatively-named 'valley of the Passion' on a ridge seven miles to the north-east of the city. In spite of the lack of time the detailed planning for the first stage of the offensive had been meticulous as usual. In a process that must have been repeated across every unit the 89th Brigade's final typewritten orders ran to more than 50 foolscap pages. The brigade major distributed 17 copies which were sent to the four battalion commanders, to the brigade's machine gun company, trench mortar battery, and signals unit, and to the artillery, the brigades on either side and in front of them, and to divisional headquarters. It was a lot of reading. Every aspect of the attack was addressed, separate sections covering co-operation with aircraft, communications by lamp, heliograph, rocket, and power buzzer, the use of gas and maps, consolidation of territory gained, traffic control in the trenches, the collection of stragglers, the evacuation of the wounded, the rounding up of prisoners, and the burial of the dead. The men were reminded that, if they were caught filching a memento from the body of a dead friend, it would be considered an act of theft from that man's relatives. They each had to carry 120 rounds of ammunition, two Mills grenades, an entrenching tool and four sandbags as well as their box respirator, gas mask, and waterbottle. They were also issued with one day's emergency rations comprising a pound each of preserved meat and biscuit, three ounces of jam, two ounces of sugar, 3/8th ounce of tea, and a quarter tin of 'M and V' (meat and vegetable ration, otherwise known as Maconochie stew). Water and charcoal for cooking was to be provided in the assembly trenches and the 20th Battalion would also be issued with 166 pairs of wire-cutters and 16 pairs of hedging gloves. As an administrative exercise it was impeccably managed: nothing was left to chance. Everything had been taken into account except the possibility of failure.

It was still dark when, shortly before 4.00am on 31 July, General Gough's Fifth Army, spearheaded by three of the four divisions in Jacobs' II Corps, launched their assault east along the Menin Road towards the German-held high ground at Gheluvelt Ridge. The 30th Division were at the point of the spear with orders to advance north–east from Sanctuary Wood across the Menin Road to the southern edge of Polygon Wood. A series of lines – Blue, Black, and Green – had been drawn on the map to mark the objectives to be taken by each successive wave of the assault. The 90th and 21st brigades would lead off, advancing in two waves through the Blue line to the Black line, which ran south from Glencorse Wood past Inverness Copse and across the Menin Road to Dumbarton Lakes. Two battalions from the 89th Brigade, the Pals' 17th and 20th battalions, advancing four hours later, would then leap-frog them and push on to the final objective of the Green line, which ran south for 1,250 yards from the corner of Polygon Wood to the Menin Road. If everything went according to plan an attempt might even be made to reach a fourth or Red line. The first wave was, however, held up by determined German defences on the Blue line at Stirling Castle and, when the Pals tried to push through, they were pinned down by savage German machine-gun fire before they even reached their final positions of assembly.

Troops inspect an old gun position in Sanctuary Wood, 25 October 1917. In
the foreground are sandbagged trenches; and in the background on the left are
the remains of Stirling Castle. (© Australian War Memorial, E01135)

Although their nerves had been badly shaken by the loss of the Messines ridge in June
the Germans had taken advantage of the subsequent delay to adjust their defensive scheme
so that it could absorb a major assault without buckling. Applying the same tactics of elastic
'defence in depth' as had lain behind the design of the Hindenburg Line, they built hundreds
of concrete pill-boxes to the rear of their lines and established a series of strategically-placed
forward machine-gun posts to protect what would now be a lightly-held front line. The
effectiveness of these tactics was borne out by events on 31 July. The 20th Battalion's four
company commanders all subsequently gave consistent accounts of their experiences when
they came up against heavy machine-gun fire and started to sustain casualties. They saw
little if any evidence of the troops who had gone before them, and those that they did find
were usually in small isolated and unorganised groups; they saw none of the red and yellow
flags that were to have been used to signal when objectives had been gained; and they saw no
sign of the enemy, dead or alive, either then or at any time over the next few days.

The brigade had been allocated a number of tanks to help it as and when the attack was
held up and to assist it in mopping up enemy strong points. They were of no use, their six-
pound shells proving ineffective against concrete. The commander of tank B27, 'Bloodstone',
reported back that he had been unable to get beyond the edge of Inverness Copse 'where
there were a large number of concrete cupola machine gun emplacements against which he

German armoured cupola and anti-tank gun near Stirling Castle with a disabled tank in the background, 20 September 1917. (© Australian War Memorial, E01411)

was unable to make any impression and that his tank had been set on fire'.[2]

Major Campbell Watson, who was commanding the 20th Battalion while Colonel Douglas was away on leave, reported back to brigade headquarters that any further advance would be futile and that he was therefore holding his position. He and the Pals hurriedly dug themselves in in a strong position near Stirling Castle. As at Arras four months earlier they would remain there for four wet and hungry days in the foulest of conditions as the weather deteriorated into heavy and persistent rain. More rain would fall in the first fortnight of August than in the whole of November, normally the wettest month of the year. The final delays in launching the offensive had cost the Pals dearly. By the time of its relief on the night of 3 August the brigade had lost 682 men: 112 officers and men had been killed with 494 wounded and another 76 missing. Among the dead was 2nd Lieutenant George Nickel whom Eric had sent out on patrol a month earlier. Major Campbell Watson, although wounded, had remained at his post: he would be awarded the Distinguished Service Order and, on his return from leave in the autumn, he was promoted to Lieutenant-Colonel and given command of the 17th Battalion.

Some at GHQ had argued before the battle that the 30th Division was no longer up to scratch after its losses on the Somme and at Arras and that it should be replaced with a fresher division. On balance it had been felt that it was too late to make a change. However, once relieved, the Pals would play no further part in the major battles of the offensive. Two days after their relief they were moved south with the 30th Division and transferred to IX

2   Report on Operations at Ypres, 31 July to 3/4 August, 1917, 20th Battalion King's Liverpool Regiment War Diary, The National Archives, WO 95/2335/4.

Corps in Plumer's Second Army. The preliminary order for the move had been issued at 9.15pm on 3 August, a quarter of an hour before the Pals had started their withdrawal from Stirling Castle.

General Gough established a Court of Inquiry as soon as the battle was over. He wanted a full investigation and explanation of the division's failure to capture the Black Line on 31 July and, in addition, an answer as to why the 90th Brigade had fallen short of its objectives and two of its battalions had lost their direction. It had been reported that they had mistaken Chateau Wood to their north, which had been captured by another division within an hour of the attack starting, for Glencorse Wood to their east, which was their objective on the Black Line and which remained heavily defended by enemy machine gun emplacements. General Williams would state in his evidence that only two companies had lost their way and that a clerical error had caused the misunderstanding; and the final report of the court reduced this further to 'elements which might have amounted to two platoons'.[3]

The three-man court was convened under the presidency of Lieutenant-General Sir Edward Fanshawe, the commander of V Corps, on 10 August and, after taking evidence from more than 40 witnesses over four days, published its findings on 19 August. It found that the division had made a determined and gallant attempt to achieve its objectives and that no blame should be attached either to its commanding officer or to the commanders of the 90th and 21st brigades. The main reason for the failure of the attack, it concluded, was the appalling state of the ground – and of Sanctuary Wood in particular – which made it impossible for the infantry to keep up with the creeping barrage. The darkness and the formations adopted by many units as the only way to traverse the broken ground only added to the ease with which units became separated and lost direction: General Williams had claimed in his written submission that 'the ground was so boggy that men could only struggle through it by pulling each other out'.[4] The evidence presented to the court also included an urgent hand-written note that he had sent to Corps headquarters on the day before the battle asking for the speed of the creeping barrage to be reduced from 25 to 20 yards a minute due to the poor weather: it was the equivalent of the infantry taking five minutes to cover 100 yards and even that, he later admitted, was too fast. The Corps commander's response had been that it was too late to make such a change. The court reminded General Williams in its concluding remarks that he should have taken more definitive action to ensure that the enemy's strong-points were shelled and that 'the preparation of barrage plans by higher authority does not absolve divisional commanders from full responsibility to obtain a barrage meeting all their requirements'.[5]

The company commanders in the 20th Battalion had their own explanation for why some units might have lost their way. They had found it impossible to take accurate compass bearings. By the end of August divisional headquarters had ordered all officers to provide themselves with oil-bath compasses. They were, so Eric told his parents, a new idea for infantry compasses, being very steady and therefore easily set 'when in the trenches where lumps of metal are flying around'. Although Eric had already ordered one through Ordnance, he asked them to find out if Chadburns in Liverpool would take his old one back. He had already written to tell them that 'the battalion distinguished themselves in the last show'.

3   Court of inquiry on conduct of 30th Division on 31 July 1917, 30th Division War Diary, The National Archives, WO 95/2312/3.
4   Ibid.
5   Ibid.

Perhaps you remember that the whole thing depended upon our capturing a certain piece of high ground and, in particular, one part of it. The attack on this failed at first and this battalion turned out of their direction and took it and held it. The battalion was mentioned in a special Army Order of the Day.

That at least was what he had been told. He had not been there to lead C Company into battle. His turn for leave had finally come up a week before the battle.

8

South of Ypres

August – December 1917

I have just realized what an infernal nuisance this war is: still it might be a great deal worse.

Eric's letter home, 14 August 1917

E ric had first mentioned leave to his parents at the end of March. With officers entitled to home leave every three months his first turn should have coincided with the start of the Battle of Arras. However casualties, officer shortages, and the frequent closing of the leave books meant that infantry officers rarely got more than two leaves a year. Each took his turn in strict rotation. At least they were more fortunate than their men whose opportunities for leave were far fewer.

By the end of May leave had become a regular topic in Eric's letters. By then he was seventh on the list. However the prospect was still remote as there was only one other officer in the company at the time and neither could be spared. By the beginning of July he was up to fourth: and his parents began to worry that, if he came home in the middle of the month, they might be away on holiday in Blackpool. Two weeks later he was up to second place; and then finally, on 20 July, only nine days after he had been given command of C Company and only eleven days before the start of the offensive, he was told that he had been granted a fortnight's leave from 25 July. 'Too good to be true', he wrote in his diary, 'but it seems strange that, having trained the company for the attack, I am not to participate. However orders provide that one company commander is to be left out and, as it is my turn for leave, I am the lucky one'.

He had mixed feelings about leaving his men at such a crucial time, and not least because he had previously complained to his parents about shirkers. 'One usually finds that there are plenty of officers in the company when we are having an easy time out of the line', he had told them in March, 'but the number dwindles down when we are in the line and, when a patrol is required, it is usually a question of one of the same three of us every time.' He would not be the only officer to miss the battle. A quarter of a battalion's officers and men were usually kept out of any battle; and, for a variety of reasons, only five of the 16 officers in the 20th Battalion's four companies on the first day of the Battle of Arras were involved again on 31 July. This time, however, both Brigadier Stanley and Colonel Douglas were also away on leave; and it is hard to believe that the absence of the brigade and battalion commander did not have at least some effect on the morale of the officers and men left behind.

Brigadier Stanley had finally agreed to take three months' leave at the beginning of June, but only after he had secured a guarantee that he would be sent back to the 89th Brigade. He would not return until the end of September. For Colonel Douglas, however, it was his second home leave since re-joining the battalion at the beginning of March. This time it coincided with, and perhaps was the result of, his selection as vice-captain of an England Army cricket XI for a one-day match at Lords on 14 July against an Australian Imperial Forces XI. The match was in aid of St Dunstan's Hostel, now Blind Veterans UK, which had been established in 1915 to care for blinded servicemen. Captain Pelham 'Plum' Warner, who was working at the War Office at the time, captained a strong English side against an Australian team that was led by Warrant Officer Charlie Macartney, the 'Governor General', who had made his debut for Australia against England in 1907 and was recently arrived in England with the Australian artillery. The Army won the match by 32 runs with Douglas scoring 20 runs and taking one wicket. He returned after the game and would be back in France by 3 August when he signed off the battalion diary for July. Otherwise all but one of the remaining team went on to represent the Army and Navy in a match against a combined Australian and South African side at Lords on 18 August.

Perhaps it was no bad thing that Major Campbell Watson had been left to lead the 20th Battalion into battle. Not only did he come from Liverpool, where his family owned a warehouse business near the waterfront, but he had also been with the Pals from the start and led from the front. 'It usually happens that he is in command of the battalion when there is anything doing', Eric told Mr. Temple, who would almost certainly have known the Watson family though business.

Eric left the battalion at the Belgian border on the evening of 24 July. After a four-mile ride to the Officers' Club in Poperinghe he caught a train to Calais shortly after midnight, arriving there early the following morning. He caught a boat back to England after lunch and was met at Victoria Station by his sister, Judy. After a night out in town they took the train back to Ormskirk the following morning for eight nights with their parents at the Ruff.

They left home again on 3 August to spend a final night in London. That evening, as the Pals were being relieved after their four days on the battlefield, Eric and his sister were enjoying a performance of Chu Chin Chow at His Majesty's Theatre. A big-budget musical based on the story of Ali Baba and the Forty Thieves, it would become one of the longest-running shows in the West End. It was especially popular with soldiers home on leave not only for its catchy songs and big dance routines but, more obviously, for its chorus of exotic and scantily-clad houris. That night the production was celebrating its first anniversary on the stage with new costumes. Pictures appeared in the Tatler the following month under a headline describing them as 'very suitable for the sultry climate of Old Bagdad'. In fact they were so suitable that they were brought to the attention of the Lord Chamberlain, who was responsible for theatre censorship and was now called upon to investigate complaints of indecency resulting from the dancers' lack of clothes and lewd movements.

Eric left early the following morning. After a night in Calais he caught a train back to Poperinghe. By a stroke of luck it happened to pass the train bringing the Pals out of the salient and, given their usual slow crawl, he was able to jump from one to the other with his kit. He was therefore back with the battalion by the time it disembarked near Steenvoorde. Six days later the Pals were moved to Bailleul for what they were told would be three weeks' rest and training before they were sent to a quiet part of the line.

Although they were now well behind the lines their camp was beside three aerodromes which were regularly subjected to enemy bombing. Their time was spent with the usual mix of training, working parties and sports. Each battalion held its own sports day as a preliminary to a grand brigade sports day which included football, tug of war, bomb throwing and sack races. Lieutenant Muir, who was almost certainly the officer that Eric had 'bumped' when

NEW DRESSES FOR "CHU CHIN CHOW"
Very Suitable to the Sultry Climate of Old Bagdad.

Photographs by F. W. Burford

THE COSTUMES OF SOME LOVELY HOURIS WHICH WERE INTRODUCED UPON THE
ANNIVERSARY OF THE FAMOUS PLAY AT HIS MAJESTY'S

Mr. Oscar Asche's great reconstruction of the days of Haroun al Raschid, "Chu Chin Chow," reached its first anniversary last Friday week and is still drawing crowded and delighted audiences to His Majesty's and may yet see its third birthday. Mr. Oscar Asche is one of the greatest manufacturers of Eastern atmosphere that the stage has ever seen, and fanciful as some of his colour schemes may perhaps sometimes appear they are not very far wide of things that can be seen to-day in almost any of the big native cities of Ajmere and Rajputana

Some of the new costumes for Chu Chin Chow that were introduced on its first anniversary
on the London stage, *The Tatler*, 12 September 1917. (Mary Evans Picture Library)

was given the command of C Company in July, had been wounded while leading it in the battle; and Captain Sutton, returned from sick leave, was once again in charge. Eric did not seem to mind: he and Geoffrey Sutton got on well and he was assured that he would not be losing his captaincy. Like many young officers, however, he needed time to re-adjust to life at the front after his first home leave.

I have been wandering about like one lost during the past ten days but I am now becoming more accustomed to it. I have just realized what an infernal nuisance this war is: still it might be a great deal worse.

My programme today was as follows. I was awakened gently at six o'clock and awakened more rudely at a quarter past and finally got up at half past. I had a bath in little more than a quart of water and was on parade at seven, then breakfast at eight and parade from 9.00am to 12.30pm. I then rode to a place about three miles away to a Corps School to hear a lecture at 2.30pm. I came back and inspected the company and put them through their work for to-morrow's inspection from 4.00pm to 6.00pm; then tea and a concert by our own experts; and then dinner and a walk of about ten minutes into the town for a game of billiards at the officers' club with Sutton. Here I am now in a tent painted to look like a clump of trees, sitting on the end of a bed made of wire netting and canvas on a wooden frame. A candle inside a biscuit tin which is continually going out completes the picture except for Sutton playing selections from Chu Chin Chow on a tin whistle. I suppose you will say to yourselves 'What more does he want?' Well – very little.

This is quite nice country although only about five miles from the line. There is an aerodrome quite nearby from which planes are always flying. There were 20 flying quite low a short time ago and it was impossible to hear oneself speak. I don't think we shall go into the line for some time. We may go for a few days but hear we are going down the line for a month or two. At any rate we shall not ourselves be doing any more fighting until next spring although this of course only applies to us. I am putting all my money on the Americans for the spring if nothing happens before. Our GOC General Plumer is inspecting us to-morrow. It is now 10.15pm so will say Bon Nuit. Love to Guy.

The following day, as Gough's court of inquiry was taking its last day of evidence on the 30th Division's recent performance, the 89th Brigade was drawn up for inspection by General Plumer, to whose Second Army it was now attached. As Plumer rode down the ranks, Eric recalled, 'he stopped in front of me and put his monocle in his eye to look at me but it dropped out so he passed on, having forgotten to say anything. Perhaps it was just as well.'

The following day, 16 August, saw the start of the Battle of Langemarck, the second stage of the offensive, when Gough's Fifth Army pushed on to the north-east of Ypres. On the second day of the battle Eric rode the three miles from Bailleul to Mont Noir to watch its progress. Along with Mont des Chats and Mount Kemmel the 500-foot Mont Noir was one of three hills to the west of the Messines ridge that gave the British a good if distant view of the salient. Eric and his fellow officers became regular visitors to the estaminet, or café, at its summit where they could see the coast from its French windows. 'With the aid of glasses I could see some 70 miles of battlefield', he told his parents. 'It was a wonderful sight – villages disappearing in dust on the far side of the broad desolate line that marks the race-course – the race-course is what used to be called and what was no man's land'.

The Battle of Langemarck would be no more successful than the Battle of Pilckem Ridge. With Lloyd George now trying to halt the offensive and transfer troops to the Italian front Haig called his generals together for a review of their strategy. Gough and Rawlinson, who commanded the Fourth Army to the north of Ypres, both felt that, as a breakout to the Belgian ports no longer appeared realistic, the offensive should be called off. Plumer, to whom Haig had spoken privately before the meeting, disagreed. He was still confident of success but argued for a change of approach. Haig closed the meeting by asking him to take over responsibility for the offensive. Plumer accepted but asked for more time to complete his plans before going back into action.

After 12 days at Bailleul the Pals started to move back slowly towards the front, first to a hutted camp at Locre and then, six days later, to Kemmel. As they moved back their training became more practical, including live grenade throwing and a major exercise to rehearse attacking under cover of a barrage. Whatever the reason for the training they would not go back into battle before the end of the year. By the end of the month they were back in the line in a quiet but uncomfortable sector south of Ypres which ran north-west from Wytschaete to the Ypres-Comines canal at Hollebeke. Subject only to minor movements and periods out of the line they would stay there until the middle of November. As part of the area that had only been recovered from the Germans in June after the Battle of Messines its defences, as Brigadier Stanley recognised, were as yet extremely poor.

> The whole system of holding the trenches was rather different to anything we had had before. Up till now our old way of holding the trenches had been a continuous front and support lines with communications trenches, but here, owing to the nature of the ground, which was in a terrible state, it was impossible to have regular trenches, and the line was held more or less in small posts of about one NCO and six men in front, and posts of rather bigger dimensions behind them. There were practically no communication trenches, and all movement had to be out in the open.[1]

It would be a major task for the Pals to bring them up to scratch. A large part of their daily routine would now be spent providing working parties, often of more than 200 men, to support the Royal Engineers and their tunnelling companies – digging and revetting the front line strong points and the support lines behind them, wiring no man's land, sandbagging dugouts, clearing roads, and creating lines of communication. In October Eric had to oversee the digging of a drain to relieve the water-logging in Ravine Wood. Dug in a single night by 170 men it was 160 yards long, 4 feet deep, and 7 feet wide at the top before tapering down to a foot at the bottom. By then the brigade had established a routine of rotating its four battalions every five days. The first battalion would man the front at Hollebeke in what was, to begin with, just a series of ten posts in a 'shell-hole line'; the second would be in support almost a mile behind between White Chateau and Ravine Wood; and the last two would be in reserve in positions west of Wytschaete. It was an area where both sides were on the defensive but were keen not to give up any ground. Apart from the occasional raid there was little fighting on the ground: artillery and aircraft, however,

---

1   Brigadier-General F C Stanley, *The History of the 89th Brigade 1914 – 1918,* pp. 228–9.

ensured that there was continuous activity in the air. When Eric went up from Kemmel for the first time to reconnoitre he thought it 'a remarkably quiet spot, even quieter than the place I was first at in the winter'. He would soon discover that it was not so pleasant.

> The battalion move tonight into position at Hollebeke. Things seem to be getting more lively and a daily feature is the shooting down of one or more of our captive observation balloons (sausages). There is a whole string of them behind our lines and the Boche uses long range guns on them but his airmen are more effective. When shelling he appears to use a kind of heavy shrapnel and it is sometimes healthy to wear one's tin hat when these are raining down – the shot seems like ¾-inch steel balls. When attacking the sausages by air the Boche plane usually comes over above a convenient cloud and then swoops down firing his incendiary bullets. As a rule he is successful if he succeeds in getting thus far and the giant balloon bursts immediately into flames – the observers jumping overboard with their parachutes. Some days many enemy planes come over and there is a general panic so that one can count perhaps 20 parachutes descending at once.

Eric had spent most of August without a proper job. He was still happy to be Sutton's second-in-command and, although he was no longer the battalion's Lewis gun officer, he was kept busy, telling his parents at the end of the month that 'I am getting all kinds of jobs in the battalion nowadays being the surplus captain'. It is likely that he also took over the battalion's musketry training as he said that he was now 'the only officer in the battalion who knows anything of musketry' and asked them to send his musketry books from home to refresh his memory. When, however, Sutton broke his ankle playing football, almost certainly helping C Company to a 5-0 victory over D Company, and was sent to the Duchess of Westminster's Hospital at Le Touquet to recover, it was not Eric who was given command of the company. He had already been lined up for another job. On his return to Kemmel after his first reconnaissance he was asked to stand in for Quartermaster Roberts when he went home on leave. He wrote immediately to give his parents the good news.

> I suppose you are picturing me living in a shell hole surrounded by thousands of shells. As a matter of fact I am out of it. The quartermaster is going on a month's leave shortly and I am to take over in his absence: so I shall have a really cushy job for some six weeks to come. I suppose they cannot find anybody who knows anything about it so I, knowing least of all, am in for it. I hear I am given it for a rest. I don't quite know why I need the rest. Still I shall have quite an interesting time dealing with the Kidney Stealers, occasionally known as the Army Service Corps.
>
> We have a grand position here on the top of a ridge. We can see the Boche for miles back and he cannot see us at all. When up there we can see our artillery shelling his back areas and towns and we hardly get a shell in return. The Boche is feeling things rather rotten and has had strict orders to economise on ammunition on account of shortages. Of course we know all sorts of things about him. I myself have seen some of his secret orders: we know the division, regiment, and battalion of the people opposite us and even the names of their officers. One company commander of theirs was holding the line opposite me before but now that I am a quartermonger I shall not have pleasure of seeing him.

Pack mules passing dead animals and a wrecked artillery limber during the
Battle of Pilckem Ridge, 31 July 1917. (© Imperial War Museum, Q5773)

Eric's new job would not be the sinecure that he had expected. Based at Kemmel he had to make sure that the battalion was supplied and fed while it was in the line. This meant accompanying the transport officer each night on the 12-mile round trip to take the mules and ration limbers up to the front, arranging for further supplies or any special work to be done in Kemmel, and securing and preparing billets for the men when they were relieved. The first stretch of their nightly journey, from Kemmel to Wytschaete, was known as Suicide Road. It only got worse after that. The water-logged ground and the lack of communication trenches mean that the journey had to be made in the open on duckboard paths. Before reporting his job done to battalion headquarters he had to ensure that the rations for the companies in the front line were taken as far forward as possible and left, when circumstances allowed, by a fallen tree at the side of the road just before Hollebeke village. After two weeks he told his parents that he had been having 'none too pleasant a time.'

When I said I had a cushy job, I did not know quite what I was in for. A week ago, having been in the line for twelve days, we moved to a different place. Although very quiet in the line it was rather hot just behind. My job has been taking the rations and stores up each night. The place was infested with guns and, when they are all firing at the same time, one's horses are not easy to manage. Though not accompanied by much danger it was nevertheless a tiring job. It is very difficult to find one's way at night when one has no opportunity of seeing the lie of the land by daylight. It is however better than living in a shell-hole for, even if one does not get back until about two in the morning, one has a bed to go to.

I have had one or two rather amusing experiences lately. I arrange to take rations up to within a few hundred yards of the front line on pack mules. This means going across country full of shell-holes with a good chance of losing one's way. One night a mule broke away from its driver and started off across country to the land of the Hun pursued by myself and the driver. Fortunately we captured it in no man's land but not without attracting the attention of several machine guns from which Very lights were sent up. Luckily we got back without any damage.

To-day I have been fixing everybody up in their new billets. I am staying inside as much as possible as I have got the first of my winter colds. It has been coming on for several days now but has been accelerated by a ducking which I got last night. I was taking rations up the line and, when I had unloaded the wagons, I walked forward to headquarters. While going through a wood I slipped in the mud and slid into a 20-foot crater, full of water.

He was lucky to get out alive. With the low water table and the onset of the autumn rains the shell-holes quickly filled with stagnant water and became contaminated with blood and poison gas. Bloated decomposing bodies, animal and human, would eventually float to the surface and explode. Many who were unfortunate enough to slip off the duck-boards could not be rescued and had to be left to drown in the liquid mud.

Troops carrying up duckboards over waterlogged ground near
Pilckem, 10 October 1917. (© Imperial War Museum, Q6049)

Life was however, as Eric recognised, better than living in a shell-hole. He was free for much of the day and he used the time to catch up with friends, reflect on the war, and send his parents detailed accounts of his surroundings and daily routine at Kemmel. Unfortunately the diary, which he had kept since arriving in France and which he later wrote up from rough notes in 1919, stops at the end of August. He tried to take it up again in 1925 but by then he was married with a young son and was busy in the family business. He found time only to add a few brief entries for September. From now on his letters are the only record of his life at the front. Although they are interesting in their own right he usually had the most time to write when there was the least going on.

At the beginning of October he wrote home from Kemmel to wish his mother a happy 46th birthday.

Many happy returns of your birthday, Mother: I only wish that I could be at home to see you. I am alone to-night and am having an evening with Gilbert and Sullivan on the gramophone. I have a song from the Mikado on at present: it is very cheery in this rather desolate place. As I expect we shall be near this village during the winter – either in front of it, in it or behind it – I will tell you a little more about it.

It is, or to be more accurate, it was an agricultural village about half the size of Ormskirk. There is a miniature railway and a tiny railway station – or at least one is led to suppose so from a pile of bricks and railway lines. There are a lot of trees in the village: the prettiest are in an avenue of copper beeches, some of which are lying across the road, and some are gone altogether. There is a brewery and at least a dozen estaminets but none with a roof and some looking proud to have one wall standing. Many of the houses have been strengthened with sandbags and there are loop holes in the walls. There are two beautiful chateaux: one is in the dust while the other is practically untouched save that the main staircase has been blown away and also the bridge over the moat. Of course the furniture is all gone with the exception of an oil painting and a safe. The stables are still left and I understand from my pony that they are very comfortable.

At the back of the village is a beautifully-wooded hill with a tower on top. From the top one can see many miles of battle line. Trained observers with powerful telescopes in concrete shelters watch the Boche all day and call down our artillery fire on the roads when they see him bringing up guns. In the village there is a continuous stream of traffic: Bunny's Corner in Church Street is not a patch on the cross roads here. In what is left of the place we are making ourselves comfortable and are organising both an officers' and a sergeants' club.

Eric also had time to read the papers and followed the news with interest. It was probably the first war where the soldiers fighting it knew what was going on. 'What do you think about the new phase in the Russian situation?' he asked his parents in September as strikes and peasant risings paved the way for Lenin's seizing power in the October Revolution.

It seems very improbable and almost impossible that she will be able to recover herself. Germany will then get the Russian fleet and all the munitions works around Petrograd while all our work there during the past six months will have been wasted. The French Cabinet seems to be somewhat muddled. One had hopes of the end coming through

Austria after Italy's brilliant efforts together with our own shows up here. Our Mess optimist has prophesied an addition of seven years to the existing fourteen to the war's duration. I myself am, in spite of it all, expecting to be able to sheathe my tin opener this year.

He was still feeling confident of a quick end to the war at the beginning of October.

Everyone is expecting the war to be over this year. I hope it will prove correct although one wonders from which direction it will come. One thing seems evident – namely that the Boche will be absolutely beaten on this front if he sticks it for another season. America is very quickly getting into swing and one hears tales of their doings each day. At one place they wanted to run a railway over the site of some houses. They offered the people what they wanted for the property and informed them that the houses would be demolished six hours later. The inhabitants were surprised at this treatment and protested: however trains were running over the spot two days later.

Eric spent much of his time, on and off duty, on horseback. When the battalion was at the front he could take his pick from the horses in the stables. He rode over to see Scott-Barrett, one of the officers from the Liverpool Rifles with whom he had travelled out to France in January, who was now a court martial officer at Corps HQ; and he began to have long conversations with Canon Linton Smith, the divisional padre, who would return to England before the end of the year to become the first Bishop of Warrington, effectively Bishop Chavasse's deputy in the diocese of Liverpool.[2] While Brigadier Stanley could find good words to say about almost every senior officer under his command, Eric was far more circumspect. It took time for him to develop any degree of respect or admiration, and then only for some of them. In Stanley's eyes the padre was a tower of strength: he was always to be found in the most dangerous places and was admired by the men, many of whom had known him before the war. Eric, on the other hand, had told his parents in one of his first letters home that 'I have not seen him yet but believe he is in our village. He is very much disliked by all and especially by the chaplains under him. He likes to hob-nob with all the generals and that I suppose is the reason for his unpopularity.'

Eric often came across him when he rode over to the officers' club at Bailleul for lunch. It was the closest that most civilians got to the front line and Eric recognised many of the famous visitors – from the portly Horatio Bottomley, the self-proclaimed 'soldiers' friend' and founder of the patriotic *John Bull* magazine, whom the Wipers Times nicknamed Cockles Tumley and who caused widespread amusement in Kemmel by insisting on wearing a tin hat, to Sir Edward Carson, whom General Plumer entertained at the table next to Eric in the middle of September. Carson had been appointed to the War Cabinet as a minister without portfolio in July and must have been sent to France to review and report back on Plumer's plans. It was then a critical moment as his renewal of the offensive was less than a week away. The preliminary bombardment had started two days before he lunched with Carson.

Plumer's plans were based on his preferred 'bite and hold' tactics where each stage in

---

2   Martin Linton Smith was subsequently appointed Bishop of Hereford in 1920 and Bishop of Rochester in 1930. When he retired as Bishop of Rochester in 1940 at the age of 70 he was succeeded by Christopher Chavasse.

'I am enclosing three snaps which I think you have seen before. In the one where we were looking at the maps, you will see the difference between a tent which has been "camouflaged" and one which has not. You can imagine what a difference the painting makes at a distance.' (Eric's letter home on 24 September 1917, four days after his 20th birthday). Eric, centre, looks much younger than his fellow officers. (Author)

a series of precise objectives was achieved and consolidated before moving onto the next. The Germans' defence in depth was ill-suited to defend against them but, at the same time, Plumer's limited objectives meant he had little chance of eliminating the enemy's heavy artillery located well to the rear of their lines. The first stage in the series, the so-called Battle of the Menin Road, commenced early on the morning of 20 September with another concentrated push along the Menin Road towards Gheluvelt. Whereas Gough had fought at the end of July with three divisions and 900 guns along a 6,200-yard front Plumer now had four divisions and 1,300 guns along a 4,000-yard front. The battle was effectively won by the afternoon. Another mile of the Menin Road was gained in an overall advance of 900 yards from the Ypres-Comines Canal in the south to the Ypres-Roulers railway in the north. Gheluvelt was now only half a mile away.

Eric got up early to watch the start of the battle from the top of Kemmel Hill. He had taken with him his sergeant-shoemaker who became extremely agitated when he saw someone below them using a torch to find his way about. He challenged him and, after issuing a severe reprimand, asked him his name. He almost collapsed when he got the reply, "Plumer – what's yours?" For Eric it was a memorable way to celebrate his 20th birthday.[3]

Six days later the Battle of Polygon Wood saw a gain of another 1,000 yards with the capture of Polygon Wood and Zonnebeke north of the Menin Road: and, eight days after that, the Battle of Broodseinde, on 4 October, proved the most successful engagement to

---

3   Eric's eldest son, Sub-Lieutenant Peter Rigby-Jones RN, my father, would have an equally memorable 20th birthday 27 years later while serving with Coastal Forces on 6 June 1944: it was D-Day and he was confined to barracks at Felixstowe although he managed to sneak out later to take his girlfriend to dinner at a local hotel. He kept the bill as a souvenir.

date with an advance of another 700 yards and the capture of the villages of Broodseinde, Gravenstafel, and Poelcapelle. British and dominion forces now held all of the ridge to the east of Ypres with the exception only of its northern spur at Passchendaele, which was now just a mile and a half away. The bad weather, however, was closing in again. A sea of mud over the whole battlefield made it almost impossible to supply the front line and to bring forward the artillery needed to support a further advance. Haig and his generals met again on 7 October to review the situation. Plumer and Gough were both now in favour of calling a halt. Haig disagreed. For him the choice lay between capturing the rest of the ridge, which would enable his troops to spend a comfortable winter on dry and defendable ground, and a general withdrawal back to a good defensive line – and perhaps even as far back as from where they had started. The high casualty count would then have been for nothing more than the wearing down of the enemy's numbers and morale, an achievement that could not be gainsaid but also one that could not be celebrated.

And so the offensive went on. Another month of muddy hell had to be endured before Australian and Canadian troops finally took Passchendaele on 6 November. Haig had to pay a price for his decision. A fortnight earlier, at Caporetto, the Italian Army had suffered its worst defeat of the war when it was forced back 80 miles to the river Piave with the loss of 800,000 casualties. The British War Cabinet's response was to order the immediate transfer of five British divisions from the Western to the Italian front. 'Italy's position is certainly not encouraging', Eric wrote home on 6 November, 'although she seems to have managed to save her and our artillery to a great extent. It will take a great deal more than that to cheer up the Boche on this front. He is having a dog's life in every way.'

Eric carried on as quartermaster until the middle of October. Any uncertainty about his future was quickly cleared up when he returned from a two-day course with the artillery to find that he was again in command of D Company. He was more than happy with his lot even though he was severely short of officers, many of whom had been sent away on courses. The Pals would stay where they were for another month before finally being relieved in the middle of November, a week after the capture of Passchendaele. The Australian 15th Infantry Brigade, who had taken part in the Battle of Polygon Wood at the end of September, took their place but, before doing so, made a preliminary written assessment of the defences. They found them much improved on what the Pals had faced three months earlier. At the front there was now a continuous and substantial band of wire along the whole line which was reinforced in front of the outposts by loose and concertina wire; the 'shell-hole' line had been reduced from 10 to five posts as it was now supported by a line of strong points which had roofed shelters and were connected by trenches; the support line, a mile behind, now had concrete dug-outs, shelters, and reinforced cellars; and, in Ravine Wood, the 177th Tunnelling Company had begun the construction of long dug-out with five shafts 40 feet below the ground. Eric's drain had substantially reduced although it had not completely eradicated the water problem; and Olive trench, the communication trench from there to the front line, was now revetted and duckboarded along its whole length. The Australians thought the area remarkably quiet and commented favourably on the quality of their accommodation which, they said, had been left in a remarkably clean and sanitary condition. It was a testament to what the Pals had been able to achieve.

The Pals meanwhile had moved back to Steenvoorde for a fortnight before they went into the line again in another sector at the end of the month. With the fighting season over Eric's thoughts turned again to leave. He was in good spirits when he wrote to his parents on the evening of 17 November.

We are now settled down in our new area and, everything considered, we are very comfortable. The men are in good barns in two farms and have plenty of new straw so have quite comfortable beds. The officers are living in the farm-houses and all have wire beds which are very easily made. I am living in luxury with an ordinary farm-house bed – one, that is, that looks as though it has been made for half a dozen. We have a large wood-panelled room for a mess and a round table with a huge oil lamp in the centre. What more could one want, if one must be at war?

I now have nine officers in the company, mostly quite new ones: they are quite an assortment, not at all like the kind of fellow one used to expect as an officer. Still, they have good intentions and one tries to pick out their good points and at any rate one has to put up with them. It is a little trying at times when I read their reports and find one mistake in grammar, two in spelling and three in arithmetic. I have, however, a commercial traveller and an ex-cavalry cook on whom I can rely if anything occurs while I am away.

I am still being used for all odd jobs going. When we moved here the battalion came in motor buses and I had to take charge of the transport column. It is usually the second-in-command's job but I suppose he preferred to ride in a lorry. Then, yesterday, we had a battalion parade for the first time for many weeks and I had to act as adjutant as the adjutant was apparently not sure of himself when taking the battalion. Before I have finished I think I shall have done everything. I don't mind it since it is all experience even if it is a trouble at the time. Sutton has been back with the battalion for some time now and is again in command of C Company. The Mess President tells me in a horribly authoritative tone that dinner is ready so must stop now.

Love to all, your ever loving son, Eric

PS Could you let me have two towels (slightly larger and thicker if possible) and up to six pairs of socks in instalments. I am sending some thin clothing home to-morrow. Also, could you arrange with a tobacconist to send me 500 packets (of 5) Woodbine cigarettes each month for distribution to the men of the company. Will you ask them to send me the bill each month? They are appreciated by the men more than anything else.

I have tried a new scheme with socks and arranged our last time in the line to wash and dry socks a short distance behind the front line. By this and a careful watch on old socks I was able to let every man in the front line have a clean pair of socks at least once a day. I don't think we shall hear of a Member of Parliament talking about the bad way in which the men in D Company of the 20th are looked after – at least, not if I can help it!

Eric had also started to make his plans for Christmas.

As regards sending something for the troops at Christmas I am counting on getting home before then so I can return with what can be got. I had intended getting a gramophone for the company as we are the only company without one. I should be very glad if you could help me out with some records. Do you know a good place in Liverpool? I have had a name given me in London – Alfred Hays of 26, Old Bond

Street. I think that Decca is the best portable gramophone and this is the kind I expect to get. I don't think it will take a record larger than 12 inches so larger records would be no use.

He gave his parents a list of the records that he wanted. It included, unsurprisingly, the Robbers' Chorus and the Cobblers' Song from Chu Chin Chow as well as Offenbach's Tales of Hoffman, Lizst's Lieberstraume, a selection of Gilbert and Sullivan with the proviso that it included 'Take a Pair of Sparkling Eyes' from The Gondoliers, 'Angels Guard Thee' from Godard's Jocelyn, 'Keep the Home Fires Burning' – the accompaniment only, he insisted, so that they could all sing along, some George Robey songs including 'If You Were The Only Girl In The World', American Patrol, and a medley of other songs including The End of a Perfect Day, Three Hundred and Sixty-five Days, Rosary, and Broken Doll. 'Rather a varied selection', he agreed, 'but one wants to suit all tastes and moods. I expect the other officers will also get some records'.

When the Pals returned to the front at the end of November it was to the Gheluvelt sector where the front line was now astride the Menin Road from Tower Hamlets north to Polderhoek Chateau. The chateau was still strongly held by the enemy which made it an unpleasant place. In the aftermath of the offensive the whole area was one of desolation, a sea of mud and shell holes. No tree remained standing, broken equipment – from steel helmets to tanks – was scattered everywhere, and the bodies of the British and German dead still lay thick upon the ground: they had either not yet been buried or had been exposed again by the savagery of the shelling.

Eric passed up a chance to go on leave on 10 December. He chose instead to wait five more days until his company had completed its tour in the trenches: that way he would be able to get home for Christmas. He did not mind that he would have to miss another of Brigadier Stanley's famous feasts. The Pals' comfort fund, which had been boosted by the profits from a series of concerts that the Optimists had given in Liverpool, had enabled the quartermasters to scour the country for pigs and turkeys for their Christmas dinner, which they then left on the farms to be fattened up. Unfortunately Brigadier Stanley's own enjoyment of the festivities was ruined when he was told on Christmas morning that the brigade would be needed for an assault on Polderhoek Chateau. It was two days before he heard that the order had been cancelled.

And so, as his first year on the Western Front came to an end, Eric found himself at home again with his family to celebrate Christmas. Four months later he was told that he had been mentioned in Sir Douglas Haig's despatch of 7 April 1918 for his gallant and distinguished service in the field during the latter part of 1917. His certificate, when he received it in March 1919, was signed by then Secretary of State for War, Winston Churchill.

9

St Quentin

January – March 1918

In this business men grow overnight like plants under glass or shrivel as if nipped by the frost.

Lord Moran, *The Anatomy of Courage*[1]

Eric left Ormskirk on New Year's Eve armed with a gramophone. Before leaving he had sent a telegram to the Adelphi Theatre to book a seat at that night's performance of *The Boy*, London's latest hit musical comedy. Unfortunately it was sold out and he had to make do with *Round the Map*, which was coming to the end of its run at the Alhambra and playing to poor houses. By chance he found himself sitting beside another Liverpool Pal, Captain Arthur Morell, one of the 17th Battalion's original officers who was now on the brigade staff. He was there with his mother who had helped organise the Optimists' recent concerts in Liverpool. After the show they found her a taxi and then walked down from Leicester Square to see in the New Year over coffee at the Savoy. 'At least I started the year on the right side of the channel', Eric told his parents.

After a rough crossing the following morning, which he claimed to have enjoyed immensely 'although most people showed a complete disregard for food economy', Eric ran into a fellow officer at Calais who told him that the Pals would shortly be leaving Ypres for 'a far more salubrious neighbourhood'. When he arrived back at the transport lines the next day he found that the battalion had already moved forward for its last turn in the line at Gheluvelt. As he was not required he spent two quiet but enjoyable evenings in the officers' mess with only his gramophone for company. They turned out to be his last for many weeks.

As the year drew to a close both sides had again taken stock of their positions and finalised their plans for the following season. Germany had had mixed fortunes in 1917. On the positive side the Hindenburg Line had proved a fearsome defensive barrier; and Chemin des Dames had been a major victory even if the German high command had not appreciated or capitalised upon the subsequent collapse of the French Army. On the other hand Plumer's capture of the Messines ridge had severely damaged morale; and significant high ground and manpower had been lost at both Arras and Ypres. The Royal Navy had maintained its blockade of German ports since the Battle of Jutland off the Danish coast in 1916 and, while U-boats still represented a major threat to British shipping, their impact had been reduced with the introduction of the convoy system. By the end of 1917 Germany faced a much graver and more immediate threat of starvation than her enemy. Morale however had been boosted at the end of the year by the decisive victory on the Italian Front at Caporetto and, on the Western Front, by the successful recovery of lost ground at Cambrai in the last

---

1   Lord Moran, *The Anatomy of Courage,* London, Constable, 1945, p. 129 (with permission of Little, Brown Book Group Ltd).

major battle of the year.

Tanks had proved useless in the mud of Ypres. When Haig's Flanders offensive stalled Lieutenant-Colonel John Fuller, the Chief Staff Officer of the British Tank Corps, submitted plans for what would be the first major tank battle of the war on the drier ground at Cambrai, 20 miles to the south-east of Arras. His aim was to restore British standing and morale by striking a drmatic blow against the enemy before the winter. On 20 November a force of almost 400 British tanks with infantry support was able to break through the Hindenburg Line and advance five miles. For the first time since the outbreak of war church bells rang out in celebration all over Britain. However the boost to morale again went unexploited; and jubilation turned to alarm a few days later when the Germans counter-attacked and won back almost all their lost territory. In the process both sides learnt valuable lessons for 1918, the British on how to exploit their tank superiority and the Germans on how to use storm-troopers to gain ground quickly.

When Hindenburg and Ludendorff met at Mons in November they knew that they had to strike early in 1918 to exploit a narrow window of opportunity. Russia's final collapse on the Eastern Front meant that they had to make the most of their numerical superiority on the Western Front before the Americans arrived in force. Lenin and his Bolsheviks had come to power in Russia only three weeks before and had immediately sued for peace. An armistice was signed in December; and, at the beginning of March, Russia was forced to accept a humiliating and punitive peace under the terms of the Treaty of Brest-Litovsk. Her surrender of Finland, Poland, the Baltic States, Belarus, and the Ukraine meant the loss of a quarter of her territory and industry, including most of her coal mines. Although the Russian war effort had been in its death throes for more than a year the signing of the treaty marked the final end of the war on the Eastern Front, enabling Germany to transfer her troops back to the Western Front. By the beginning of March 1918 her 192 divisions there outnumbered the allies' 169. Her plan was to put everything into an overwhelming offensive to win the war as soon as winter was over.

Like Great Britain at the start of the war it would take the United States more than a year to put a large army into the field. Her recruits had to be trained, equipped, and transported and her war industries geared up to supply them. By the end of 1917, nine months after President Wilson had declared war, American troops were still thin on the ground in Europe and often reliant on their French and British allies for essential kit and equipment. There were only 14,000 by the end of June, 62,000 by the end of September, and 175,000 by the end of the year. Their numbers then increased dramatically in the new year from 319,000 at the end of March to 874,000 in June, when they made their first appearance on the battlefield, and 1,705,000 in September. By the time that the armistice was signed in November there were almost two million American soldiers in the field. Meanwhile Great Britain and France had somehow to survive until their new ally was up to battle strength.

Great Britain had ended 1917 in much the same position as in 1916. The Somme and Flanders offensives had both resulted in campaigns of extended attrition when the promised break-through had failed to materialise. The capture of the high ground at Ypres, while it had given the French Army the breathing space to recover from its mutinies, had come at a high price. British casualties in 1917 were higher than they had been in 1916. The 420,000 casualties on the Somme were exceeded by the 160,000 at Arras and 310,000 at Ypres. 'We have won great victories', Lloyd George commented in November in a widely-reported speech at a lunch at the war ministry in Paris a week after the creation of the Supreme

War Council: 'when I look at the appalling casualty lists I sometimes wish it had not been necessary to win so many'.[2]

When the British Prime Minister took stock of what he had achieved in his first year in office he could claim to have succeeded in only one of his three main objectives. Although he had created an effective war cabinet and secretariat he had been taken in by Nivelle in the spring and then, critically, had failed to impose his will on the conduct of Haig's Flanders offensive. He had also made little progress on unifying the allied command on the Western Front and on developing other battle fronts. The military triumvirate of Field-Marshal Haig, Sir William Robertson, and Lord Derby had survived the challenges to their authority; and the removal of any one of them, however much the Prime Minister might have wanted it, might result in the loss of them all, which he probably could not afford.

In September 1917 Lloyd George had formally proposed for the first time the setting up of a supreme allied war council to control military operations. The council, he suggested, should comprise three representatives from each of the allied nations – the prime minister, a second politician, and a military representative. When he met the French prime minister privately at Boulogne at the end of the month they agreed that France's Chief of General Staff, Ferdinand Foch, was the right man to head the council's military command. The following month Lloyd George also asked two generals, Sir John French and Sir Henry Wilson, to prepare an independent review of the strategic options at what was seen as a turning point of the war. While the 65-year old French was an obvious choice – he had commanded the British Expeditionary Force before Haig – the appointment of Sir Henry Wilson was more overtly political. Lloyd George must have known not only that he could manipulate the younger and less experienced man, whose career had faltered since the outbreak of war, but also that he was 'persona non grata' to the military triumvirate. A committed Francophile, Wilson had spent many of his leaves before the war cycling around Belgium and Northern France and so had been the obvious choice for British liaison officer at French headquarters in the spring of 1917 when Haig was placed, albeit temporarily, under Nivelle's command. The appointment still rankled and ensured Haig and Robertson's continued distrust of the man.

Lloyd George's new supreme war council came into being at a conference in Rapallo in early November shortly after the disaster at Caporetto. The British delegation comprised Lloyd George as prime minister, General Smuts as a member of the war cabinet, and Robertson as Chief of the Imperial General Staff. Lloyd George, however, also asked Wilson to attend and, at the end of the conference, he put down a clear marker of his future intentions when he appointed Wilson and Lord Milner as Britain's military and political representatives at the Paris-based Council. Although he held no ministerial portfolio Lord Milner had been appointed to the war cabinet by Lloyd George when he became premier and had quickly established himself as his most loyal and effective political lieutenant. Lord Derby considered resigning when he heard the news. Although he was Secretary of State for War he did not sit in the war cabinet and was rarely given the chance to participate in key strategic decisions. At the end of the month, and only shortly after he had heard of the death of his son-in-law, the younger son of Lord Rosebery, while on active service in Palestine, he expressed his dissatisfaction in a letter to his friend, Lord Esher. In a quick sketch of the key figures involved he admitted that, while he liked the Prime Minister and admired his determination to win the war, he could sometimes be infuriated by his methods; Smuts

---

2   *The Times*, 13 November 1917, under the headline 'The Lessons of the Past', pp. 7-8.

and Carson were the only members of the cabinet for whom he had any respect; Milner he found intolerable; and he was deeply suspicious of his being in Paris with Wilson.[3]

Wilson's new role and responsibilities clearly clashed with those of Sir William Robertson as Chief of the Imperial General Staff. However, when Lord Derby attempted to resolve the issue in a private discussion with Lloyd George, he quickly realised that the Prime Minister was intent on making wholesale changes to the supreme military authorities both at home and abroad. His sights were set mainly on the targets at home. As the commander in the field Haig was the least dispensable of the triumvirate. Not only did he stand apart from the politicking in Whitehall but there was also no obvious candidate to take his place. Plumer's recent successes probably made him the front-runner but in Lord Derby's view, although he was sound, he did not have the imagination for which the Prime Minister was looking. Lord Derby also tried to protect Haig by transferring criticism of the recent offensive to General Charteris, his over-optimistic Director of Military Intelligence. Haig felt that he was left with little choice but to comply with the earl's request to sack him.

Shortly after Christmas the war cabinet came to the conclusion that removing Robertson was the best way to resolve the conflict between him and Wilson. Lloyd George gave him the impossible choice of either staying on in his position as Chief of the Imperial General Staff, albeit with some trimming of his authority, or taking over as the British military representative at the Supreme War Council in a direct swap of roles with Wilson. Robertson believed with some justification that the two roles were best combined as they had been for his French counterpart, Foch. He refused Wilson's job when it was offered to him formally on 11 February and was told later the same day that he had been replaced by Wilson as Chief of the Imperial General Staff. General Rawlinson, the commander of the Fourth Army, would take Wilson's place on the council. After 40 years' service it was an undignified and discourteous end to the career of a man who could claim the unique distinction of having risen from the ranks to the highest military position in the empire.

Although Lord Derby always believed that one of his main jobs as Secretary of State for War was to stand up for his generals he was ineffective and out of his depth when faced with the practiced scheming of the Prime Minister. He resigned or threatened to resign several times – at one stage, according to Lloyd George, three times in the space of a single day – and each time it became a blunter weapon. In January Lloyd George mischievously dangled in front of him the carrot of the British Embassy in Paris. It was an offer that the earl would eventually accept in April. He would leave for Paris within the week and remain there after the war during the negotiation of the Treaty of Versailles. It was no surprise when his place as Secretary of State for War was taken by Lord Milner. Haig, alone of the triumvirate, would remain in post. Over the winter he had become increasingly frustrated not only by the political manoeuvring but also by Derby and Robertson themselves. He accepted that one could not be a soldier and a politician at the same time and that, in the final reckoning, military leadership was subordinated to political authority. His focus was exclusively on defeating the enemy.

The creation of the new Supreme War Council delayed the finalisation of the allies' plans for 1918. At its first full meeting at Versailles on 1 December the military representatives were asked to revert at the next meeting with detailed strategic studies and proposals. They had to consider not only their own offensive plans but also how best to meet the anticipated

---

3   Letter from Lord Derby to Lord Esher, 25 November 1917, in R. Churchill, *Lord Derby; 'King of Lancashire'*, p. 293.

German offensive and how and when to include the Americans in their planning. Their proposal to establish a joint allied army reserve to meet the increased threat on the Western Front was presented and approved at the next full meeting of the council at the end of January. The establishment of this reserve, which would report directly to the military representatives under Foch's presidency, was the first practical step towards the unification of the allied command on the Western Front. The commanders in the field, however, agreed with it more in principle than in practice. Although they all appreciated the need for such a reserve they were loath to weaken their own increasingly scarce troop numbers to staff it.

Haig, like most of his colleagues, expected the German offensive to fall in the French sector where the fighting spirit of the French Army had not been tested since the mutinies of the previous summer. Haig had always been capable of close co-operation with his French counterparts when left to his own devices. As a result, when political pressure forced him to take over more of the line from the French at the beginning of 1918, he was able to secure an undertaking from General Pétain that he could call on French reserves in the event of his being attacked. The British front had already been significantly extended since August 1914 when it covered only 25 miles in Flanders. By February 1917 it stretched 107 miles from the Belgian coast to the River Omignon just north of St Quentin. Now, in January 1918, it was extended another 30 miles, first to just south of St Quentin and then, a fortnight later, on to the village of Barisis, five miles south of the medieval fortress town of La Fère on the river Oise. In two months General Gough, who had only taken over command of the British right wing at the end of November, would see the length of his line increase from 12 to 42 miles and his Fifth Army from four to 12 infantry divisions.

Two days after his return from leave Eric was told that this was where the Pals were headed. After his success as quartermaster in the autumn he was asked to stand in as staff captain and lead the brigade's advance party on the first stage of the journey. It took them two days to reach Amiens by train, 80 miles away on the river Somme, where the Pals were to be billeted in adjacent villages south east of the city.

When we arrived at this station I saw the outgoing division and secured two motor lorries which conveyed us to our area. I then went round each village in turn ending up at the village in which I had decided to place our battalion. It was now fairly late and I went to the adjutant of the battalion then in the village and he fixed me up with a billet after which I had dinner with them. They were an Ulster division and I was very surprised to find that one of their company commanders was an ex-corporal from the Rifles named Bryan whom I knew quite well. We had a long chat together and I think he was glad to hear what little news I could give him of the old battalion.

This regiment left the village early next morning and I spent the day fixing up the billets of the battalion. This is quite a long business if one is to do it well and if one is unaided by an interpreter. However I managed to get along with the local people who seemed quite pleased to have troops, especially when I explained that we were an English regiment. As a rule they like the English best, then the Irish and the colonials, and last of all the French. By 5.00pm I had fixed up billets for the men and officers including a nice bedroom for the CO and second-in-command, quartermaster's stores, shops for pioneers, tailors and shoemakers, a sick bay, officers' mess rooms, sergeants' club, recreation room and canteen, orderly room and office, and a number of other minor places which are useful but which of course one cannot always get. I was about to find room for our transport which comprises some 50 animals when I saw an interpreter (pronounce as "interrupter") coming along the road. He was rather late but came in very useful in a long and somewhat heated conversation with the Mayor.

The next morning I and the brigade interpreter, a little timber-merchant from Paris named Rathaux who held the rank of sous-lieutenant in the French Army, tramped round the rest of the brigade area to see that the various billeting parties had fixed everything up alright and to settle any little troubles which had arisen. The villages are very scattered and I soon discovered that we had a very long day in front of us. There was already two feet of snow on the ground and twice we were caught in a very severe blizzard which blotted out the whole landscape from our view. At one point I persuaded my friend to take a short cut over the now frozen marshes on the side of the little French river which some time ago became so famous to English people. We went for about a quarter of a mile across the ice when we heard the ice crack and he refused to budge until I had assured him that I could swim and would be able to save him if we both fell in. I also pointed out that we were quite near the bank at the other side of the bend. As we went on the ice continued to crack and it was very amusing to watch his face and hear his remarks when we at last reached solid ground. Eventually we completed our days work and reached the new brigade HQ where I had decided to remain until the arrival of the brigade on Friday. It was by then 8.00pm and, as we had altogether covered 24 kilometres or 15 miles in the snow, we were glad to turn in after a very welcome cup of tea produced by the ever ready Tatlock.

That was yesterday. To-day we did not get up until after 9.00am and after some breakfast I enjoyed myself looking round the chateau in which we are staying. It is the residence of a judge and is quite a large place. All the furniture is left in the place though the family are not living here at the moment. There is a large billiard room among other things, which is quite useful: also there is stabling for about 30 horses. I am now in the dining room of the place and have just had some dinner. You would be amused to see us sitting in such a gorgeous room at a little table in one corner without a table cloth with two plates, one glass and a cup from which to eat and drink.

Before lunch this morning we walked into the town which is about three miles away. It is the largest town I have yet visited in France and is known to Grandpa who often speaks, I think, of its beautiful cathedral. We had lunch here and visited the cathedral and saw the main shops and buildings in the place: after this we had a bath and then some tea. At 7.00pm we got a train back here. I doubt whether we shall stay in this district and, when we go forward, we are not going to the place where there has been recent fighting. In fact we shall be going further south than any British troops have been before and, if I know anything at all about the French, I think that the war there will be quite passable.

The brigade arrived by train on 12 January. For all Eric's hard work they stayed only one night before starting out on a 50-mile march eastwards. It would take more than a fortnight to reach their final destination as they stopped en route for several days' intensive training at both Rosières and Solente, where General Gough paid his first visit to brigade HQ. Eric was kept busy from early morning to late at night. 'We have had an extraordinarily busy week spent on training', he told his parents to explain why he had not written before.

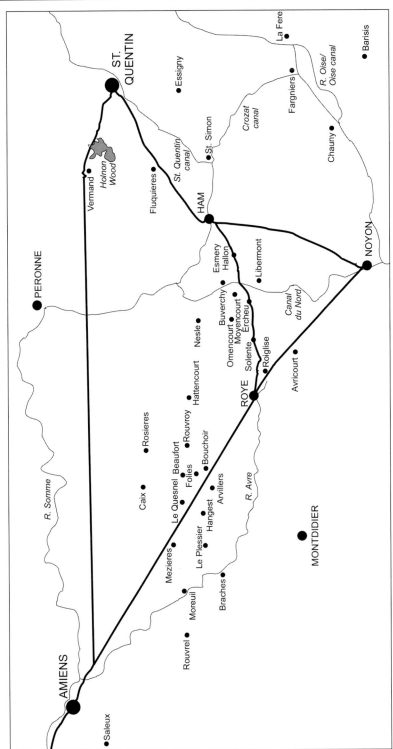

The area between Amiens and St Quentin.

I have always longed for more freedom as a company commander in the matter of training and it has at last come. The Corps Commander insists that the training of companies shall be entirely under their commander as regards the scheme and arrangement. This makes it necessary for one to train one's junior officers to do more and so on: consequently the initial period of training has involved quite a lot of work.

Even so he and Sutton found time to walk over to a French aerodrome where they cadged their first flight 'in a big French bombing machine, having previously attired ourselves in the usual fur caps and coats'. Eric said that he enjoyed it immensely as well as learning a great deal about what could and could not be easily seen from the air.

It would not be the last that the Pals saw of Rosières and Solente and the other places on their march. They could not have imagined that less than ten weeks later they would be retracing their steps over the same ground in very different circumstances. Almost as soon as they started their march the Pals found themselves in an area where no British troops had previously been and which, from Rosières onwards, had been held by the Germans until their withdrawal to the Hindenburg Line the previous spring. At first the villages through which they passed had suffered almost no damage from either artillery or occupation. However, as they moved eastwards, they found that more and more of them had been destroyed in the German withdrawal. As Eric told his parents, everything that could be taken had been taken, down to the very last brass door knob.

We are now in country which a year ago was in enemy hands and from which he retired. Most of it has not been under shell fire and the inhabitants have lived here during the whole of the war. Before leaving the Boche tried to destroy as much as possible and I must say that he has succeeded very well. In the larger towns, in which he gathered the population, the houses are more or less intact. Elsewhere there is hardly a house in the place which is not destroyed. All large houses, schools, and buildings are levelled to the ground: only a few cottages remain. He appears to have effected this destruction by placing explosives in the cellars. All railway lines and sleepers have been removed to Germany as well as telegraph poles and anything portable which is useful. He even took bed linen and washing tubs. Those fine avenues of old trees which line nearly all the roads in France have been felled and removed. All fruit trees have been cut down, stack-yards burnt, and cattle and horses taken. Many traps were left. There was a coal stack on the station of the largest town near here where, after a number of loads were removed, certain mechanisms would be set into action and the station would be blown up. Fortunately a friendly prisoner gave this away and the station was saved.

And still the people remain in the place and carry on. It is hard to realise how much they have to put up with. I was talking today to a poor woman whose husband is fighting at Verdun and whose little girl was very ill but she could get no medicine because there are no doctors in the town. It is marvellous how they manage to keep their spirits up. Not even the churches have escaped this wanton destruction. The old village priest even did his bit by hiding such local documents as related to information of military importance. When he refused to hand these over to the enemy he was placed against a wall and threatened with shooting. He did not give in but the Boche did not shoot him – why I cannot conceive for they shot 17 other men for minor offences. All

The ruins of the bridge at Chauny after the German withdrawal to the
Hindenburg Line, spring 1917. (From Eric's postcard collection)

able-bodied men and women were deported before the evacuation to work for the
Hun. Things like this should make us think twice about peace terms.

The Pals reached Chauny on the banks of the Oise, seven miles south-west of La Fère,
by the end of the month. Once an important town it had been razed to the ground by the
Germans in a three-week spree of bombing and burning that left it, according to Brigadier
Stanley, as 'the most awful scene of wilful destruction imaginable'.[4] Two days later, on 31
January, the Pals took up their new positions south of the river on the extreme right of the
new British line. Although their accommodation was poor it was the quietest place that
they had ever been. Any comparison with Ypres was, in Brigadier Stanley's view, 'simply
laughable. Here there was absolutely not a shell hole.'[5] The French division that they relieved
was sorry to be going. They had had only 27 casualties in six months, nine of which had been
during a single raid. The Pals hoped they would have as quiet a time. The Oise formed a
strong natural barrier north of La Fère. All the bridges over the river had been destroyed and
the open fields on its banks were marshy and prone to flooding in the spring. The Germans
chose to hold their line well back on drier ground more than a mile east of the river. It did
not seem the obvious place from which to launch an attack. The Pals' only concern was
their lack of manpower. The three brigades in the 30th Division had seven miles of front
to defend.

After more than three years of war Britain, like all the combatant nations, faced a
manpower crisis. The French, whose soldiers were killed during the war at almost twice the
rate of the British, had already introduced conscription for men up to the age of 50. Haig
desperately needed reinforcements. Outnumbered by the German forces ranged against him

4   Brigadier-General F C Stanley, *The History of the 89th Brigade 1914 – 1918*, p. 246.
5   Brigadier-General F C Stanley, op. cit., p. 245.

he had more calls on his limited resources than ever before. He not only had to make good the casualties from his Flanders campaign and the divisions that had been transferred to the Italian Front but had also to find the extra men needed to defend his extended line and to contribute to the new inter-allied reserve. He knew that there were 500,000 trained soldiers being held back in Britain as a last reserve; and he also had his eyes on the 300,000 men that were still stationed, unnecessarily he thought, in Salonica in Greece. He was unable however to convince Lloyd George to release them. The Prime Minister never reconciled himself to the level of slaughter on the Western Front and was always mindful of its effect on the electorate. He had also to ensure that Britain herself was defended and that the output from her farming, shipping, mining, and munitions industries was sustained.

The manpower crisis would become a cause celebre in the aftermath of Germany's Spring Offensive when the completeness and accuracy of Lloyd George's statements to the House of Commons on the matter were publicly challenged. In a speech of 9 April, in which he savaged the performance of Gough's Fifth Army, the Prime Minister claimed that at the beginning of 1918 the British Army on the Western Front was considerably stronger than it had been a year before. Statistically it was true – the total number had increased from 1,533,000 to 1,751,000 men – but what Lloyd George chose not to make clear was that the non-combatant labour corps now accounted for 335,000 of them and that the fighting strength of the infantry had fallen sharply from 904,000 to 630,000 men. Major-General Sir Frederick Maurice, who was privy to the facts as Sir William Robertson's Director of Military Operations, was so outraged by the Prime Minister's wilful misrepresentation that he wrote to the national papers to correct it. Shaken by the threat of a parliamentary enquiry, Lloyd George retaliated in an oratorical tour de force two days later during a debate on the issue in the House of Commons, where he accused Maurice not only of flouting King's regulations but also of having had some responsibility for the figures that he had been given. Discredited, Maurice had no alternative but to take early retirement.

Although it would not resolve the underlying issue of overall numbers one simple way of bringing individual units back up to strength was to disband and redistribute some of the existing units. It was not a new idea. Haig had himself suggested disbanding fifteen infantry divisions in November: and six months earlier, in what Lord Derby even then called an old argument, Lloyd George had proposed that divisions be reduced from twelve to nine battalions, that the remaining three battalions be used to create a reserve, and that the loss of rifles be made good by an increase in the number of machine-guns and heavy artillery. The proposal had merit in that it acknowledged the lessons learnt in three years of trench warfare. However it was no more than a whitewash if its only purpose was to paper over a shortage of men.

On 10 January the War Office ordered the immediate reduction of every infantry brigade from four to three battalions. Although the number of machine-gun companies was increased at the same time overall troop numbers were not and no new manpower was identified for the inter-allied reserve. The order was carried out at the beginning of February. More than 100 battalions disappeared almost overnight in a badly-timed blow to the morale of all the junior officers and other ranks who were affected. For them the battalion more than any other unit was their home: it gave them their collective pride and sense of identity. On 1 February, a day after it had taken up its new position south of the Oise, the 20th Battalion heard that it was to be disbanded. Eric wrote home that night with the news.

I am rather worried tonight about things in the future. Owing to the shortage of men many units of the army in France will shortly be disbanded and their personnel distributed among the remainder. This division has had hard wear during the past year and especially this brigade. The battalion is going to be split among the three others very shortly. Whether it is because we are the smallest or the most recently formed I do not yet know. You will understand how I feel at the moment. I have had command of this company almost continuously for nine months and have spent all my energy on it and I shall undoubtedly lose it now. I don't yet know which battalion I shall be sent to. I shall of course lose my acting captaincy. The CO had intended for some time past to get my rank confirmed, ie made permanent, but he did not hurry about it as he was waiting to be able to put another promotion through at the same time. This will now be impossible. I am undecided at the moment what to do – whether to transfer to the Tanks or to the Flying Corps or back to the Rifles or to take what comes here. Although I thought little about a captaincy when I got it I do not desire to give it up or to undertake any subordinate work if I can help it. I want to get some sort of a job: I don't like the life of any ordinary subaltern with nothing in particular to do. I will let you know how things go on: at the moment I am feeling thoroughly 'fed up'.

Eric had returned from his leave at Christmas in great heart and with his captaincy and command of D Company apparently assured. It was still only two weeks since he had asked his parents to send him some new company and platoon roll-books as well as an ink pad and a rubber stamp inscribed with the words 'D Company, 20th Battalion, the King's Liverpool Regiment'. Now it looked as though he would lose both his company and his rank. It was no consolation that his battalion had been selected not because of its poor performance – Brigadier Stanley made sure to praise its fine record and spirit – but simply because it had been the last of the Pals' four battalions to be formed.

On 3 February Brigadier Stanley met with his battalion commanders at Brigade HQ to decide how the officers of the 20th Battalion should be redistributed among the remaining battalions; the next day the battalion was relieved by the 2nd Bedfords and marched back to Chauny; and on the following morning, 5 February, it was formally disbanded in a small ceremony in the ruined town. The men paraded at 11.00am and were addressed in turn by Colonel Douglas, in what would be almost his last act as their commanding officer, General Williams, the commander of the 30th Division, and, finally, Brigadier Stanley himself. The next day they were marched off to their new battalions. About 12 officers and 250 men were allocated to each of the 17th and 19th battalions. Colonel Douglas signed off the final entry in the battalion's war diary on 13 February and then went on leave. The only fillip to the Pals' morale was that, after two years, the 2nd Bedfords were to be transferred back to the 90th Brigade and replaced by the Pals' 18th Battalion. Although now down to three battalions the Liverpool Pals would once more be fighting together as the 89th Brigade.

In spite of his earlier antipathy towards the Pals Eric found it hard to come to terms with the loss of his company and comrades.

I am very sorry that I have not written to you for so long but I have not been able to settle down to do it. At noon today the battalion ceased to exist and naturally everybody feels it very much. Sixty men of my company left for another battalion this morning and some more this afternoon. I am now in the 17th Battalion with only a very few of my old crowd: all my officers have gone to the 18th. It was a hard task saying goodbye to them all. It has done me up entirely. I have lost a hundred of the best friends I ever had today. I have seen many sad spectacles during my year in France but I have seen the saddest today. I know it may be hard for you to understand but out here, where one meets troubles every day, friendship is very dear. Still one has to meet everything with a smile and I hope things will very soon brighten up for all.

The 17th Battalion is the 1st City Battalion and is at present commanded by Colonel Campbell Watson. Emery, who is now major in command of the brigade school, is transferred with me. I have not yet joined the battalion so am still captain but I expect to be told tomorrow to take one star down. Please address my letters to the 17 KLR. I am very proud to have been in this battalion for it has had a very fine record as the history of the war will show when it is written. I must really stop now. I will let you know everything when I get to my new battalion. By the way I received your two parcels.

Eric signed his name in full at the bottom of the letter before crossing it out and substituting just Eric. 'Sorry, I am upside down today', he added by way of explanation. He wrote again four days later.

On Thursday we marched away from the town in which we left what remained of the battalion and a sadder spectacle I never want to see as everyone was leaving behind some friends. We joined the 17th Battalion that evening and moved with it again yesterday. Today we are going to our new companies. I am taking command of A company and am pleased to get a job but I don't much like the idea of taking somebody else's company off them. It is not, I understand, Colonel Watson's idea for, though he probably wishes to do the best for his old battalion, he also does not want to put any of his officers down. I understand however that it is a brigade arrangement.

From what little I have seen so far I can see that it will take some work to make another company as good as the one I have just lost but I think I shall get along alright. I have succeeded so far and I can do the same again. It is up to all of us to work and train like mad now for what we have got before us – what I believe will be the last of battles in this war. It will be a tremendous blow but we have reason for every confidence. The war is not going to be won on the Western front but we are going to prevent it being lost. The war is going to be won in the homelands of the nations who are fighting and not on their battlefields. If the people at home will only face what they have at present to contend with and perhaps a little in addition then we shall win. Germany is absolutely tottering I am sure.

I think your soup kitchen idea is a glorious one: I wish more people were doing similar things. Such things are going to win the war. Of course everyone has lost that enthusiasm about the war which was common to all when we started. Still most of the men here are determined to see the thing through. Nothing makes the men more pessimistic than to hear about troubles at home – food queues, etc. The so-called reverse at Cambrai did not worry us much. We are able to understand these things better than people at home. If the people at home and the men out here will each do their utmost and trust each other then nothing can stop us. I am afraid I am writing a lot of rot but one cannot help thinking about it. We have undoubtedly reached the crisis and everybody knows it and we have all to put our backs into it. Don't imagine from this letter that we think that the British Army is done for – far from it. It is a case of the British alone now against Germany's last resources and the Boche hasn't got a look in. His army on this front has been demoralised and his Russian Army is not worth two straws.

Please excuse this queer letter but it is hard to write when a gramophone is playing the latest ragtime about two yards away.

Clearly a decisive moment was approaching. Although no-one yet knew where or when the enemy would strike experience told them that it would come sooner rather than later. Once more Eric found himself in command of a new company only weeks before he had to take them into battle. He was possibly never aware that on 8 February, three days after the demise of the 20th Battalion, he was formally stripped of his acting captaincy. The announcement did not appear in the *London Gazette* until the summer but was quickly followed by another confirming his re-appointment with effect from 25 February.

Eric joined up with the 17th Battalion at Fargniers, just west of La Fère, where it was in the middle of four days of working parties. Two days later the whole brigade was relieved and withdrawn to Avricourt, near Roye, for a fortnight away from the front to re-organise. There it was finally reunited with the 18th Battalion. While there they had to march seven miles in the rain to be inspected by Field-Marshal Haig, who wanted to see for himself the results of his re-organisation. On his return that night Eric wrote home to tell his parents about his new battalion.

My second-in-command is Lieutenant Ashcroft who is with his father in Hutchinsons: I don't know whether he is a distant relation. He is much older than me of course and a very nice fellow. He went on leave yesterday so you may hear from him. My best platoon commander is 2nd Lieutenant Gill, MC, MM, a Wesleyan minister who was at St Johns for a time. Grandpa and Grandma will know him. He is a glorious fellow and very keen: he was out here for many months as a stretcher bearer before taking a commission. Another was in my company in the Rifles in England and I recommended him for his commission. I am not therefore an entire stranger.

The second-in-command of the battalion is Major – or rather 2nd Lieutenant Acting Major – Pitts. He came from a regular battalion and is a very good officer. The adjutant is Captain Holmes who is also much junior to me on commission. In fact all the officers are junior to me with exception of the CO but, as I was not confirmed in rank, I am now junior to three others. My sergeant-major is an ex-guardsman and my quartermaster-sergeant a man called Potter from the Bank of Liverpool. He is one of the original 17th KLR men and is a glorious man to have in such a position. He is an elderly man and I should imagine that he held a good position in the bank. He asked me if I was related to a firm in Dale Street who once banked with a branch of the bank. He remembers it as one of the most business-like firms with whom he came into contact and said their accounts were exceptionally neat and tidy!

By the end of the month Eric was able to tell Mr Temple that, although he was still bitterly upset by the loss of the 20th Battalion and his old company, he considered himself lucky to have struck such a good crowd and, in particular, to be back with Colonel Campbell

Watson. His opinion of his commanding officer had improved considerably since his arrival the previous year when he had described him as a man who was 'unpopular with both his officers and his men and who never fails on all possible occasions to show his extreme dislike for war and his supreme contempt for red hats and generals'.

The Pals found themselves in a new sector when they moved back to the front on 23 February. They were now based at Fluquières, half way along the main road that ran south-west from the German stronghold of St Quentin to the town of Ham on the Somme. Although they were under constant enemy observation from the burnt-out shell of St Quentin cathedral Brigadier Stanley thought it 'not at all a bad spot and up till now very quiet indeed. Nothing whatever to complain about.'[6] His optimism would not last for long. Although the British and French high commands may have remained unconvinced until the last minute it quickly became clear to those on the ground that this was where the Germans were planning to launch their offensive. German officers were regularly spotted looking at the British line with maps and binoculars; by the end of the month reconnaissance planes had started to report increased activity behind the enemy lines; and, shortly afterwards, they noticed the build-up of ammunition dumps even though they could not at first identify precisely what they were.

Hindenburg and Ludendorff had taken some time to decide where to launch their offensive. They had looked at four places – Verdun, St Quentin, Arras, and Ypres – but had eventually chosen St Quentin because they thought that the allied line was thinly held there, the ground was likely to dry out quickly after the winter, and the Hindenburg Line provided good cover for their preparations. It was also the point where the British and French sectors had met before the last extension of the British line; and the Germans hoped to split the allies in a drive westwards to take the key city of Amiens before moving on to the coast. The only drawback was that they would be advancing over the same ground that they themselves had devastated the year before. The plan then was to follow up with a second assault, this time on the British supply lines south-west of Ypres in order to take Britain out of the war and thereby force France's surrender. A date of 14 March was originally fixed for the start of the offensive but this was later postponed by a week to enable final preparations to be completed.

Gough's Fifth Army now found itself in a desperate race against time to bring its defences up to scratch. There was a lot to do and there were days rather than weeks in which to do it. The French had left behind an incomplete system of trenches and almost no road and rail links to and from the front. Although the Fifth Army's labour corps grew from 17,000 men at the beginning of January to 68,000 when the Germans launched their offensive almost half of them did not arrive until March: and, as Gough later admitted, 'no amount of labour – nothing short of a fairy wand – could have prepared all those defences in a few weeks'.[7] If the manpower shortage was a problem for the British Army as a whole then it was most acute for Gough's Fifth Army at St Quentin. His 12 infantry divisions, in which the strength of each brigade had now been reduced from four to three battalions, held 42 miles, or almost a third, of the extended British front. To his north the 14 divisions of Byng's Third Army held only 28 miles while at Ypres Plumer's Second Army, whose 12 divisions held only 23 miles, had almost twice Gough's manpower per mile of front. No one suggested that this was wrong. The St Quentin sector had been quiet for some time and had been expected to

---

6   Brigadier-General F C Stanley, op. cit., p. 249.
7   General Sir Hubert Gough, *The Fifth Army*, p. 225.

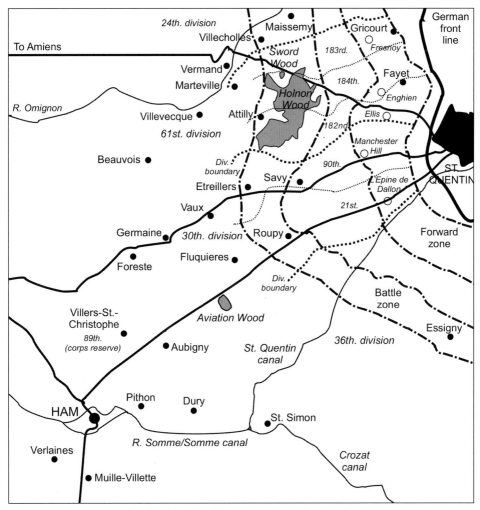

The British defensive scheme west of St Quentin.

remain so. Everyone, including Gough, agreed that Haig's priority was to concentrate his troops in the north and to defend the territory nearest the Channel at all costs.

Gough's shortage of men and the poor state of the trenches forced him to adopt a new defensive system. Applying the same scheme of elastic defence in depth that had proved so successful for the Germans on the Hindenburg Line and at the start of the Flanders offensive he divided the Fifth Army's front into three zones – a forward zone, a battle zone, and a rear zone. The forward zone itself had three elements – a forward observation line, a so-called line of resistance that comprised a series of lightly-held machine gun posts, and, towards the rear, a cordon of fortified redoubts on what higher ground there was. The whole zone was expendable inasmuch as its only purpose, according to the 30th Division's provisional scheme of defence, was to 'hold on, break up, disorganise, and exhaust the enemy's attack'.[8]

8   Provisional Defence Scheme, March 1918, 30th Division War Diary, The National Archives, WO 95/2312/5.

At best the attack might be brought to a standstill; at worst it might be held up until divisional reserves or reinforcements from other parts of the line could be brought forward. Thereafter the only option for the troops stationed there was to fall back. They did not have the manpower to counter-attack: and the isolation of their positions meant that they could not rely on any immediate help from their own units. Brigadier Stanley was in no doubt that, if the enemy attacked in force, then the men in the forward zone would be lucky to survive. The troops, who had not had the time to be fully trained in the new tactics, saw themselves as 'sacrifice units'.

Situated more than a mile behind the forward zone, the battle zone was a well-chosen and strongly-defended position of up to a mile in depth which was seen as the main line of resistance and therefore to be held at all costs. Time prevented the completion of the rear zone, behind which were stationed the heavy artillery and infantry reserves.

Gough was reminded that he could call on the six French divisions that Haig had been promised by Pétain when he agreed to the extension of the British line; and, although his orders were to stand and fight, he was also given a written assurance that he could, if necessary, make a strategic withdrawal as long as he fought a robust rearguard action. As he later wrote:

> Haig was, therefore, absolutely sound in his judgement to keep his reserves in the north and to leave the Fifth Army to do the best it could with its divisions to hold up and perhaps exhaust the German forces. I understood this conception perfectly and in my discussions with Haig it was clearly understood by both of us that the role I was to play was to retire gradually and to delay and exhaust the enemy without exposing my army to annihilation.[9]

Sadly this understanding was forgotten when Gough was made the scapegoat for the failure of his heavily-outnumbered Fifth Army to halt the German advance: and, by the time the British and French high commands accepted that the offensive would be at St Quentin, the French divisions that Haig had been promised had been withdrawn to reinforce the French line further east.

Within Gough's new defensive system the 30th Division – comprising the 21st, 89th, and 90th Brigades – was responsible for two and a half miles of front almost due west of St Quentin. Their sector was split into a northern and southern half with one brigade responsible for each and the third held to their rear in Corps reserve. Within each half one battalion would man the forward zone while the other two held the battle zone. In the forward zone itself two companies would be used to man the observation line and machine-gun posts, with about six men at each post; the third would be in support; and, at the rear of the zone, the fourth would be responsible for garrisoning a redoubt – Manchester Hill in the north and L'Épine de Dallon in the south – where battalion headquarters would also be based. Duties were rotated each week as the final preparations were made. The 17th Battalion spent its first week back at the front at Flusquieres – digging trenches, laying wire in the battle zone, and rehearsing its routines for when it was ordered to 'stand to' or 'man battle positions'. Then, on the night of 1 March, it relieved the 18th Battalion for a week in the forward zone at L'Épine de Dallon. Eric joined it there the following evening, having

---

9   General Sir Hubert Gough, op. cit., p. 238.

L'Épine de Dallon, looking south from Maison Rouge near Manchester Hill. (Author, 2016)

spent the previous three days at corps headquarters in Ham on a course to learn more about the new defensive system. Although Eric described it as the usual 'instructive holiday', it had clearly been more intense than usual.

> It is quite a relief to get away from things even for a day or two: I am quite enjoying myself here and at the same time learning a good deal of useful instruction. It is rather an exceptional thing for a company commander to be sent on a course. We are subjected to a series of lectures and demonstrations by generals and others during the three days over which the conference extends. It is rather an 'Irishman's conference' for, after the day's lectures when we are invited to ask questions and make remarks, anyone who dares to say anything is entirely squashed. I ventured a remark yesterday and very soon wished for a trap door or some other easy and immediate means of exit. Now I sit still and try if possible to persuade the man next to me to ask the question I want asked myself – or else I enjoy the spectacle of a brigadier or colonel being sat on by the Corps commander. The Corps commander is, by the way, Sir Ivor Maxse, a brother, I believe, of the editor of the National Review. He is a great enthusiast and has a most capable staff – at least it appears so to me who sees things only from the outside fringe.

The battalion spent the next week hard at work in a desperate effort to fortify the redoubt and to ensure that it had enough weapons, ammunition, food and water to hold out for two days. Just before dawn on their fourth morning they had to see off a large enemy raiding party of about 150 storm-troopers in 10 minutes of heavy hand-to hand fighting. All the men in one of the forward posts were wounded or reported missing. According to one German who was taken prisoner after being seriously wounded the storm-troopers had been brought up especially for the raid. It was a warning of what was to come.

The eastern edge of L'Épine de Dallon, looking north-west with
Manchester Hill in the background on the right. (Author, 2016)

It was only when the battalion was relieved on 9 March and moved back into support
in the battle zone at Vaux that Eric finally accepted that he needed medical treatment. He
had found it difficult to stay fit and healthy since his return from leave at Christmas and had
already felt 'rather rotten' by the end of January when a bout of flu and rheumatism in his left
knee made it painful to move. Now, he told his parents, he was 'unfortunately in a bad way'.

> I have a boil on my face due to knocking into a piece of corrugated iron in the dark. It is
> just at its best so I am feeling a little less than A1: it has completely closed up my right
> eye which is a nuisance. Also I have got a touch of gum disease due, according to the
> Medical Officer, to my teeth not fitting properly now. I am going to see a dentist at the
> first opportunity. You will understand that, when I have a moment to spare, it takes no
> little effort to write a letter. I am going on alright and there is nothing to worry about
> though the discomfort is considerable.

As the boil had turned septic he was taken by car to a field ambulance to have it properly
dressed. Here, for the first time in a week, he could take off his boots, bathe, and change
his clothes. Although he had expected to be discharged immediately – he didn't want to
be away from his men at such a critical time – he was transferred the following day to the
officers' rest station at Ham. It would only be much later that he came to realise how poorly
he was. In the meantime he told his parents that he was not unhappy with his lot.

> It is a glorious place and one which you would hardly believe existed over here. It is a
> very large house in the town which was used previously as a hospital by the French. The
> old doctor in charge of the place looks after us like children – there is nothing that he
> cannot do for us. We are allowed to do exactly as we like and there are very few rules
> and regulations which are often so annoying. The only rule that I have stuck to is the
> one which forbids us to get up for breakfast. When you do get up you can either go for
> a walk in the town or in the woods or sit in one of the rooms downstairs where there
> are plenty of books and papers and also a gramophone and all kinds of games. At eleven
> o'clock an orderly comes in and implores you to have a cup of cocoa or milk and some

biscuits. The dining room is a beautiful old oak-panelled room and is usually lit up with a lot of silver candlesticks. We get top-hole food, always fish and often game for dinner. Altogether I don't think one could live as well anywhere else at the present time.

Eric was kept there for four days before returning to the battalion in Vaux. In his absence all available men had spent every day improving the defences in the battle zone; and all the officers and NCOs had been up to the forward zone to make sure they knew the lie of the land. The expected German offensive was now only a week away. As Brigadier Stanley acknowledged, its time and place were no longer in doubt. On the night of 19 March he was summoned to a conference at divisional HQ after two German deserters had revealed during interrogation that the offensive would start on the morning of 21 March. A quiet and uneasy wariness fell over the British lines. The Germans had not launched a major offensive against the British on the Western Front for three years. It would be a new and terrifying experience for almost every Tommy. Eric's letters reflect the change in mood. At first his confidence had been boosted by attending the course at corps headquarters.

There is quite a lot of interesting news in the paper just now: everybody seems to have the wind up. One has every reason to have full confidence in ourselves for the forthcoming season. There is certainly nothing to fear in this neighbourhood but a great deal to be ready for. A tremendous amount of work has been and is being done while the organisation is wonderful. The secret of it all is that everybody is working together. None of us have any fears for what we may have to put up with here in the very near future. We have seen what the Hun can do and no further methods of frightfulness, if he has any, are likely to trouble us. One only wishes that everyone had the same confidence as we have without belittling what we have up against us. There is so much in the papers now that one can hardly grasp the importance of each event.

He was less confident a week later when he was laid low by his boil.

I hope you received my field postcards as I have not had much of an opportunity of writing. You can probably guess where I am: we are having a quiet time for the most part but a busy one and to a certain degree anxious. The news at present is not too encouraging and Germany is doing her best to persuade us that she is in a very strong position – but I think it is mostly bluff. Undoubtedly we shall have a lot of trouble especially in the east but she looks like hastening her destruction by being too ambitious – I hope so.

He then fell silent in the final week before the offensive. He scribbled only one brief note home with a few scraps of news for his parents about people that they knew and had asked after. Easter was now only two weeks away; and it looked as though Harry and Alice would again be desperately short of news when they visited her family at Edingale for the holiday. It would be Easter Monday before Eric wrote again.

The 89th Brigade was relieved on the morning of 18 March to take its turn in Corps reserve four miles behind the battle zone in the village of Villers St Christophe. At the same time the 90th Brigade took over the northern half of the sector, with the 16th Manchesters providing the garrison for Manchester Hill, while the 21st Brigade took over the southern, with the 2nd Wiltshires at L'Épine de Dallon. Eric's continuing good fortune meant that the Pals would not be in the front line on 21 March.

It was a time of high tension. These last few days of waiting form the backdrop not only to the climax of the third of John Buchan's Richard Hannay adventures, *Mr Standfast*, but also to RC Sheriff's play, *Journey's End*, which is set in a company dug-out at St Quentin over the three days leading up to the German offensive. Sheriff wrote from experience, having served as a captain in the East Surrey Regiment. His play's five main characters are the company's officers – Osborne and Trotter, two older lieutenants; Hibbert, a younger man with the wind up, who hopes to use a bout of neuralgia as an excuse for avoiding action; the recently-arrived schoolboy Raleigh, whose first time it is in the trenches; and Captain Stanhope, played by a 21-year old Laurence Olivier in its first performance in 1928, an outwardly daring young captain who hides his funk with a bottle of whisky a day. Osborne is killed on the day before the offensive in a suicidal and unnecessary daytime raid on the German trenches; Raleigh, who accompanied him, chooses to spend his last evening outside with the men; but the other three officers remain in their dug-out to enjoy a dinner to celebrate a successful raid. They drink champagne and are served chicken, followed by jam pudding made with boiled ration biscuits, before finishing their meal with whisky and cigars.

The play resonates with Eric's own experience. Like condemned men before their execution he and the nine other officers in his company also enjoyed an excellent dinner that evening in their Nissen hut, listening to the gramophone, talking of Blighty, and doing their best to convince themselves that the Germans were not about to attack. Such dinners must have been repeated all along the line. Elsewhere in the same village Brigadier Stanley organised another of his famous parties at brigade headquarters. It was a somewhat grander and more exclusive affair where Colonel Campbell Watson and the brigade's other senior officers were royally entertained with a concert by the Optimists. When they turned in at around midnight there had still been no sight or sound of a preliminary bombardment. Many of them must have begun to hope that the enemy might not after all attack the following morning.

10

The German Spring Offensive

21 – 22 March 1918

The people of Great Britain, not to say those of all the allies, owe the officers and men of the Fifth Army a debt of gratitude which neither words nor deeds can sufficiently repay. Unfortunately, owing to a variety of causes ... my countrymen, with few exceptions (confined principally to those bereaved ones who lost their dearest and best), have not shown an appreciation of the splendid deeds of these men.

General Sir Hubert Gough[1]

The German Spring Offensive of 1918 was characteristically bold in its conception and scale. Launched against the weakest 50 miles of the British line it dwarfed the allies' 16-mile front on the first day of the Somme. Two British armies would bear the brunt of it – Byng's Third Army to the north towards Arras and Gough's Fifth Army to the south around St Quentin. Their 25 infantry divisions, all of whom were battle-weary from Ypres or Cambrai or both, and whose brigade strengths had now been reduced from four to three battalions, were up against 76 German divisions. Gough's Fifth Army had the most daunting task. It had the fewest men, with the three divisions in Maxse's XVIII Corps facing 14 German divisions, it was defending a new line, and it had not had the time either to complete its defences or to become proficient in its new tactics.

In order to conceal the time and place of their offensive the Germans' chief artillery tactician, Lieutenant-Colonel Georg Bruchmuller, had foregone the allies' usual preliminary bombardment lasting several days. He opted instead for the 'shock and awe' of a short hurricane bombardment that did not start until 4.30am on the morning of 21 March. For the next five hours 6,500 German guns fired an average of 4,000 shells a minute in a deep and systematic barrage of all three zones of the British defences. The troops in the forward zone were cut off immediately.

Their infantry assault followed on immediately at 9.30am. Instead of the allies' steady advance in line German storm-troopers, some armed with flame-throwers and light machine-guns, had been trained to advance as far and as fast as possible at identified weak points. Their orders were to avoid any strongly-held defensive positions such as redoubts which, once isolated, would be mopped up by the main infantry when they followed up in strength. Hindenburg's aim was to push through the whole of the British battle zone and to capture the artillery to its rear by the end of the first day. He had kept his troops well behind the front line before the offensive not only to provide protection but also to escape the notice of British aircraft reconnaissance. They had only begun to move forward to within five miles of the front on 16 March and had then stayed under cover for three days before

---

1   W. Shaw Sparrow, *The Fifth Army in March 1918*, p. viii.

finally moving into the front line on the night of 19 March.

Once again the weather favoured the enemy. Spring arrived early that year and, although it had rained the day before, the eve of the battle turned out sunny and windless. Bruchmuller would be able to use his gas shells to full effect. A ground mist then developed as his bombardment started which by daybreak had turned into a thick fog covering the whole battlefield. Visibility was down in places to twenty feet. It caused the Germans some problems. Their observers were unable to report back on the accuracy of their artillery fire and there were difficulties co-ordinating the movements of the infantry. One of the abiding British memories of the battle is of the eerie sound of the enemy communicating by bugle amid the fog and shells. However it also allowed the German storm-troopers to get into their jumping-off positions in front of their trenches without being seen. The isolated machine-gun posts at the front of the British forward zone had no means of communicating either with each other or with those behind them. The fog only compounded the problems caused by the pall of gas and cordite and the restricted visibility of the men's gas masks. Often they would not see their attackers until they were upon them when further resistance was futile and surrender was the only option. Nearly all the outposts along the line fell within an hour. Within ten minutes of starting their attack the German storm-troopers had penetrated the 30th Division's line of resistance in the forward zone. The British had other problems as well. Their guns were also firing blind and their reconnaissance aircraft were unable to take off but, when the fog finally cleared in the afternoon, the pilots reported back that the roads behind the German lines were clogged for 10 to 15 miles with reinforcements moving forward.

The German storm-troopers were able to push on rapidly past the redoubts at the rear

German stormtroopers advancing during the Spring
Offensive. (© Imperial War Museum, Q47997)

of the British forward zone. If the weather had been clear the garrisons there could have used their machine-guns and trench mortars to devastating effect. As it was the defence of the redoubts quickly turned into a series of isolated sieges as each was surrounded by the main German forces when they followed up. There had never been any lines of communication between the redoubts and those with the rear had in many cases been cut off by the bombardment. Brigade and divisional commanders in and to the rear of the battle zone had little idea of what was going on in front of them and no way of co-ordinating a response. All too often the desperate and heroic actions of the officers in charge of the redoubts left them dead or missing and their garrisons without any chain of command.

At some redoubts the defenders fought to the death, at others they either surrendered when they recognised the impossibility of their situation or eventually fought their way back to the battle zone. At least 11 redoubts were still holding out at mid-day; and, although the redoubts on Maxse's Corps' front were all still holding out an hour later, they were coming under sustained attack. They were encouraged to stick it out and hang on until dark. Contact with L'Épine de Dallon was lost at 1.45pm: it was probably captured less than an hour later. The last telephone contact with Manchester Hill was at 3.30pm, half an hour after the Germans had launched their final assault. Its garrison of the 16th Battalion of Manchester Pals would hold out for another hour in what would become one of the most famous actions of the day. Their commanding officer, Lieutenant-Colonel Wilfrith Elstob, had told his men that they were to fight to the last round and to the last man. He would be awarded a posthumous Victoria Cross for his valour. His body was never found. By nightfall all the redoubts in the forward zone had been lost. The plan had been for them to hold out for two days and, with their stocks of weapons and supplies, they could probably have done so had it not been for the fog. For those in the redoubts who were still there to receive it a general order came through at 4.00pm for them to break out and withdraw at nightfall. For most it was too late.

The British Third and Fifth armies lost a fifth of their fighting force, the equivalent of 47 battalions, in the battle for the forward zone. Although some were killed or wounded the majority were taken prisoner: either way they were lost to the already outnumbered British forces. Two-thirds of the losses, the equivalent of 32 battalions, were sustained by Gough's Fifth Army; and a third of those were in the first hour and a half of the battle. The exact details were never established. As the 30th Division's subsequent report on the offensive made clear, 'any account of the fighting in the forward zone must of necessity be vague: few men came back, of those that did their accounts are limited to their own particular vicinity'.[2] According to the Official History only 50 men from the eight battalions in Maxse's forward zone got back to the battle zone – and half of those were wounded. Elsewhere in XVIII Corps the fate of two battalions of the Kings Royal Rifle Corps would remain a mystery for two months until news of them filtered back from a few survivors in German hospitals. When, at the beginning of April, the 16th Manchesters sent in their casualty report for March the battalion's acting commanding officer who signed it off was a 2nd lieutenant rather than a lieutenant-colonel. Wilfrith Elstob was still listed on it as unofficially wounded and missing; and, although no officers or men were reported as killed and only 13 were reported as wounded in the first three days of the offensive, over 600 were reported as missing.

Most of the battalions responsible for defending the battle zone were asleep in their

---

2   Narrative of the 30th Division, 21 to 30 March 1918, 30th Division War Diary, The National Archives, WO 95/2312/5.

German troops concentrating in St Quentin, 19 March
1918. (© Imperial War Museum, Q55480)

billets at the start of Bruchmiller's bombardment. Within 20 minutes they had received
their orders to 'man battle stations', a manoeuvre that had been rehearsed repeatedly, and, by
the time the forward zone was lost, they had all reached their fighting positions. Where the
forward zone was weakest or the gap between the forward and battle zones the narrowest
the Germans had often broken through to the battle zone within half an hour of leaving
their jumping-off points. Although the resistance in the battle zone was more robust the
defenders were again heavily outnumbered. In a repetition of events in the forward zone
some units held out while others surrendered, were taken prisoner, or withdrew. Some of the
strongest resistance was offered on the six-mile front held by Maxse's 30th and 61st divisions.
The gap between the forward and battle zones was at its widest here, at over two miles,
and the fog had cleared by the time the Germans reached the battle zone. Although both
divisions were still holding out at the end of the day their situation was already precarious.
By early afternoon the enemy had been reported massing east of Savy and Roupy in the 30th
Division's northern and southern halves that were manned by the 90th and 21st brigades
respectively; and by 3.00pm there was fighting along the whole front of the battle zone. The
disparity in numbers was only exacerbated by the fact that the Germans had committed
only half their forces at the start of the battle against three-quarters of the British. It could
only be a matter of time before the battle zone was also lost.

   General Gough had found it difficult at first to get any news of what was happening.
By early afternoon however he was left in no doubt about the seriousness of his situation.
Recognising the impossibility of holding the battle zone, he realised that his only hope
of salvation, as he had already agreed with Haig, was to carry out a delaying action using

whatever reserves were at his disposal until British and French reinforcements were able to come to his rescue. The alternative was the complete annihilation of his Fifth Army. By then he had already been made aware that he could count on no immediate help from the French. General Humbert, the commander of the French Third Army whose line he had taken over at the beginning of the year, had visited him at lunch time and told him that Pétain had already taken his men away: all he had left with him was his headquarters staff. Pointing at the pennant on his car he told Gough that he had nothing to offer him but his flag.

Gough reckoned that, in addition to the two infantry divisions that he already had at his immediate disposal in GHQ reserve, he could probably count on two more British divisions and three French divisions arriving by the fifth day of the battle. All in all he thought that he might have to hold on for at least eight days. Having already lost significant numbers of men in the forward zone, he could not afford to lose any more. His approach and orders over the next few hours and days must be seen in the light of this realisation: it probably saved Eric's life. Gough spoke to all four of his corps commanders on the telephone to tell them that his strategy was 'to fight a delaying action, holding up the enemy as long as possible, without involving the troops in any decisive struggle to hold any one position'.[3] Then, before going round to see each of them in person, he brought up what limited reserves he had. The scale and speed of the German offensive meant that he had some difficult choices as to where and how best to use them.

His first concern was for Butler's III Corps, on the 30th Division's right flank, in his southern sector down from the St Quentin Canal to La Fère. Butler was the first commander that he visited. With the dry weather making the terrain less marshy than usual the Germans had had no difficulty in crossing the River Oise and making rapid progress against III Corps. With Haig's agreement, Gough now ordered Butler's four divisions, which he reinforced with a cavalry division, to fall back under cover of darkness to the protection of the Crozat Canal, which ran north-west from La Fère to St Simon where it met the St Quentin canal. Unfortunately it was a manoeuvre that would create a dog-leg in his line and leave the 30th Division's right flank in the air.

Gough also brought up the two divisions in GHQ reserve, allocating the 39th Division to Congreve's VII Corps in the north and the 20th Division to Maxse's XVIII Corps in the south. He would use the 50th Division, which he was expecting to arrive the following day, to support Watts' XIX Corps in the middle. The 20th Division had started the day 14 miles behind the front at Libermont, on the banks of the Canal du Nord. Rather than using it to counter-attack or to reinforce the battle zone Gough ordered it to take up a position at the front of the rear zone so as to provide a protective cordon in front of the bridgehead over the Somme at Ham through which Maxse's troops in the battle zone could then withdraw.

When darkness fell at 8.00pm on 21 March it looked like being a cold and frosty night. The day had seen the heaviest fighting to date on the Western Front in terms of overall numbers and casualties. Although not known at the time, the casualty figures were remarkably even. German casualties have been estimated at between 35,000 and 40,000, British at 38,500: of the latter 7,500 had been killed, less than 1,000 of whom now have an identified grave, 10,000 had been wounded, but 21,000, or more than half, had been taken prisoner. The Germans had nevertheless clearly won the day. They had advanced up to four and a half miles, captured almost 100 square miles of ground, most of it from the Fifth

---

3   General Sir Hubert Gough, *The Fifth Army*, p. 266.

British troops taken prisoner during the Spring Offensive. (© Imperial War Museum, Q23831)

Army, who were now withdrawing from a further 40 square miles, and were bringing up fresh troops. When, however, Gough spoke on the telephone that evening to Haig's chief of staff, General Lawrence, he was unable to convince him of the seriousness of the situation. Lawrence did not believe that the enemy would 'come on again' the following day: they would, he thought, be kept busy clearing the battlefield and reorganising and resting their tired troops.

Eric's own account of the first two days of the German Spring Offensive forms the opening chapter of this book. He clearly felt it important to keep a record; and, although his account is undated, the immediacy of his description, his hand-writing style, and the paper on which it is written – the same cheap lined paper that he used for many of his letters – all suggest that he wrote it only shortly after the event while it was still fresh in his memory. There are places where his accuracy can be questioned or where his account is at variance with brigade and divisional records; but there are also places where those records are themselves imprecise, incomplete, or inconsistent. It is clear from the various unit diaries that the reports received of the fighting were often inaccurate and the timing of orders misleading. There was often a considerable time lag between an order being issued by a corps or division and it finally being received and carried out by a battalion or company. Facts, to the extent that they can be established, are always blurred in the psychological and, in this case, physical fog of combat. The story of a major battle is a mosaic of the myriad tales of every combatant, each with his own perspective and place in the whole; and the last concern of anyone caught up in the maelstrom is to make sure that an accurate and comprehensive account is written up for the battalion diary. Even then it would not have been Eric's story nor indeed, on this occasion, that of his company or of any of the Pals' battalions. They were all temporarily transferred to other units; and two of the three battalions would lose their commanding officers. The interest and value of Eric's story lies in the fact that it was his and his alone to write.

The 89th Brigade was lucky to be taking its turn in corps reserve in the village of Villers St Christophe when Bruchmiller's bombardment opened early on the morning of 21 March. As such it was under the orders of Maxse's Corps HQ rather than Williams' divisional HQ. However, although the Pals were safely to the rear of the rear zone, they had a good idea of what might be expected of them. A detailed appendix to the 30th Division's scheme of defence, which had finally been issued less than a week before the start of the offensive, made it clear that their primary purpose was to counter-attack to recover lost ground; and, in particular, in the event of an enemy break-through they might be called upon to 'restore the situation' in the battle zone around Holnon wood. Three scenarios had been specifically envisaged, one relating to the area south of the wood and the other two based on the enemy's capture of the high ground to the north of the wood around the ruined mill on Villecholles Hill. They were predicated, it would appear, on the assumption that the Germans' most likely line of advance on Amiens was to break out north-west from St Quentin to Vermand and then head due west along 40 miles of straight roman road. It was the most direct route. The southern and less direct approach, which meant crossing the Somme at Ham and then moving on through Roye, appears to have been of less concern. Although Holnon Wood lay outside and to the north of the 30th Division's own sector, the other two brigades in the division had had the opportunity to reconnoitre the area while they were in corps reserve. The 89th Brigade may not have been so lucky. After three weeks in the line they had only arrived back in corps reserve three days before the start of the offensive and had then been kept busy cleaning up, training, and laying cables. For a reason that he doesn't fully explain Eric spent one day trying to find a suitable site for a rifle range and also sent some of his officers into Ham for a change of surroundings.

Although Eric claims that Bruchmiller's bombardment started to their north at midnight, only shortly after he had and his fellow officers had turned in after their dinner, he must have lost track of time. Every other account confirms that it started at 4.30am and that the orders to man battle stations were issued at 4.50am. The first German shell hit Villers St Christophe at 6.00am. Seven minutes later, Eric says, they received their orders to move. The bombardment was still in full swing as they went forward. Eric thought it the most spectacular artillery display that he had ever seen. After marching five miles the Pals reached their 'stand-to' positions at the front of the rear zone by 9.00am, half an hour before the German storm-troopers began their assault on the forward zone. Eric and the 17th Battalion were stationed alongside brigade headquarters in the village of Beauvois with the 19th Battalion on their right in Germaine and the 18th Battalion ahead of them both in Vaux.

As soon as they arrived Brigadier Stanley sent a scout forward to get in touch with Colonel Poyntz, one of the Pals' former battalion commanders who was now acting commander of the 90th Brigade, to try to find out what was happening. Shortly after 10.30am he heard back that, although the garrisons at Manchester Hill and L'Épine de Dallon were still holding out, the enemy had broken through between them and had already reached the front of the battle zone at Savy, only two miles east of Vaux. Stanley ordered his battalions forward to dig in in front of their villages and reported his position back to divisional HQ. 'It was very lucky that we moved the 17th Battalion', he remembered, 'as only a few minutes after they had gone a big shell landed in a building where one of their companies had been, and they would undoubtedly have lost a lot of men.'[4]

Eric and his company spent the rest of the day in their hastily-dug trenches. Although they knew that the battle was getting closer, and not least when they saw gunners running past them, carrying the breech blocks that they had removed from their guns to incapacitate them, they received no further orders before nightfall. Their sector of the battle zone had managed to hold out all day. Shortly after 9.00pm however, and almost an hour after the order had originally been issued from corps to division, Brigadier Stanley was told to split up the brigade and send his three battalions forward to reinforce the battle zone. As soon as he had received confirmation that they had reached their destinations he withdrew his headquarters back to Villers-St Christophe where he had started the day. At dawn the following morning he was ordered to follow divisional HQ back to Ham. He would be out of touch with his men for the next 24 hours.

The 18th and 19th battalions were sent forward to reinforce their divisional comrades in the 90th and 21st brigades respectively. With the two halves of his sector to defend and his third brigade in corps reserve General Williams had, unlike other divisional commanders, no divisional reserves of his own on which to call. When L'Épine de Dallon was lost in the afternoon and the enemy moved on to attack Roupy, the next village along the road to Ham, he had pulled together what spare troops he had from his pioneer corps and the Royal Engineers and sent them forward to Aviation Wood, near Fluquières, to support the 21st Brigade. The situation had then deteriorated in the evening. At 7.00pm the 2nd Yorkshires, who were defending Roupy, sent up an SOS flare to signal that they were under severe attack. Although they were still holding out at Stanley redoubt to the west of the village, they reported their situation as precarious and developing rapidly. The Pals' 19th Battalion would be sent forward to counter-attack there later that night. Half an hour after the SOS at Roupy the enemy were reported to have captured a quarry to the west of Savy in the northern half of the sector held by the 90th Brigade. Although his brigade would recover it two hours later, Poyntz asked divisional HQ for support, reporting that, with the enemy advancing in large numbers, the pressure on his battle zone was continuous and severe. Although he was given the Pals' 18th Battalion, which was stationed only two miles to his rear at Vaux, it was made very plain to him that there were no more reserves available.

At the same time the 17th Battalion was temporarily attached to the 184th Brigade, one of the three brigades in the 61st Division, which was stationed immediately to their north and responsible for the defence of Holnon Wood. Eric's orders were to report with two companies to the brigade's commanding officer, the 56-year old Brigadier the Honourable Robert White, at his headquarters at Attilly on the western edge of the wood. By the time they arrived at 1.00am the weather had turned very wet and cold.

The fourth of the five sons of the 2nd Baron Annaly, Bobby White was a one-time professional soldier with a history. At the end of 1895, while serving as a major with the Rhodesian Volunteers, he had been, along with his older brother Henry, one of the leaders of the unauthorised and ill-conceived Jameson raid into the independent Boer-controlled Transvaal. If Eric realised who his new commander was he is unlikely to have been reassured. As Hugh Marshall Hole, Jameson's former secretary who wrote the definitive account of the raid in 1930, made clear in his opening pages:

4   Brigadier-General F C Stanley, *The History of the 89th Brigade 1914 – 1918*, p. 256.

Jameson and some of his officers on their way back to Britain: in the back row
are Henry White (3rd from left), Jameson (4th from left), and Robert White
(6th from left). (© National Portrait Gallery, London, P1700(20b)

No study of the chain of events which culminated in the Raid can be complete without
a study of the characters, the temperaments, and the psychology of those who guided
the rank and file, and, with what appears to be an utter disregard of the ordinary canons
of good sense, compassed the ruin of their own cause.[5]

Encouraged almost certainly by his friend Cecil Rhodes, the prime minister of Cape
Colony, and perhaps even by the British government, the administrator and chief magistrate
of Matabeland, Leander Starr Jameson, had taken it upon himself to raise a force of imperial
troops with the aim of leading a mounted raid into the Transvaal in support of a planned
uprising there by the Uitlanders. The influential Uitlanders, or foreigners, although forming
a majority of the Transvaal's population and contributing a large proportion of its tax
revenues through their extensive gold and diamond mining operations, had nevertheless
been repeatedly denied the franchise by the ruling Boers. Unfortunately Jameson jumped
the gun and was left in the lurch. By the time that he found out that the Uitlanders had
drawn back from their armed protest, he and his 600 men had already crossed the border.
After riding for three days they were held up by Boer forces just west of Johannesburg and
forced to surrender. Imprisoned in Pretoria they were, after two weeks of negotiations,

5   H Marshall Hole, *The Jameson Raid,* p.2.

handed over to the British governor of Natal and escorted to Durban where they boarded a troop ship to take them back to England to stand trial.

Jameson and fourteen of his officers were remanded on bail at Bow Street Magistrates' Court on the day after they arrived home at the end of February. Although nine of them were subsequently discharged the six ringleaders – Jameson himself, Lieutenant-Colonels Sir John Willoughby and Raleigh Grey, Major the Honourable Charles Coventry, the son of the Earl of Coventry, and the White brothers – were committed to trial in July under the Foreign Enlistment Act 1870, accused of having launched a military expedition against a friendly state from within the Queen's dominions. Popularly acclaimed as heroes rather than criminals – Jameson's Ride, Sir Alfred Austen's first poem as Poet Laureate, had been published in the Times while the raiders were still in prison in Pretoria – all were convicted after an eight day 'trial at bar' – a legal process reserved for 'causes celebres' and criminal cases of exceptional public importance – and given jail sentences ranging from five to 15 months. As the raid's senior staff officer Bobby White received the harshest sentence after Jameson himself and Willoughby, its military commander. The five officers were also all stripped of their commissions and discharged from the army only to be re-instated on half-pay a year later by the Secretary of State for War. All would return to Africa on military service, four of them to fight in the Boer War. Rehabilitated and later revealed by Kipling as the inspiration for his poem, If, Jameson would go on to be prime minister of Cape Colony from 1904 to 1908 and to be awarded a baronetcy in 1911.

As soon as the 17th Battalion arrived at Attilly Brigadier White placed two of their companies, along with Campbell Watson and his battalion HQ, in the railway cutting north-west of the village: according to the 30th Division's scheme of defence it was the designated place of assembly for the troops in corps reserve in the event of the enemy's occupation of the high ground north of Holnon Wood. The other two companies he sent forward to counter-attack positions in Sword Wood, a copse on the north-western edge of Holnon Wood in the valley below the high ground at Villecholles Hill. Although they are not specifically identified in the battalion diary they were almost certainly Eric's A and C companies.

Eric must have had a good idea of what lay in store for him even before he received

The old railway cutting and level crossing at Attilly looking west with Holnon Wood on the right: the modern water tower at Vermand is visible on the horizon. (Author, 2016)

his orders from Brigadier White. He had had two and a half hours to think about it on the march forward from Beauvois. Even so, as he later admitted:

> Never before had I received such an order and it came as a blow. I had been in tight corners and had always before had a sporting chance but this I soon realised was nothing short of suicide. It took me quite a few minutes to collect my thoughts and recover my senses before I left the deep dug-out in which were the headquarters.

Nevertheless he reacted with remarkable stoicism and resolution for a 20-year old, keeping his knowledge of their likely fate away from both his officers and his men. He must have thought that his luck had finally run out. It was only six weeks since the 20th Battalion had been disbanded and he had lost the men that he had come to consider his closest friends – perhaps it was some consolation that he would not be leading them to their deaths; he had been out of hospital for only a week; and, although he had been lucky enough to find himself behind the lines in corps reserve at the start of the day, he had now been transferred to another brigade in another division and had been given what were likely to be his last orders by a brigadier whom he had never met before and whom he did not know, except possibly by reputation.

Although the thought might have crossed Eric's mind it would be wrong to assume that, if, as he thought, the loss of a few men was a price worth paying to save the many, then Brigadier White might have had fewer qualms about sending men from another brigade on such a mission. Rather he was almost certainly using every resource available to him in a desperate effort to stall the enemy's advance and prevent a major breakthrough on his left flank. He may have earned a reputation as a maverick, a dandy, and a martinet but he was not a commander who stayed safely behind the lines while his men were in the thick of battle. He himself had already received a nasty shrapnel wound that morning when his dug-out received a direct hit from a shell; and he would be wounded in the head again the following day as he waved encouragement to his men with his tin helmet.

White's 184th Brigade was, along with the 182nd and 183rd brigades, one of the three brigades in the 61st Division which formed the left flank of Maxse's XVIII Corps to the north of the 30th Division. Together they were responsible for defending the approaches to Holnon Wood. White's brigade covered the central section, its forward zone running from Fayet to Gricourt with Enghien redoubt at its rear. The 2/4th Battalion of the Oxfordshire and Buckinghamshire Light Infantry offered the same stout resistance at this redoubt as did the garrisons at Manchester Hill and L'Épine de Dallon. However by mid-day they were unsure whether the German storm-troopers had got round behind them and captured the village of Holnon in front of Holnon Wood, thereby cutting them off. Colonel Harry Wetherall, their commanding officer, sent out a number of unsuccessful patrols before deciding to go out himself to investigate. He did not come back. He was taken prisoner by the Germans but managed to escape later that night while being escorted back to St Quentin. The redoubt was finally abandoned at 4.20pm. According to one report only one officer and two privates made it back to the battle zone: the Official History says there were none. By then the 61st Division, although still holding on in its own battle zone, was seriously threatened on its left flank where the Germans had broken through against the 24th Division in Watts' XIX Corps around the village of Maissemy. Any further advance along the Omignon valley towards Vermand and Marteville would not only cut off Holnon

Looking south from the ridge east of Villecholles Mill towards Sword Wood on the left, with Holnon Wood behind it, and Marteville on the right: cars travelling on the road from St Quentin to Vermand are just visible in the middle distance. (Author, 2016)

Wood from the rear but also open up the road to Amiens.

Maissemy was lost in the early afternoon. Along with Essigny in the south and Ronssoy in the north it was, according to Gough, one of only three breaches in the Fifth Army's battle zone on the first day of the battle. Although the Germans were then held up midway along the Omignon valley, the high ground to the north of Holnon Wood and to the east of the ruined mill at Villecholles was reported lost by the 183rd Brigade by 3.00pm.

While the second of White's three battalions, the 2/5th Glosters, was still defending the battle zone in Holnon Wood his third, the 2/4th Royal Berkshires, which had been in reserve at Marteville at the start of the day, had already been transferred to the 183rd Brigade to his north. It would be used now to try to restore the situation. At 4.30pm it was ordered to make a counter-attack to regain the lost ground. It would be a heroic but sadly quixotic failure. The battalion's commanding officer, 34-year old Lieutenant-Colonel Jack Dimmer, who had been awarded the Victoria Cross at the First Battle of Ypres in November 1914 and who had been married for only two months, decided to boost his men's morale by leading the attack on a white charger. When he and his batman reached the crest of the ridge they were silhouetted against the darkening sky and quickly picked off. They fell not far from Villecholles mill along with 40 other men.

When, however, the Germans pressed forward their advantage, they came up against the determined defence of the 1/8th Battalion of the Argyll and Sutherland Highlanders in the 183rd Brigade. It was an action for which 25-year old platoon commander 2nd Lieutenant John Crawford Buchan, who was originally reported as wounded and missing, was posthumously awarded the Victoria Cross. His medal citation states that, although he had already been wounded, he insisted on staying with his men and, with an utter disregard for his personal safety, continued to go round their posts to give them encouragement.

Eventually, when he saw the enemy had practically surrounded his command, he collected his platoon and prepared to fight his way back to the supporting line. At this point the enemy, who had crept round his right flank, rushed towards him, shouting out 'Surrender'. 'To hell with surrender', he replied, and shooting the foremost of the enemy, he finally repelled this advance with his platoon. He then fought his way back to the supporting line of the forward position, where he held out till dusk. At dusk he fell back as ordered but in spite of his injuries again refused to go to the aid post, saying his place was beside his men. Owing to the unexpected withdrawal of troops on the left flank it was impossible to send orders to 2nd Lt Buchan to withdraw, as he was already cut off, and he was last seen holding out against overwhelming odds.[6]

In spite of Buchan's valour the Germans had by nightfall firmly established themselves to the north of Holnon Wood. They were expected to press forward again the following morning before dawn. Brigadier White was desperately short of men when he ordered Eric and his two companies forward to Sword Wood in the early hours of the morning. He had already lost two of his three battalions, one in the forward zone and another when it was transferred to the 183rd Brigade. Eric and his friend, Captain Norman Henry, were convinced that they too were now facing certain death. Like both Buchan and Dimmer, they had been placed under the command of another brigade. After what must have been a terrible night they shook hands, wished each other luck, and waited until they could see the German storm-troopers advancing through the fog before giving the order to open fire.

Eric never doubted that his last-minute orders to withdraw, and the intrepid runner who delivered them, saved his and his men's lives. What he does not make clear, and perhaps did not know, is who exactly gave them and when.

With the exception of the 19th Battalion's counter-attack at Roupy in the early hours of the morning the rest of the night had passed relatively quietly for the men of the 30th Division. However, as part of Gough's plans for his army's orderly withdrawal, General Williams was told shortly before midnight to pull his divisional HQ back from Dury to Ham first thing the following morning. Once he was established there he would in turn order his three brigade headquarters to withdraw towards the town. When he arrived Williams took advantage of the chance to talk briefly to Maxse before Maxse's own corps HQ was withdrawn from Ham to Ercheu behind the Canal du Nord. He had some serious concerns. Unlike other divisions he had no divisional reserve under his command, his third brigade having been lost to corps reserve; his right flank was in the air following the withdrawal of Butler's III Corps behind the Crozat canal; his left flank was in danger of being turned north of Holnon Wood, and within his own sector the situation at Roupy was particularly hazardous. If or, as was more likely, when the village was lost then the road to Ham and the bridgehead over the Somme would be open. It seems that he was able to convince Maxse. At 10.00am, two hours after the enemy had first been seen massing that morning and an hour after they had renewed their assault in the fog along his whole divisional front, Williams was informed by corps HQ that the Pals' 17th Battalion was once more at his disposal. It took eight minutes to track it down to Attilly and another two to pass the order on to the headquarters of the 61st Division. They were asked to order the Pals to march immediately to Fluquières and to send an officer in advance to report to the 21st Brigade's headquarters in front of Aviation Wood: it was a task that Colonel Campbell Watson probably undertook himself. The 17th Battalion's own diary did not record their receipt of the order until 10.30am, by which time Eric and his men had been under attack for an hour and a half; and it was another half hour before divisional HQ let the 21st Brigade know that the battalion

Aviation Wood on the left beside the main road from St Quentin to Ham. (Author, 2016)

would be available to them by 2.00pm and asked them for suggestions as to how it might best be used if the brigade's line broke. Once Roupy fell, Fluquières and Aviation Wood, which were on the so-called Green line that marked the front of the rear zone, would be the next and final line of defence.

By then it was already clear that Gough was proceeding with his plans for an orderly withdrawal. At 10.45am he issued orders by telegraph to his corps commanders confirming his previous day's decision.

> In the event of serious hostile attack corps will fight rear-guard action back to forward line of rear zone and, if necessary, to rear line of rear zone. Most important that corps should keep close touch with each other and carry out retirement in complete co-operation with each other and corps belonging to armies on flank.[7]

An orderly retirement is, however, a delicate and difficult manoeuvre to accomplish. It requires a steady and co-ordinated withdrawal in line to prevent any unit being left behind or cut off. In the coming days units would often fall back just to stay in touch with those retreating at a faster rate on either side of them. They had to learn the rules as they went. The general staff had decided before the battle that it was undesirable to provide such training: they did not envisage such an eventuality and thought it would damage the troops' morale.

And so Eric's good luck had held once more, although this time it had been at the last minute and might not last for long. Unfortunately the order came through too late to save his colleague, Captain Eric Beaumont, who was in command of D Company. 22-year old Beaumont, the son of the congregational minister of Rock Ferry in Birkenhead, had

---

7   General Sir Hubert Gough, op. cit., p. 266.

interrupted his studies at Oxford to join up and was the only officer in the 20th Battalion to have led his company into battle at both Arras and Pilckem Ridge in 1917, the latter resulting in his being awarded the Military Cross. Like Eric, he had been transferred to the 17th Battalion in February when the 20th Battalion was disbanded. At 6.30am that morning he had been sent by Brigadier White with his company to reinforce the 2/5th Glosters in Holnon Wood. The Glosters would manage to hold on there until the middle of the afternoon by which time both their flanks, north and south of the wood, had been turned. Beaumont, however, was wounded in the fighting and, having been carried out of the fighting by his men when they were almost surrounded, would die in hospital at Rouen 11 days later. Campbell Watson considered him one of his best officers and a born leader of men.

Meanwhile Brigadier Stanley had arrived back in Ham with his brigade headquarters shortly after General Williams. The atmosphere in the town was now very different from the 'glorious place which you would hardly believe existed over here' that Eric had written about only a week earlier when he was recovering from his septic boil at the officers rest station. Maxse's corps HQ was already clearing out; Williams' divisional HQ, having arrived that morning, would leave that night. The town was in chaos. In the morning a makeshift party of some 400 men was pulled together from, among others, the corps cyclists and the Royal Engineers to defend the bridgeheads over the Somme at Ham, Pithon, and Dury. Then, in the early afternoon, Stanley was summoned to a conference at divisional HQ and placed in charge of the defence of the town. As a senior officer without a command he was an obvious choice. He set every available man he could find to guard the bridges and to prepare for their destruction as and when the Germans arrived. 'But', as he admitted, 'there was little more that could be done for the good reason that there was nobody to do it with, and no time to do it in.'[8] At the same time he was told to reform and resume command of the 89th Brigade and to bring it back to defend the town. By then the 21st and 90th Brigades had also been told that, if they were forced to retire from the battle zone, they should withdraw through the 20th Division's cordon directly to Ham without getting involved in any further rearguard action.

It would take some time for the orders to get through to the Pals' three battalions and for each of them then to extricate themselves from their positions. The 17th Battalion had started to arrive at Aviation Wood at around 2.30pm only to find that, in accordance with the divisional orders issued earlier that morning, the 21st Brigade's HQ had already withdrawn two miles further back to Aubigny. Colonel Campbell Watson managed to make contact with the troops in front but, without specific orders or the manpower to counterattack, he decided to dig in and hold his position. The Pals knew the ground well. They had spent a week there when they first arrived in the area at the end of February after their re-organisation. They had a glorious position, Eric thought, and were prepared to hang on to it against almost any attack. Then, at around 6.30pm, and just as the Germans were coming within range as they pushed forward from Roupy, they were told that the 30th Division had been ordered to withdraw to Ham. When he later had time to reflect Eric must have realised what an extraordinary stroke of luck it was to have been rescued at the last minute twice in one day.

Already there had been every sign by early afternoon that the battle zone was about

---

8   Brigadier-General F C Stanley, op. cit., p. 258.

The cemetery north of Roupy, still showing the bullet holes
from the fighting in March 1918. (Author, 2016)

to be lost. The dam was about to burst with consequences that were difficult to foresee. It was a terrifying situation. To the north the 61st Division had reported shortly after midday that, having lost their battle zone trenches, they were withdrawing to Vaux and Villeveque, leaving one battalion behind to cover the 90th Brigade's left flank. To the south reports of the 36th Division's withdrawal from the battle zone started to come through at 2.00pm but would not confirmed for another two hours. Sandwiched between them, General Williams chose to keep his 30th Division in the battle zone for as long as he could. The 90th Brigade was still desperately trying to hold on to its strongly-defended series of redoubts at the rear of the battle zone around Étreillers while the 21st Brigade was still fighting a long but losing battle to keep control of Roupy. By 6.00pm however both brigades had started to withdraw; and at 7.45pm Williams informed corps HQ that his troops had evacuated the battle zone and were withdrawing south of the Somme. The river would be Gough's next line of defence.

The 17th Battalion got back to Ham at 9.30pm. When Brigadier Stanley was re-united with them later that night, all he knew of their activities was that they 'had been marching about all over the place and had had quite a lot of fighting to do'.[9] The 18th Battalion had arrived back two hours before them. After their attachment to the 90th Brigade, they had been rushed forward from Vaux in the morning to help with the defence of Étreillers. When Eric and his men passed through them on their way to Aviation Wood both villages were already, he said, 'a mass of flames'. When Savy was lost in the early afternoon the 18th Battalion's acting commanding officer, Major Robert Villar, went forward to see what chance he had of making a counter-attack. He was not seen again. His body was never found. The battalion managed to hold out without him until they were ordered to withdraw to

9   Brigadier-General F C Stanley, op. cit., p. 259.

Ham at around 4.00pm.

The Pals' 19th Battalion, however, had had the worst time. Those of them that were left only managed to struggle back to Ham in the early hours of the morning. Having been attached to the 21st Brigade the previous night, they had immediately been called upon to make a counter-attack at the small cemetery just north of Roupy. Although they managed to recover most of the ground that had been lost the divisional diary would describe their attack as no more than 'useful': it was never going to be enough to turn the tide. The precise details of what followed are unclear. The high casualty count meant that there were few men left to tell the story: Roupy, having been one of the first places in the battle zone to be attacked on the first day, would be one of the last to be lost on the second. The Pals held out at the cemetery until 4.00pm when they were finally ordered to withdraw to Stanley redoubt on the western edge of the village. Although the enemy broke through here at 4.30pm it would be another hour and a half before they overwhelmed the final defences. In an echo of Elstob's orders at Manchester Hill the Pals had been ordered not to retire but to hold their positions until either captured or killed. The statistics are uncertain but over 200 men were reported lost in the engagement, up to half of whom are now thought to have been killed. The battalion's commanding officer, Lieutenant-Colonel John Peck, was himself originally reported to have been killed in the final fighting when he mounted a parapet at Stanley redoubt to assess the situation. It was discovered later that he had just been wounded and had been taken prisoner along with seven other officers. According to Stanley the battalion lost all but one of its officers – and he was wounded and would be killed in action the following day. Although Stanley does not mention him by name it was almost certainly Eric's friend and former company commander, Geoffrey Sutton, who had been transferred to the 19th Battalion when the 20th Battalion was disbanded.

11

Retreat

23 – 31 March 1918

The fate of France, of Great Britain, of Europe rested with those few men who comprised the Fifth Army and who, perforce scattered and unsupported, were worn and exhausted by strain and fatigue for nights and days in succession yet still fought on against the numbers which tried to overwhelm their defence.

General Sir Hubert Gough[1]

Ham would offer the Pals no respite or sanctuary. Threatened from three sides, the town was already in a perilous position when they re-grouped there on the night of 22 March. It would fall to the Germans early the following morning

The Pals were immediately pressed into action to defend the town. The division's original orders had been for all three of its brigades to take part in its defence. Now, in a last minute change of plans, the 89th Brigade would be the only unit left north of the Somme canal to defend the town itself and it northern approaches. The other two brigades were ordered to take up positions south of the canal at Muille-Villette and Verlaines.

The 17th Battalion established its headquarters near the bridge at the northern edge of the town where it was joined by 2nd Lieutenant Robert Petschler, one of the Royal Engineers to whom Brigadier Stanley had given the task of blowing the four bridges over the canal. Petschler had drawn the short straw. His bridge was on the main route south for the retreating troops and would almost certainly be the last to be blown. Like his colleagues at the other three bridges he had been given written orders by Stanley making him personally responsible for ensuring that the enemy did not cross his bridge but also that it was not blown up prematurely or unnecessarily. By early evening the bridge was crowded with a slow but constant stream of troops and materiel: the traffic would not begin to ease until just before dawn. By the time that the Pals' 19th Battalion finally got back at 2.00am the 20th Division who had covered the withdrawal was itself retiring, bringing with it the news that the enemy had broken through at Aubigny, less than three miles away, and were now marching on Ham along the main road.

By 6.00am reports had reached divisional HQ from the artillery that the enemy had penetrated the town. The hastily dug defences of the previous day were necessarily limited and incomplete and did not stretch right back to the canal on both sides of the town. They allowed the Germans to infiltrate around their edges in the fog and also to capture Pithon to the east of the town. The Pals were finally forced to withdraw when they came under machine gun fire from their rear. They had to fight their way back through the town to the canal. They must have been among the last to leave. Enormous quantities of food and

---

1   W. Shaw Sparrow, *The Fifth Army in March 1918*, pp. vii-viii.

Ruines du Moulin de HAM — Pont sur la Somme   Visé Paris 956

The bridge over the Somme on the north side of Ham. (From Eric's postcard collection)

supplies had to be left behind. Although some had already been loaded on to trains these had to be put out of action when no train drivers could be found.

The bridge to the north of the town was blown at 7.00am, followed shortly afterwards by the blowing of the last of the other bridges over the canal. Although he had heard the Germans cheering when they entered the town Petschler held off blowing his bridge for another half an hour to allow the last of the Pals to withdraw. Then at the last minute, when he caught sight through the fog of a small party of Germans starting to rush the bridge, he detonated his charges. A burst of enemy machine gun fire stopped him hanging around to see the results. The original bridge over the canal had been destroyed by the Germans in their retreat to the Hindenburg Line but had been replaced by the British with a temporary girder bridge. These girders now fell only six feet onto the lock below. While men could still scramble across, it was for the time being impassable for horses and transport. However, as Petschler recognised, the canal had little water in it at the time and could be forded without too much difficulty. In any event it would take the Germans less than a day to construct a pontoon bridge further downstream.

The defensive line on the Somme had shattered quickly in the face of the strength and speed of the German offensive. By mid-morning Gough had told his senior commanders that their new line, which was to be held at all costs, was five miles further west along the Canal du Nord, which ran south from the Somme east of Nesle to Noyon on the Oise. Described by the Official History as a great excavation, the canal was still under construction and so not as much of an obstacle as Gough would have wished.[2] Although it was 60 feet wide and 20 feet deep there were only rushes and a couple of feet of water at its bottom.

The 30th Division's headquarters had already withdrawn west of the canal early that morning: and at 9.30am Maxse ordered it to withdraw a further five miles to Roiglise.

2   Construction of the canal was called off at the start of the war and would not be completed until 1965.

The modern bridge over the Somme canal on the main road going south out of Ham: it still lies only a few feet above the narrow canal lock. (Author, 2016)

The Canal du Nord looking south from the bridge at Lannoy Farm: Libermont is just visible in the distance on the left. (Author, 2016)

Similarly Brigadier Stanley had withdrawn his brigade headquarters back to Verlaines in the early hours but, by the time the Pals re-grouped there after the fall of Ham, he had already left and the village was in enemy hands. Stanley was now three miles further back at Esmery-Hallon where he joined up with Colonel Poyntz and the headquarters of the 90th Brigade. The two commanders decided that their brigades should work together to cover each other's withdrawal. By the end of the day they would have withdrawn their headquarters twice more, first to the east and then to the west bank of the Canal du Nord at Lannoy Farm, midway between Buverchy and Libermont.

The Pals meanwhile, having found a good position on the crest of a hill near Verlaines, had dug in for the rest of the day. The 90th Brigade were dug in behind them straddling the road in front of Esmery-Hallon to provide cover in the event that any further withdrawal was required. Various counter-attacks were hastily organized to make good their defensive line but otherwise, although they were subjected to heavy artillery and machine-gun fire and to harassment by enemy aircraft, the rest of the day passed relatively quietly for the Pals. Having secured Ham the Germans advanced only as far as the railway line just south of the canal before halting to re-group.

The position looked rosier for the Pals at the end of the day than it had done at the start. Although their defence of Ham had lasted for no more than a few hours the German advance had, at least temporarily, been brought to a halt. In the afternoon Stanley received his first good news since the start of the offensive when he was told by corps HQ that, after almost three days of fighting and in accordance with Pétain's original undertaking to Haig, four French divisions were now coming to their aid. It was imperative, he and his fellow brigade commanders were told, that they hold on until then. Although the French were expected to start arriving during the night they did not actually appear until late the following afternoon.

By then the Germans had pushed forward again early the following morning. With their left flank exposed by the enemy's crossing of the canal by pontoon bridge and their right reportedly turned and driven back during the night, the Pals were ordered to make a fighting withdrawal to Esmery-Hallon where they would make a stand. However, when General Williams ordered Brigadier Stanley shortly after noon to pull together his reserves for a counter-attack, Stanley effectively refused, saying that he had no available men and that those that he did have had had no food or water for two days and were in no state to fight. By now the men of the Fifth Army were absolutely exhausted, their units were mixed up and short of officers, and stragglers were clogging the roads.

The order to withdraw to the Canal du Nord came through early in the afternoon. Once there the 90th Brigade took over the northern half of the sector from Lannoy Farm up to Buverchy with the 89th Brigade taking over the southern from the farm down to Libermont. When the French finally started to arrive in the early evening they took over the southern half from the Pals, who then withdrew north to Moyencourt to support the 90th Brigade. Here they were also re-united with the 21st Brigade. After the trauma and exhaustion of the previous four days the 30th Division was finally back together again and was able to disentangle and reorganise its brigades, to provide some respite for the men, and to bring up food, water, and ammunition. General Williams reminded his brigade commanders that, although they had now been partly relieved by the French, their orders to hold on to the canal at all costs still applied, at least for the time being. He added, however, that if any further withdrawal became necessary due to the exhaustion of the men, it was to be made in good order – and then only as an absolute last resort – to a line three miles further back

British and French troops manning newly dug rifle pits near Nesle, about four miles north of the Pals, 25 March 1918. (© Imperial War Museum, Q10812)

between Solente and Omencourt. It would not be until the following afternoon that the 30th Division was finally taken out of the line and the defence of the canal handed over to the French 62nd Division.

Although the French had confirmed that they were happy with their dispositions, Brigadier Stanley was concerned, as he would be again later, that they were taking over prematurely and with a weaker force. Haig later acknowledged that this was so, writing in his dispatch on the offensive that 'while the exhaustion of my divisions was hourly growing more acute, some days had yet to pass before the French could bring up troops in sufficient strength to arrest the enemy's progress'.[3] He and Pétain had kept in close touch as the disaster unfolded. When they met after the fall of Ham on the afternoon of the third day they had agreed that the French should take over south of the Somme as quickly as possible. Accordingly Gough was informed in the early hours of the morning after the Pals' relief that, while all British units north of the Somme would now come under General Byng, the commander of the Third Army, he and his Fifth Army south of the river would be subordinated to the French forces whose general, Fayolle, had only been recalled from Italy at the beginning of the month to head up the French Army reserve.

Angry and bitter, Gough felt cast aside by GHQ. Although he saw the decision as an abdication of Haig's responsibilities, he otherwise played down its significance. 'Placing the Fifth Army under Fayolle's group of armies made no material difference', he wrote later: 'he

---

3   Field Marshal Sir Douglas Haig, Despatch of 21 October 1918, recorded in the *London Gazette*, supplement no. 30963, 18 October 1918, page 12425 onwards, para. 34.

issued no orders to me and I only saw him once for a few minutes'.[4] He did not yet know that his days were numbered. In the meantime he had more immediate and serious concerns. He was afraid not only that there might now be a potentially disastrous lack of communication between the allied forces north and south of the Somme but also that the French might have different defensive priorities. Indeed Pétain had already told Haig when they had met late the previous night that, although he was aware that one of the German objectives was to defeat Gough's army and to open the way to Amiens, his priority was to defend Paris. The Germans were now less than 70 miles away from the French capital; and only the previous morning their first long range shell had fallen on the city. The gun, which was stationed 75 miles away, caused panic among the civilian population, killing 16 and wounding a further 29 on that first day and bringing home to them just how exposed they were. If necessary, Pétain made clear, Fayolle's relieving forces would fall back south-west to defend Paris rather than west, as the British wanted, to defend Amiens. It would create a dangerous gap between the two armies.

There was also a developing problem of resources. The agreement was that the British forces south of the Somme would come under French orders as and when the French arrived in each area and but that they would then revert to British command when they were relieved. While this was largely uncontentious for the infantry the French had arrived too quickly for their own artillery to follow and so tried to keep hold of the British artillery even when their infantry were relieved. It meant not only that the British artillery, which had done sterling work to date to cover the infantry's retreat and to slow down the speed of the German advance, might now be ordered to fall back with the French to defend Paris rather than their own comrades but also that the infantry units of the Fifth Army, when relieved, might be left without adequate artillery support.

Although the morning of 25 March began quietly the situation became more precarious as the day went on as the 89th and 90th Brigades were threatened on both flanks. The Germans started to push forward towards the canal at 10.00am, by 11.00am troops were seen retiring to the Pals' north, and by midday the enemy were advancing on Buverchy in strength. However there was worse news early in the afternoon when reports started to come through that the French had given way on their right. By 4.00pm the reports had been confirmed. Overwhelmed by the strength and determination of the German assault – one French captain claimed to have counted at least 16 waves of enemy infantry – the French had lost not only Libermont but the whole line of the canal south of Lannoy Farm. They had already withdrawn to a line behind the Pals' position at Moyencourt and would in due course, and in compliance with Pétain's orders, fall back south-west on to and beyond the road from Roye to Noyon.

Unfortunately the timing of the enemy's assault coincided with the final relief of the 30th Division, which the French had chosen to start at 3.00pm. At 4.30pm the Pals were finally ordered to withdraw to Solente, the village where they had spent a week at the end of January when they first arrived in the area from Ypres. Heavy enemy shelling made it difficult for them to get away. The 90th Brigade, who followed them out from the banks of the canal, had a much worse time. They lost many men when they were subjected to savage machine-gun fire from what was now their exposed right flank.

Although the Pals had hoped to find motor transport waiting for them in Solente the

4   General Sir Hubert Gough, *The Fifth Army*, p. 292.

heavy shelling of the village had prevented it from getting through. They were left with no choice but to march on another three miles to Roiglise, just south-east of Roye, where the local inhabitants were already making their own hurried preparations to leave. Brigadier Stanley thought his men a very poor little party when they arrived there that evening after a five-hour march: however he was proud that, after five days of desperate fighting, their resolve was undimmed. 'All the fellows were splendid', he recalled: 'they were dead tired but their tails were not a bit down and I think they were rather amused at having held up the Boche for so long and then having just got away'.[5] For Eric it was another lucky and last minute escape. An hour and a half later, after they had been given some hot food, the Pals were loaded on to buses for the 14-mile journey to Le Plessier, a village halfway along the main road from Roye to Amiens, where they arrived shortly after midnight. A charming chateau was waiting there as Stanley's headquarters and comfortable billets had been arranged for the rest of the men. It would be their first sight of a bed, and their first chance of a night's rest, for almost a week.

Any hopes that, having been relieved by the French, they were now out of harm's way were quickly dashed. At 9.30am the following morning they were rushed back into the line to defend the road to Amiens. With the French falling back south-west towards Paris after the loss of the Canal du Nord a four-mile gap had appeared overnight in the line between Roye and Hattencourt. From Hattencourt north to the Somme the line was now held by Watts' XIX corps who had retired there overnight from their previous line on the Somme when both their flanks were exposed. With the separation of the command north and south of the Somme Watts would now find his left flank on the river repeatedly exposed over the next few days when the Third Army to his north withdrew independently and at a faster rate, enabling the enemy to cross the river and get round behind him. It would have significant repercussions further south.

Roye fell to the Germans some time in the early hours of the morning of 26 March, only a few hours after the Pals had passed through the town. After five days they were now halfway to achieving their objective. Only 25 miles of straight and currently undefended road lay between them and Amiens; and, once they reached Amiens, it would be an easier task to move down the lower reaches of the Somme to Abbeville and then on to the English Channel. The British Army in Flanders could then be rolled up from the south. It was vital that the gap in the line was plugged as quickly as possible.

Watts ordered the 72nd Brigade on his right flank to fight their way back to a new line between Rosières and Rouvroy where they would link up with the 89th Brigade. With the Germans already pushing on from Roye the Pals had been unable to get as far forward as they had intended. However by 1.00pm they were established in the old French trench systems from 1914 in a line that ran south from Rouvroy to Bouchoir on the Roye-Amiens road. South of the road the line was picked up first by the 90th Brigade as far as Arvillers and then by the 36th Division from there down to the river Avre, where it met up with the French. Cast adrift, with his command in limbo and without any artillery cover, Gough was grateful that Maxse still had the men to fill the gap. 'Maxse's firmness and decision in keeping his corps together and moving it westwards and north-westwards,' he wrote, 'saved the Fifth Army, and in fact the whole British Army and the allied cause, from a disaster: for a complete separation of the French and British armies would have been nothing else'.[6]

5   Brigadier-General F C Stanley, *The History of the 89th Brigade 1914 – 1918*, p. 265.
6   General Sir Hubert Gough, op. cit., p. 296.

The Crossroads of the Dead at Rouvroy, looking east. (Author, 2016)

Although no further attack developed during the day the Germans were able to secure their positions in all the villages immediately in front of the British line. They were expected to press forward in strength again the following day. It was clear that another critical moment was approaching. With significant events having taken place elsewhere that day on the political and strategic front it was made clear that the defence of Amiens was once again the foremost priority for both the French and British forces. No further ground was to be given. In the early evening General Williams issued detailed orders to all his units: they were to patrol actively throughout the night and ensure that that all roads and tracks leading to their positions were barricaded against armoured cars. Attached to his orders was a special note from General Maxse to each of his brigades.

> The Corps Commander thoroughly recognises the gallant effort the brigade has made during the last six days and appreciates how much they must be worn after their hard and splendid fighting. He nevertheless asks for a final spurt on the part of the British troops to hold on to the present position at all costs until the concentration and deployment of large French forces behind us is completed.[7]

Stanley's staff had agreed at the outset with their opposite numbers in the 72nd Brigade where the boundary between them at Rouvroy should be. However it was not until after dark that it was discovered that there was a gap of some 300 yards between them at the apex of what threatened to become a dangerous salient in the defensive line. Ominously the place was marked on the map as the Crossroads of the Dead. As the 17th Battalion was in support at the time at Folies, Eric was given two companies, amounting by then to only about 100

---

7   Narrative of operations, 21 – 30 March 1918, 90th Infantry Brigade War Diary, The National Archives, WO 95/2338/3.

men, and sent to fill the gap. It is difficult now to assess just how significant or dangerous this move was or how long he had to stay there. Eric makes no reference to it himself; while Brigadier Stanley confirms that he sent up two companies to fill the gap he gives no further details on what then happened to them; and Everard Wyrall, who based his history of the regiment on battalion diaries, has nothing of substance to add, limiting himself to a passing comment that there was little of interest to report in the records of the 17th, 18th, and 19th battalions on 26 and 27 March. And yet it is worth noting that it is one of the few times that Eric is mentioned in the battalion diaries, and the only time that he is given a specific order by name. Indeed he and Eric Beaumont, the commander of D Company who was sent by Brigadier White to Holnon Wood early on the second morning of the offensive, are the only two officers to be named in the 17th Battalion's diary during the March offensive.

The fighting the next day, 27 March, on the wide flat plain of the Santerre south of the Somme, where machine guns could be used defensively with devastating effect, was intense and desperate. Eric was still at Rouvroy when the Germans made their first unsuccessful attempt on the village at 7.30am but that is the last we hear of him there. The enemy attacked again at 10.00am and took the village, only to lose it again two hours later when Brigadier Rosslewin Morgan led a counter-attack with three companies from the 72nd Brigade. It was a microcosm of the fighting that day which by mid-morning had developed along the whole front. The 30th Division's subsequent report on the offensive summed it up briefly with the comment that 'our defences were shaken and some retirement took place, only to be restored again almost immediately. By 1.00pm the attack had been broken and the situation was well in hand all along the line.'[8] Although they had been forced to give some ground they had probably ended the day on a stronger defensive line.

At times it had been touch and go. The 90th Brigade's own account of the fighting that day includes the following statement, which was later widely quoted by Gough and others:

> The troops were dazed and weakened by their long period of fighting without rest and it was difficult to keep them in position under the heavy shelling. There was no sign of panic and any attempts to withdraw were quite orderly and the men obeyed willingly when ordered to return to their positions, but they appeared to have lost the sense of reasoning and it was difficult to make them understand.

Although there were now clear signs that the German advance was beginning to lose momentum the more immediate worry for Gough was that withdrawals on both his left and right flanks had left his troops on the Santerre plateau even more exposed, and in particular at the head of the salient between Rosières and Rouvroy. Further withdrawals by the Third Army north of the Somme had left a six-mile gap along the river which the Germans were able to exploit until Watts pulled back his left flank. South of Roye the French had been forced to concede further significant ground. Their falling back south rather than west led that night to the loss of Montdidier, a key railhead for the deployment of their reinforcements. The town was given up without a fight. Once more there was a gap between the French and British forces, this time along the river Avre. But it was one that the Germans again failed to exploit.

The Pals had now had to hold out for another two days after their initial relief by the

8   Narrative of the 30th Division, 21 to 30 March 1918, 30th Division War Diary, The National Archives, WO 95/2312/5.

French at the Canal du Nord. However news came through that evening, albeit an hour before the loss of Montdidier, that they would once more be relieved by the French. No time had yet been fixed for the relief but it was expected to be late that night. Although some of the units in reserve were indeed relieved before midnight, the two French officers whom Brigadier Stanley had been told to expect never appeared. He waited up until 3.00am before ringing divisional headquarters to protest: and, when he and Brigadier Stevens, who had resumed command of the 90th Brigade the day before on his return from leave, found out the following morning that they were again to be relieved by a smaller French force they dug their heels in. They had been ordered the previous evening not to leave the forward zone before ensuring that they were properly relieved. They now made it clear that they were not prepared to withdraw unless they first got proper authorisation from their commanding officer.

It would late in the morning before a senior staff officer finally turned up with the two French officers. By then the Pals were again under heavy attack and, although they were holding their ground, they were in danger of being cut off. Their only hope of escape was to retire along the main road to Amiens. The Germans already occupied the villages of Caix and Hangest, which were well behind them on either side of the road, and they could see troops withdrawing on both their flanks even though the French tried nonchalantly to claim that this was only because they had just been relieved. At 11.50am Colonel Hoff of the French 133rd Division gave both Stanley and Stevens notes written in French confirming that he was satisfied that the units of the 30th Division in the sector from Folies to Beaufort could leave without upsetting his arrangements and asking them to withdraw as quickly as possible.

It would be another two hours before their relief was complete and the Pals were able to start back towards Amiens. 'We came away not a moment too soon', Stanley remembered, 'and had a pretty near shave of it. We then retired according to orders, though Mézières to Moreuil, and so to Rouvrel – a very ticklish time it was, too. The Boche might have done us much more harm than he did; in fact, he might quite easily have got the lot of us.'[9] The 72nd and 90th Brigades had an equally difficult time, being harried by machine gun fire and sustaining heavy casualties as they also extricated themselves from the salient. Once again the French followed them out. They had been forced to give ground almost as soon as the relief was complete. With fewer troops they had already decided that their main defensive line was to be further back between Hangest and Le Quesnel but by now even this line was threatened by the German advance. At 4.30pm the French were forced to withdraw another half a mile before quickly falling back a further mile along the road to Mézières. The Pals got there only just before them before cutting off west on a final seven mile march to their billets at Rouvrel. They arrived at around 6.30pm, their progress having been made slow and difficult by the congestion. The main road to Amiens was now clogged not only with troops, transport, and ambulances but also with French civilians evacuating their homes and taking all their most precious belongings with them in wheelbarrows and any other carts that were to hand.

Brigadier Stanley was full of admiration for his men. 'I don't think I have ever seen anything so fine as when we marched to Mézières from Folies and re-formed up as a brigade', he claimed in what would be his final speech to the brigade just over a week later. 'It was something grand. I cannot tell you how proud I was, and those who saw us pass said nothing

French refugees near Béthune, April 1918. (© Imperial War Museum, Q10899)

could be finer than the spirit of the brigade; although the enemy forced us back and caused us to withdraw, but the spirit was there all the same.'[10]

It was bitterly cold and raining by the time the Pals reached Rouvrel. They were now only ten miles from Amiens and the village was packed with troops and civilians heading west. General Williams, who had been told by Maxse's corps HQ that the 30th Division would now be under French command until further notice, received an order in French from General Lavigne-Delville shortly after their arrival asking him to keep his troops in the village that night but to ensure that they remained in a state of preparedness and were ready to intervene, if necessary, at a moment's notice. The French general added a personal note in his own hand at the bottom of the order – 'I hope to be able to leave you in peace all day on the 29th and on the night of 29th/30th for you to rest and re-organise. All is going well on my front.'[11]

Apart from a couple of false alarms no further orders came through either that night or the following day. The Pals were left to enjoy their first full night's rest since the start of the offensive. Once more Eric had managed to get away. Not all the Pals had been so lucky. More than 200 had now been killed since the start of the offensive, more than half of them from the 19th Battalion which had been told to fight to the death at Roupy. Many more had been wounded, were missing, or had been taken prisoner in the opening hours of the offensive

10   Brigadier-General F C Stanley, op. cit., pp. 275-6.
11   Narrative of operations, 21 – 30 March 1918, 90th Infantry Brigade War Diary, The National Archives, WO 95/2338/3.

Troops from the 17th Division regrouping after their withdrawal at Hénencourt,
three miles west of Albert, 26 March 1918. (© Imperial War Museum, Q8621)

or left behind as stragglers during the retreat. A roll call at Rouvrel in the morning revealed
that the 89th Brigade, which had been in corps reserve at the start of the offensive, had
suffered a 50% casualty rate and was now down to less than 1,000 men. The 21st and 90th
Brigades, which had manned the forward and battle zones on the first day, had fared much
worse. They both had a 75% casualty rate and could muster fewer men between them than
the Pals. The highest casualties had been in the two battalions defending the forward zone
and garrisoning the redoubts at Manchester Hill and L'Épine de Dallon. When the three
brigade commanders met after the roll call they decided to reform each of their brigades into
a single battalion which together would form a composite brigade. It meant that, in the two
months since the disbanding of the Pals' 20th Battalion, the strength of the 30th Division
had been reduced from twelve to three battalions.

The Pals spent the rest of the day and night in Rouvrel. In the afternoon the Optimists
put on an impromptu show in their mud-spattered battledress. They had been forced to
abandon all their props and costumes in the retreat. Their performance was interrupted
repeatedly as news came through that the enemy was continuing to press forward. By the
end of the show they were reported to be less than five miles away in the village of Braches.
Eric himself found time to scribble a brief note home, his first for almost a fortnight.

Dear Father and Mother
I am afraid you will be wondering what has happened to me as I have not written for so

long. We have been hard at it for a week and have really had no opportunity for writing. I am quite well although my teeth are still troubling me. I have not seen the papers at all but from all appearances things are going on as well as possible. Must stop now and get some work done.

Best love to Ju, Guy, and yourselves – your ever loving son, Eric

It was not the first news that Harry and Alice had had of their son. It seems extraordinary now – and a tribute to the efficiency of the Army Postal Service, which handled 12 million letters and a million parcels a week during the war – that Eric had been able to send home three field postcards since the start of the offensive. The first is dated 21 March, the opening day of the offensive; the second is dated 25 March, when the Pals were first relieved by the French at the Canal du Nord; and the third was sent from Rouvrel on 29 March, presumably before he found the time to write his letter. Nothing could be written on these small pre-printed cards that measured only 4½ by 3¼ inches and were sent home from the front in their millions. The senders could only cross out the sentences that did not apply. On all three cards Eric erased all but the first sentence which stated simply that 'I am quite well'. The precise meaning of 'quite' was perhaps left to the reader's interpretation.

The Pals were finally withdrawn from the battlefield the following morning. It was raining hard, and the roads were still crammed with troops and civilians, as they slowly trudged the 12 miles back to Saleux on the outskirts of Amiens. There, at 6.00pm, they were packed like sardines into two trains for the 40-mile journey to St Valery at the mouth of the Somme. By the time they arrived there six hours later, at midnight, they were too exhausted to march the final five miles to their billets. They bedded down at the station wherever they could find a space. It was only the following morning, 31 March, that they reached their final destination. It was Easter Sunday, and almost a year since the previous Easter when Eric had spent the day under cover in a field south of Arras waiting for his first experience of battle. It was a miracle that he was still alive after a year in which 1,000 Liverpool Pals had died.

Three weeks later Eric heard that he had been awarded the Military Cross. The medal had been introduced in 1914 to honour gallantry shown in the presence of the enemy by

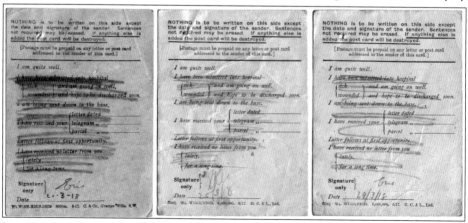

The three field postcards that Eric sent home during the Spring Offensive dated 21, 25, and 29 March 1918. (Author)

Exhausted troops asleep at Hénencourt, 26 March 1918. The Pals
would have to hold on for another two days before they were finally
relieved by the French. (© Imperial War Museum, Q8635)

warrant and junior officers whose rank made them ineligible for the Distinguished Service
Order. The equivalent Military Medal was introduced for other ranks in 1916. Over 37,000
officers were awarded the medal during the war, 2,800 were awarded it a second time,
receiving a 'bar' to their original medal, but fewer than 200 received it for a third time
and only four for a fourth. By comparison the Victoria Cross, the highest British award for
gallantry and one which was open to all ranks, was awarded only 600 times during the war;
and almost a third of those awards were posthumous.

Eric's citation – 'Heaven knows what for', he told his parents, 'I have done so little
compared with the many who have been hit' – would not appear in the *London Gazette*
until the end of July.

> Lieutenant (Acting Captain) Eric Rigby-Jones, Liverpool Regiment – for conspicuous
> gallantry and devotion to duty during lengthy operations. He held on to positions with
> great tenacity and, although almost surrounded on several occasions, he continued to
> exercise complete control over his men, fighting his way back to new positions. The
> fine behaviour of all ranks was largely due to his splendid example.[12]

Eric had his medal inscribed 'St Quentin, 21 – 28 March 1918', thus making it explicit

---

12   *London Gazette*, supplement no. 30813, published 23 July 1918, p. 8838.

that the award covered the whole period of the offensive, from his being sent to Sword Wood by Brigadier White on the first night through the defensive stands at Ham, the Canal du Nord, and Rouvroy to the Pals' final relief at Rouvrel. On 19 April he received a signal of congratulations from General Williams to which Colonel Campbell Watson had added his own heartiest congratulations. Campbell Watson himself had been honoured with the award of a bar to the Distinguished Service Order that he had received at Ypres the previous summer. When, however, Everard Wyrrall came to write his history of the regiment during the war, he not only listed both men as being from the 19th rather than the 17th Battalion but also transcribed Eric's name incorrectly from the battalion diary as Captain E Rigley-Jones. It is, as far as I am aware, the only time that my grandfather is mentioned in any published history of his unit or the war.

12

St Valery-sur-Somme

April 1918

Three weeks ago today the enemy began his terrific attacks against us on a fifty-mile front. His objects are to separate us from the French, to take the Channel ports and destroy the British Army. In spite of throwing already 106 divisions into the battle and enduring the most reckless sacrifice of human life, he has as yet made little progress towards his goals. We owe this to the determined fighting and self-sacrifice of our troops. Words fail me to express the admiration which I feel for the splendid resistance offered by all ranks of our Army under the most trying circumstances ...

Field Marshal Sir Douglas Haig's Special Order of the Day, 11 April 1918

The allies' political and military leaders had watched with growing alarm as Gough's Fifth Army was pushed back towards Amiens. After meeting on 23 March Haig and Pétain met again late the following night to decide a plan of action. Lloyd George sent over his two most trusted lieutenants, Lord Milner and Sir Henry Wilson, now Chief of the Imperial General Staff. Both spent the following day in a series of meetings with the British and French high command and with the French president and prime minister. By the end of the day arrangements had been made for an emergency meeting of the French and British political and military leadership at Doullens the following day, 26 March. The situation was still critical.

With the exception of Lloyd George, whose place was taken by Lord Milner, all the major players were at the meeting. The French were represented by President Poincaré, who chaired the meeting, Prime Minister Clemenceau, Marshal Foch and General Pétain. Those who travelled from Paris must have had a nervous journey skirting round the advancing German Army. The British delegation was led by Milner, Wilson, and Field-Marshal Haig. There was unanimous agreement that Amiens had to be defended at all costs and that Foch should be appointed commander-in-chief and generalissimo of the allied armies on the Western Front. It had taken a crisis for Lloyd George to achieve what had been one of his three main goals when he became Prime Minister.

Doullens, 20 miles north of Amiens, was not the easiest or most obvious place to meet. It had been chosen only because Haig had already arranged to meet his generals there that day. Plumer came from Ypres, Horne from Béthune, and Byng from Arras: only Gough was absent. Plumer was surprised and disappointed that Byng had not chosen to stay with his Third Army which was still involved in a desperate fight north of the Somme. Gough, on the other hand, had not been invited. Indeed he had not even been told that the meeting was taking place. He and his Fifth Army had been placed under French command the previous day, although Pétain could not resist a caustic comment that so little of it remained that in truth it could hardly be said to exist anymore. When the British delegation met separately

173

Stained glass window commemorating the British and French conference on 26 March
1918 in the Salle du Commandement Unique at Doullens town hall. (Author, 2013)

after the conference they agreed that Gough should be removed from his command. He was
the obvious scapegoat for the success of the German offensive. His removal and subsequent
treatment ranks as one of the shabbiest episodes in the history of the war and was almost
certainly instigated at the highest levels of government.

Although he remained reticent about his approval of Gough's plans for an orderly
retirement, Haig acknowledged in his later dispatch that the Fifth Army had faced
impossible odds. To his credit he also tried to put a chivalrous slant on Gough's removal by
claiming that the offensive had put an unbearable strain on the general and his staff and that
he needed to be replaced to avoid any loss of efficiency. Other officers at every level in the
Fifth Army had also reached breaking point. Poyntz, who had commanded the 90th Brigade
at the start of the offensive, was admitted to hospital on 29 March – he was 'absolutely done'
according to Brigadier Stanley; Campbell Watson collapsed at the beginning of April; and
Eric himself admitted that at one stage it was a struggle to stay sane. But for Gough, a career
soldier whose father, uncle, and brother had all been awarded the Victoria Cross – they
remain to this day the most highly-decorated British family – it was an undisguised personal
humiliation that would not be put right for many years. At the end of the war he was the
only army commander not to be invited to the victory celebrations; and he received none of
the honours and decorations that were showered upon his colleagues. Unlike the ennobled

Earl Haig and Viscounts Plumer, Byng, and Allenby – of Messines, Vimy, and Megiddo respectively – Gough was passed over for generous financial awards and had to wait almost twenty years to be invested as a Knight Grand Cross, Order of the Bath (GCB). Inviting him to a private ceremony some weeks ahead of the official investiture, King George VI is reported to have commented that, as Gough had had to wait so long, it would be unfair to keep him waiting any longer.

Lloyd George was altogether less chivalrous when he addressed the House of Commons on 9 April. Although he made it clear that, with the battle still being fought, it was too early to make any final judgements, he had no compunction in singling out Gough for criticism. He praised Byng's Third Army for never having given ground; he congratulated the French for the remarkable speed with which they had brought up their reserves, a statement that Brigadier Stanley and others might have challenged; but he also made it clear that he was looking for an explanation of the Fifth Army's retirement and why it had failed to hold the line of the Somme and to destroy all the bridges over it. 'Until all these are explained', he said, 'it would be unfair to censure the general in command of the army—General Gough. But until those circumstances are cleared up, it would be equally unfair to the British Army to retain his services in the field.'[1]

In the meantime Gough had to endure four days of humiliation. He and his Fifth Army south of the Somme had already been placed under French command the previous morning. Now Foch's first port of call as generalissimo after leaving the conference at Doullens was Gough's HQ at Dury, just south of Amiens. It was a short, frosty, and brutal meeting. Gough, who had been warned by GHQ to expect a visit from Foch in the afternoon, was taken aback both by his attitude – he described him as 'peremptory, rude, and excited in his manner' – and by his tirade against the performance both of the Fifth Army and of himself as its commander. 'There must be no more retreat, the line must now be held at all costs', Foch shouted as he left to go back to his car.[2] It was only that morning, after five days of fighting, that the Pals had been rushed back into the line at Rouvroy to plug the gap left by the withdrawal of their French relief from the Canal du Nord.

The following afternoon Gough had a visit from Haig's military secretary, General Ruggles-Brise, who told him that he was to be replaced as commander of the Fifth Army by Rawlinson. Rawlinson, the recently-appointed British Military Representative at the Allied Supreme Council, arrived with his staff and their lorries the following day. Gough described it as 'the last day of my career as a soldier'.[3] In less than a week he was back in England on half pay. He would have smiled if he had known that one of Rawlinson's first orders from Haig was to ensure above all else the safety of the forces under his command. Haig himself had already been informed by Sir Henry Wilson in London that every fit trained man was being sent to France.

By then the German advance on Amiens had begun to run out of steam. Its success had unintentionally re-created the problems that had been resolved a year earlier by their withdrawal to the Hindenburg Line. The greater strength and resilience of Byng's Third Army in the north had resulted in a bulge in the German front in the south. It was now 50 miles longer than it had been at the start of the offensive. Troops had to be diverted south to cover it. The absence of a road and railway infrastructure, which the Germans had themselves

---

1   Hansard, *House of Commons Debate, 9 April 1918, vol. 104 c. 1343.*

2   General Sir Hubert Gough, *The Fifth Army*, pp. 306-7.

3   General Sir Hubert Gough, op. cit., p. 318.

German troops looting a captured British ration dump during the
Spring Offensive. (© Imperial War Museum, Q61539)

destroyed in their withdrawal, caused havoc with their transport and communication lines and made it increasingly difficult to get essential supplies to the vanguard of their advance. Water in particular was in short supply. German troops, who themselves had sustained high casualty rates, were as exhausted and hungry as their enemy. When they came across the supply dumps abandoned by the British in their retreat they were shocked by the quantity and quality of the supplies that were still available to the British Tommy: they had long been deprived of them by the blockade of the German ports and shortages at home. They fell greedily on the food and fine wine and helped themselves to British trench coats, jackets and leather boots. Pushing on no longer seemed quite so urgent. There was time, they thought, to taste their victory and to enjoy the fruits of their labour.

The German High Command was forced to take stock. Although they had come close to making a breakthrough they had not yet won the war and their line was now mis-shapen and difficult to hold. On 28 March they decided to re-invigorate the offensive by shifting its focus back to its northern end at Arras. The change was short-lived. This time they had no fog to help them. The German storm-troopers were mown down by British machine-guns as they moved forward. The attack was called off the same evening and the focus returned to Amiens where French reinforcements were now arriving in numbers. On 4 April the Germans made a final attempt to take the city. When this failed Hindenburg and Ludendorff decided to turn their attention to Flanders and to the second stage of their offensive. By then they had taken 1,200 square miles of territory and captured 90,000 prisoners, 1,000 guns, and vast quantities of stores.

Eric, meanwhile, was out of the line and trying to come to terms with what he had been through. On Easter Monday, 1 April, the day after the Pals arrived at their billets at the mouth of the Somme, he was able to write his first long letter home for a fortnight.

Dear Father and Mother

At last I can sit down and write you a proper letter. I am now properly clothed and in my right mind again. We are right back on rest and getting our strength back again. I have, I think, experienced more in the past ten days than in the whole of my life so far. I shall have a tremendous lot to tell you all when I see you again. My brain is working better now but at one time I had a job to keep myself from going clean off my head. I have been in all sorts of places from which I never expected to come out alive. I have a tremendous lot to be thankful for.

Poor old Tatlock was killed quite early on. I must write to his wife: perhaps Mother would write also. I will put his address in at the end of the letter. I miss him more than I can tell you as he has been such a wonderful friend. I have lost a great deal of my kit. Some I can get here but I would like you to send me the following as soon as ever possible: two shirts, two pairs of pants and two vests – slightly thinner than before, four pairs of thick socks – not too large, and a trench cost (Zambrene). I only had one change of clothes in my valise, which is safe: the others are lost. The clothes that I had in action are worn away. My feet have let me down rather but they are feeling better now. It is a beautiful place here and we are all dazed with the quietness and peace. I have not had any word from you since your letter of 18 March but expect a mail to-morrow. I will write to you again to-morrow.

Love to you all, your ever loving son, Eric

PS Things over here are looking brighter now. You will soon see the Boche out of France altogether.

Eric's batman, 29-year old Private James Tatlock, had been a warehouse foreman in Bolton before the war. He was killed on 24 March during the Pals' withdrawal from Verlaines to the Canal du Nord. His body was never found. His name is now engraved on the Pozieres memorial alongside more than 14,000 other men who died near the Somme between 21 March and 7 August 1918 and who have no known grave. He had been with Eric since his arrival in France. As Eric had told his Aunt Lu after the battle of Arras, they had quickly developed a close relationship.

You can imagine how glad I was to see your parcel and a cup of tea that my orderly had ready for me. He's a wonderful chap, this orderly. He can always manage to get a cup of tea ready wherever he is. Of course he does ordinary duty when we are in the line but we generally manage to keep together. I thought I had lost him on Easter Monday. On two occasions he was lifted off his feet by a 5.9 but it didn't upset him in mind at all except that he lost a Boche helmet he was carrying as a souvenir.

A year later and Eric had lost his friend. His death was the final blow after losing so many friends with the disbanding of the 20th Battalion in February. Eric's mother not only wrote to Mrs. Tatlock, as he had asked, but also went to see her in Bolton a few weeks later. The following day Mrs. Tatlock wrote to tell Eric how much the visit had meant to her.

After two weeks without a letter Eric was desperate for news from home. He also had

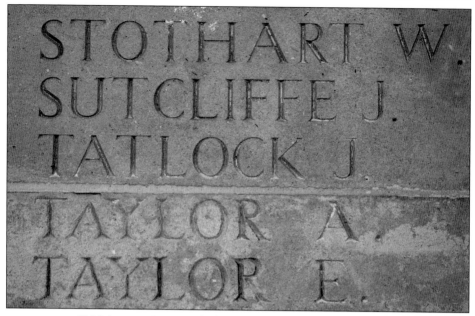

Eric's batman, James Tatlock, one of the 14,000 names inscribed
on the Pozières memorial. (Author, 2013)

time to catch up on his own letter-writing and wrote home every day for the next week.

I was longing for a line from you when your letters dated 21, 22, 23, 24, 25, and 26 March were delivered to me late last night. I sat in front of the fire and enjoyed them immensely. I am very sorry that I have not sent news of Norman Winder in my previous letters. He is and has been quite alright and I suppose for that reason alone I did not mention anything about him: his father will no doubt have had letters from him by now. We have been quite near together during the battle and at one time lived in the same hole which we dug for ourselves. During the show we must have dug ourselves in at least 20 times as of course it is the only way to get protection from shells and bullets when you are fighting in the open.

We had a pretty stiff time for 10 days. We were at it continuously and I laughed last night when I read in one of Mother's letters that she expected that we should be relieved on Sunday the 24th. Now that the situation is clearer one can be more hopeful of future events. When in a fight one only sees the position on a very small sector of the front and one is apt to judge the whole situation from one's own position. The latest news is very good and I hope it will continue so. I think if everybody continues to put their best into it we shall soon see something for our work. At any rate it is worthwhile. The more I see of the Hun, and I have seen a little of him lately, the more convinced I am that it is worth anything to win the war properly.

We are now in the most delightful billets I have known in France in a delightful neighbourhood only a mile or two from the sea: the air is wonderfully bracing and the weather is beautiful. It is the ideal place for us to get back our strength which we are doing rapidly. We are living in a little bungalow on the top of a hill: it belongs to some people in Paris who apparently only use it during the summer months. There are quite nice bedrooms, a drawing room, dining room and a kitchen so we are well off. The old concierge and his wife live in a little lodge at the gate and she has done the washing of what few clothes we have left. The old man tells me that the place belongs to me for the present and that he is there to do whatever I tell him. There are only three officers left in the company out of the original ten and one more is coming back from hospital to-day so we are quite a small family now, though larger than most company messes. I am not sure what has happened to Sutton: he is a prisoner I know but I fear he was killed. I met Bampton during a fight and did not recognise him at first and am afraid I had not time to say much to him. He looked very well and was very cheery.

I am feeling much better now: it is wonderful how soon one recovers after these things. The officer I referred to above as returning from hospital has just come in. It is Gill: he had a bullet through his neck at the beginning and had a very narrow shave but seems OK now. Ashcroft is quite alright and so is Colonel Watson although heaven alone knows why we are all still alive. Another thing which I have found is my miniature chess men and board so I will be able to have a game with Gill this evening. My old gramophone has survived and is the only one in the battalion and I still have most of the records so am quite lucky there.

I have managed to get my trench coat back but it is practically done for although it will do until I get a new one. I rode over to a town a few miles away and managed to get a pair of rather, in fact very, inferior French socks, a pen-knife and a pair of gloves. These I was without: I now need only underclothes and then I shall be alright again. My feet are still raw but I am looking after them and hope to get them right again soon. Naturally there is a lot of work to be done but everybody is cheerful and optimistic, which is the most important thing. I have just been out to see the company on parade for a few minutes before they dismiss as I have been indoors writing all day. It is a big job re-organising and sorting out, reporting casualties, etc. The job which I am on with now and which I loathe is the writing to the parents and wives of the poor fellows who have gone under. Fortunately there are few but I have lost a great number of men wounded from the company, many only slightly, and I hope to have them back soon.

I do hope you have enjoyed your Easter as I have done. Must stop now and get a cup of tea before I start to pay the men.

As well as maintaining their regular stream of food parcels Harry and Alice now started to work through Eric's shopping list of urgent requests. When, however, they tried to help by sending him a newspaper cutting which explained how one could claim for the recovery of lost kit, he felt he had to put them straight.

As regards the extract from the paper re. recovery of lost kit everything looks quite easy but, when the ordnance stores itself is lost and one is landed in a place as near the Boche as it is to an ordnance store, things become more difficult. Then, if one did get to a store to refit, one has to pay for the things and reclaim later. I have got my things from home and shall reclaim the money, if lucky, in the ordinary way. I don't expect the claim will take more than a year to go through after having been subjected to several divisions and subtractions and other alterations.

Even though the 89th Brigade was now much reduced in size Brigadier Stanley was still feeling gung-ho about the future. 'All that were left were in splendid form', he said, 'and there was no question of our tails being down – the very reverse. If only we could be given the chance we were only too anxious to get at the Boche again and this time push him back.'[4] Work began immediately to bring the brigade back up to scratch. The composite battalion was disbanded and the three Pals battalions resurrected and replenished with new recruits. However they were given almost no time to recover from their ordeal and to complete their re-organisation. On 4 April, after only three nights in their billets at the mouth of the Somme, they were on the move again, marching four miles to Woincourt to board a train back to Flanders. Haig had had to send reinforcements south to meet the German threat: now he needed his battle-weary troops from the south to take their place. The Pals were optimistic that the Ypres salient was and would remain quiet. For them, if not for Brigadier Stanley, the chance to get back at the Boche would come rather sooner than they anticipated.

Eric quickly recovered his fighting spirit. His hackles, however, were raised when reports of the growing criticism of General Gough and the Fifth Army began to filter through from home, especially in the aftermath of Lloyd George's speech to the House of Commons on 9 April. Eric told his parents what he thought a fortnight later.

> The criticisms of the Fifth Army and of many individuals are enough to make anyone almost too fed up to carry on. I shall be glad to hear the whole story when it comes out but meanwhile I wish the non-combatants would shut up. Of course we do not know what goes on in higher commands but I for one am proud to have fought amongst those comparative few who had to bear the brunt of the Boche's first and fiercest outburst. I just hope there is a strong enough man in Parliament to run the show at home: that is all we are worrying about. I think Ireland and conscientious objectors, etc are proof of the extraordinary weakness of our politicians. It is appalling to think that Ireland and many in England are still neutrals in this terrible struggle. We at any rate are all still as cheery as ever and shall be whatever happens.

General Gough would not be the only senior officer in the Fifth Army who had to fall on his sword. As soon as the Pals arrived back in Flanders – it was still only a week since their relief at Amiens – 47-year old Brigadier Stanley was replaced as their commanding officer. 'I cannot tell you how it hurts me. It fairly breaks my heart', Stanley told his men when he gathered them together before Church Parade on Sunday, 7 April. General Williams, he said, had decided that a younger man was required and so 'unfortunately, it falls to my lot to go to the wall.'[5] Stanley, however, was certain that he too had been made a scapegoat for the retreat from St Quentin. In particular, in the light of Lloyd George's comments in parliament, he may have been held responsible for the collapse of the bridgehead at Ham and his failure to destroy all the bridges over the Somme. Although he was never a great fighting brigadier he had always been a most loyal and popular commander, and concerned above all else for the health and well-being of his men. Eric told his parents how he felt three days later.

> Colonel Watson has gone down sick to-day: I fear he is rather broken in health after the enormous strain. General Stanley has also left us. We are all not too grand. I have

---

4   Brigadier-General F C Stanley, *The History of the 89th Brigade 1914 – 1918*, p. 274.
5   Brigadier-General F C Stanley, op. cit., p. 275.

been having a lot of trouble with my inside and had an attack of cramp this morning but am really alright and shall soon get over it. It is a case of the survival of the fittest now – at any rate as far as front line troops are concerned. I rather regret coming out of hospital when I did as I was certainly far from fit when it all started. But I would not have missed it for the world. It was a wonderful experience though costly and cruel. It is something to have experienced real hunger and thirst and all that; and it is glorious when one gets out of it all.

It would be another five days before Brigadier Currie arrived to take over command of the brigade. The following week Brigadier Stanley's brother, Lord Derby, stepped down as Secretary of State for War on his appointment as British ambassador in Paris. The Pals would however have little time to reflect on their loss of the Stanley connection. Only a few hours after the brigadier's final Church Parade they received their orders to return to the front.

13

The Battle of the Lys

April 1918

... Many amongst us now are tired. To those I would say that victory will belong to the side which holds out the longest. The French Army is moving rapidly and in great force to our support. There is no other course open to us but to fight it out. Every position must be held to the last man: there must be no retirement. With our backs to the wall and believing in the justice of our cause each one of us must fight on to the end. The safety of our homes and the freedom of mankind alike depend upon the conduct of each one of us at this critical moment.

Field Marshal Sir Douglas Haig's Special Order of the Day, 11 April 1918

Five days after the failure of their final attempt to take Amiens Hindenburg and Ludendorff moved on to the second phase of their Spring Offensive. Their plan now was to strike west of Armentières to seize Hazebrouck, the major terminus 17 miles south-west of Ypres through which ran half of the British Army's supplies of food and munitions. Its capture would cut off Ypres and lay open the route to the Channel ports.

The Germans once again made immediate and significant territorial gains. On 9 April, the first day of the offensive, they struck south of Armentières and advanced six miles to the banks of the river Lys, which would give its name to the battles that month; on the second day they struck north of the town and by noon had reached the southern slopes of the Wytschaete Ridge and retaken the town of Messines; and by the end of the third day they had consolidated territorial gains up to eight miles deep along a 20-mile front from Ypres to Béthune.

Haig was quick to recognise the speed and scale of the threat and the weakness of his own forces to meet it. On 11 April he entrusted the defence of the new front to the ever-reliable Plumer and issued his famous order of the day to all British troops serving on the Western Front. Eric had clearly read it when he wrote to his parents a few days later.

The Boche appears to pushing all along the front but with little measure of success. It looks like an admission of his failure to achieve his final objectives in his first effort. I think his wickets will soon fall in the second innings.

We are still carrying on with our backs to the wall with the faith in the righteousness of our cause that will live until the tide turns. Your cheery letters do a great deal to keep one going. Possibly you may have thought from my letters that I have been one of those foolish optimists that have done so much harm in preventing all from realising the odds against us. Possibly I have been, but not to so great an extent, for I have seen enough to know what the Boche is worth. I think all now realise that only by everyone putting their utmost into the fight shall we come out victorious. The light way in which

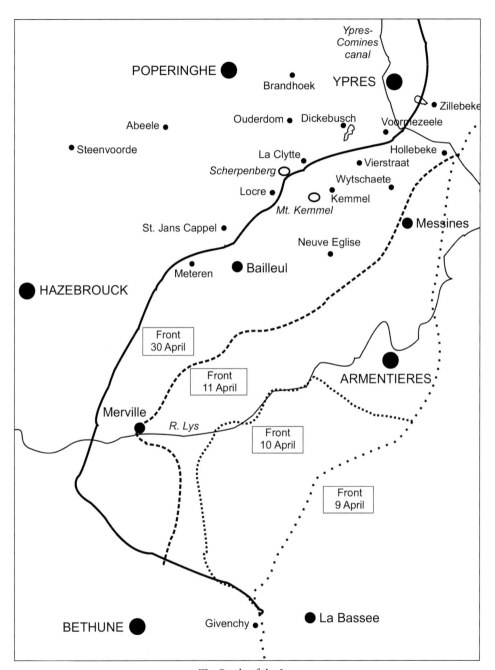

The Battle of the Lys.

the papers treat our defeat in the first battle makes one feel sick. The odds were very heavy against us and, as far as I am concerned, I have a clear conscience that I have not withdrawn an inch unless ordered to do so because of our flanks being in danger or when we were actually surrounded.

I feel very annoyed that I am not up to the mark but I shall not give in, for I am not as bad as some and I can keep my spirits up. I have just had a visit from Colonel Watson: he is a marvel and I don't know how he carries on. Do not worry for my bodily safety: that is worth little. As long as I can put everything into it up to the last I am content. We must take a lesson from France who is keeping her end up wonderfully. We shall do the same and soon we shall see a turn in the scale.

The Boche is nearly done. History shows us how often a country has gone under when, by sticking to it but a little longer, she would have emerged victorious. In the Russo-Japanese war we know that, had Russia withstood a little longer, she would have won because Japan was utterly exhausted, having put her last ounce into the struggle. So it is now and I am convinced that we shall pull it off but not without a supreme effort.

The British Army fell back reluctantly in the face of the German onslaught, fighting for every inch of ground. In order to shorten their line and to release more troops to defend the greater threat south of Ypres Haig and Plumer made the desperate decision to withdraw from Passchendaele and the ridges to the north and east of the city. The withdrawal began on the night of 12 April and was completed three nights later with the establishment of a new line that ran along the Steenbeek stream in the north-east and then around to Wytschaete in the south-east. It took just a few days to evacuate the positions which had been won at such cost the previous autumn.

At a conference in Abbeville on 14 April Haig pressed the new generalissimo, Marshal Foch, for reinforcements. Foch hesitated at first. He was hoping that the German advance would soon flounder of its own accord for lack of reserves. He was keen to keep his own troops back as he was still expecting an attack on the French line towards Rheims. However the scale of the immediate threat was driven home to him later that day with the loss of Neuve Église and then, over the next two days, of Bailleul, Meteren, and Wytschaete. With the Germans now only five miles from Hazebrouck Foch ordered Pétain to send a French division to the area immediately. Another three would follow three days later.

On 17 April the Germans made their first assault on Mount Kemmel. It was where Eric had been based the previous autumn when he stood in as quartermaster and where he had bumped into General Plumer on his 20th birthday at the start of the Battle of the Menin Road. If the Germans took the hill they would have a commanding view over the whole salient and would be able to monitor all activity behind the British lines. Mercifully their assault did not succeed. A second assault was expected two days later but was thwarted by heavy artillery barrages from both sides. On the same day German attacks were seen off further south at Merville and Givenchy. They were the first signs that the second stage of their offensive was faltering. For almost a week thereafter there was an unexpected lull in the fighting while the Germans re-grouped. By then they were as exhausted as their enemy and running short of supplies; and the British withdrawal to strong positions on a shorter front around Ypres meant that German casualties were mounting in the face of murderous machine-gun fire. French infantry and artillery reinforcements were also beginning to arrive and by 21 April they had taken over the whole of the Kemmel sector from the British.

The Pals had arrived back in the Ypres sector on the night of 5 April. Two nights later, after Brigadier Stanley had taken his farewell at his final church parade, they found themselves back in the front line to the north of the city. They were now on the end of the British line between Poelcappelle and the Yser canal: to their left, on the west bank of the canal, was the Belgian army. In the space of only ten weeks the Pals had now been on both the left and right wings of the 120-mile long British front.

On 11 April, two days after the start of the German offensive, the 17th Battalion took over the forward zone east of the Steenbeek. Although they were now in a quiet sector and well away from the fighting their line was only thinly-held. Their orders, as before, were to hold their position at all costs and to withdraw only if they faced overwhelming and sustained pressure from the enemy, and then only they if they contested every inch of ground. They were to patrol vigorously each night and to provide prompt and detailed reports of all enemy activity. Eric was given a printed card 'giving points to be attended to when reporting enemy shelling with a view to obtaining immediate neutralizing fire'. These cards, he was reminded, were issued as an aide-memoire and were not be used for writing his reports on. He was required to report immediately on the area shelled, the calibre of shell ('Don't exaggerate', the card warned), the time when the shelling started and ceased, the interval between shells, and the direction from which they came. In spite of all this he received a written reprimand from the adjutant on 14 April, saying that the battalion's commanding officer was not satisfied with his reports.

The following night, in line with Haig and Plumer's decision to surrender the ridges to the north and east of the city, the battalion was withdrawn behind the Steenbeek. As they left they destroyed all their dug-outs and pill-boxes, and the crossings over the stream. Bailleul fell the same night; and on the following day the Pals were temporarily attached to the 34th Division and ordered south to help defend the line between Meteren and Mount Kemmel. The 18th and 19th battalions were rushed there immediately by bus: the 17th followed the next day. By the time they arrived Meteren had been lost, Mount Kemmel was facing its first assault, and the weather had taken a turn for the worse. They now had to contend with intermittent hail and snow showers. They were sent immediately to St Jans-Cappel, the first village that the enemy would encounter if they pushed on north-west from Bailleul. They had orders to send out patrols to find out all they could on German troop positions and movements. Eric however found time to write a quick note to his aunt Frieda, his father's youngest sister who was only eight years older than him and was still living with her parents at Claremont, to thank her for her parcel of clothes.

> I managed to get a clean change yesterday, the first after a fortnight. You will guess what a boon it is to have fresh clothes to get into although I have been wet through several times since. Of course I am also covered with mud again by now but then that is only to keep oneself warm. Please excuse this untidy scrawl but, if you saw the little hole, 2 feet x 4 feet x 3 feet deep, which constitutes my residence, you would understand.

Eric was sure, during the lull in the fighting that followed the Germans' failure to take Mount Kemmel, that his men's spirits were as high as they had ever been. Nevertheless the Pals' patrols soon began to take their toll. 'Brown of the 20th was wounded yesterday', Eric told his parents, 'and Emery got a nice piece at the same time. Lucky fellows! – although I want to be in it until we push the Boche back again. The situation is well in hand as far as

I can see and the Boche is at last getting it in the neck.' His chess partner, Lieutenant Gill, the former Wesleyan minister who had been wounded in the neck in the retreat from St Quentin, was now wounded again and missing: it would not be confirmed until much later that he had been killed in action. Eric's parents were still asking for news of him in October. Eric told them all he could.

> This is all I know about Gill. He was ordered on the afternoon of 19 April to take out a patrol and go up a narrow country lane which led from our lines to a farm-house where there was known to be an enemy post and which he was, if possible, to capture. He took a sergeant and four men and started off at dusk in a diamond formation, he being in the centre. When near the farm the leading man came back and reported a strong party of enemy ahead. Then about twenty Germans rushed out and a bit of a scrap ensued. Gill was shot and rolled into the ditch and our men were driven back. These men got away wounded but Gill was taken in for no sign of him could be seen when we visited the place later in the night. He was undoubtedly badly wounded but there is a good chance of his being safe.

2nd Lieutenant Harry Crook was also badly wounded while leading another patrol later that night and could not be rescued. He died the following day. His and Gill's bodies were never recovered. Their names can be found today on the Memorial to the Missing at Tyne Cot cemetery.[1]

The Pals were relieved the following evening when the French took over the Kemmel sector. After a night bivouacked in a small wood they moved back to their new camp near Ouderdom, two miles south of the main road from Poperinghe to Ypres. Although they were now in reserve their orders were to be ready to move wherever and whenever they were required. 'Once again we are out of things for a short time', Eric wrote home. 'How long one can never tell: last time it was only six and a half hours.' Only 2nd Lieutenant Arthur Ellis, a former corporal from the Northamptonshire Regiment, was still with him out of his company's original complement of ten officers at the start of the Spring Offensive. 'We are rather lonesome', he confessed.

The battalion's relief had been marred by one final tragic accident. Colonel Campbell Watson was hit by a shell while showing his French counterpart around the front line. One of his legs was blown off and the other was badly shattered. Brigadier Stanley could only wonder how he had escaped for so long 'because he never spared himself in the least bit, and was always taking chances'.[2] He was the man that Eric had probably grown to admire more than any other. 'He was as brave as a lion', he told his parents, 'and very proud of his battalion. He was no soldier and he knew it: he relied on his officers to run the battalion

---

1   The 33-year old Reverend Rowland Gill was an exceptional man. The son of a Methodist minister, he himself had been appointed minister of Aigburth Vale Methodist church in Liverpool a year before the outbreak of war. Determined to play his part he enlisted immediately in the Royal Army Medical Corps and in 1916 was awarded the Military Medal during the Battle of the Somme when, for five days, he helped to evacuate the wounded under heavy fire. Keen to play a more active role, he requested a transfer to the infantry and was commissioned as a 2nd lieutenant before joining the Pals' 17th Battalion in the middle of June 1917. Only six weeks later, at the Battle of Pilckem Ridge, he was awarded the Military Cross when, wounded but refusing medical attention, he continued to lead and encourage his men in the face of enemy shell and machine gun fire without any thought for his own safety.

2   Brigadier-General F C Stanley, *The History of the 89th Brigade 1914 – 1918*, p. 280.

but at the same time he saw that they did it.' It had been only the previous day that he had congratulated Eric on his Military Cross and been told of the bar to his own DSO. His second-in-command, Major James Pitts, who had joined the battalion in November, now took over. At 25 he had already had a remarkable career. Having enlisted originally as a 14-year old bandboy in the Bedfordshire Regiment in 1907, he had fought as a private at Mons in 1914 before getting his commission in the 2nd Bedfords in 1916. Now, as soon as he was confirmed in his command of the 17th Battalion, he would become one of the youngest colonels in the army and be used as an example, in an information booklet for the American forces now arriving in Europe, of how far an ordinary man could progress in the British Army.[3] Pitts would remain in command even when Colonel Douglas was attached to the battalion on his return from the two months' leave that he had been given after the disbanding of the 20th Battalion. Douglas stayed behind at the transport lines – 'as usual', Eric reflected – and so would be one of the few Liverpool Pals who took no part in the German spring offensives.

After almost a week of inactivity the Germans launched their third and final assault on Mount Kemmel early on the morning of 25 April. By 7.10am they had reached its summit and by 7.40am they had taken Kemmel village. It had taken little more than an hour to capture the best British observation post in the salient. Although the British line north of Kemmel remained unbroken and reinforcements were being rapidly deployed, Haig and Plumer immediately withdrew their forces south of Ypres into a tight defensive cordon that ran west from Hill 60 through Voormezeele and Vierstraat to La Clytte, where the British and French lines now met. After more heavy fighting the following day, as the Germans pressed forward their advantage, they withdrew the cordon still further to within the western end of Zillebeke Lake. The British front line had never been so close to the city. With their own army exhausted and their reserves running out Hindenburg and Ludendorff knew that they had one last chance to take Ypres. They had to succeed if they were to win the war. Everything was now in the balance.

The last four days of April, which saw the final fighting in the Battle of the Lys, would be some of the most momentous in Eric's life. However it is difficult now to be sure of all the details. The Battle of the Lys has never inspired the same level of interest as the first stage of the German Spring Offensive, many accounts of which stop at the end of March with their failure to capture Amiens. General Gough and Brigadier Stanley had both lost their commands and so were no longer in a position to provide personal accounts. Stanley relied instead for his history of the brigade on the diaries of Colonel Rollo, one of his senior officers and another Liverpool Pal whose family had strong connections with the city's maritime economy. His grandfather, David, had founded a well-known firm of marine engineers and ship repairers, Grayson Rollo and Clover Docks Ltd, which Rollo would take over as managing director after the war. However, as the Pals' three battalions would again be split up, even Rollo's understanding was limited. The entries in the battalion diaries on which Everard Wyrall relied for his history of the regiment are, understandably, all too brief. And Eric had stopped writing up his own diaries the previous autumn. He wrote no separate account of the Battle of the Lys as he had of the opening days of the offensive at St Quentin.

---

3   Frederic William Wile, *Explaining the Britishers*, pp. 96–7. Published in London by William Heinemann in autumn 1918, the book is subtitled 'The Story of the British Empire's Mighty Effort in Liberty's Cause', as written by an American for American soldiers and sailors. Wile dedicated it to 'my fellow Yanks who are streaming into Europe for the worthy purpose of Kanning the Kaiser'.

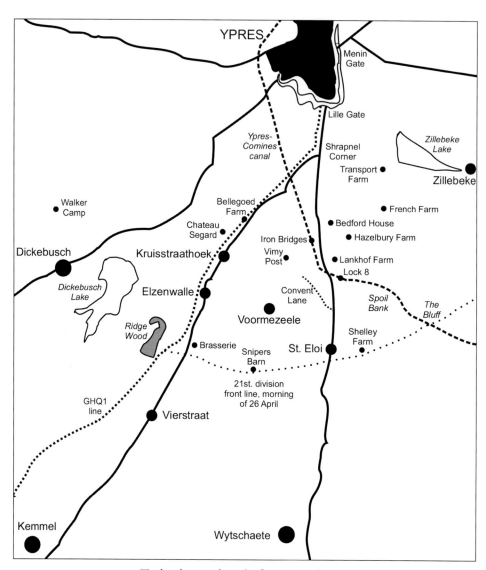

The battleground south of Ypres, April 1918.

He would later tell his parents that he could not remember exactly what happened. What he did keep, however, and later pasted into his cuttings book, were a number of the orders and signals that he received: he probably still had them with him when he left the battlefield. They bring a haunting immediacy to his experiences.

Held in divisional reserve as a counter-attack force, the Pals had been out of the line for four days when the Germans captured Mount Kemmel on the morning of 25 April. Although they had been warned in the early hours to be ready to move at half an hour's notice, it was not until the afternoon that they were called forward to a position of readiness north of Dickebusch Lake. They were not called into action but, when they arrived back in camp at Ouderdom late that night, they were told that they had been placed under the orders of the 21st Division. They would follow the same routine the next day, but this time they had to take up positions nearer the lake by dawn. Again they were not called into action.

The Germans had quickly pushed on north after their capture of Kemmel to take Vierstraat. By the morning of the next day, 26 April, the 21st Division's defensive front line ran south-east from Stirling Castle on the Menin road to the Bluff on the Ypres-Comines canal and then due west past Shelley Farm, St Eloi, Snipers Barn, and the Brasserie to Ridge Wood. Although the enemy continued to push forward on the second day they met stubborn resistance from the 39th Composite Brigade. This exhausted brigade, which had been pulled together from what remained of the 39th Division after the March offensive, had now spent almost a fortnight holding the southern end of the divisional line between the canal and Ridge Wood where, although not called upon to fight, they had been heavily and repeatedly shelled while they worked desperately to improve their defences. The Brasserie was now lost in the morning only to be recovered by the brigade in the early afternoon; although Ridge Wood was subjected to heavy bombardment the enemy's subsequent infantry assault was successfully seen off; and Voormezeele, probably wrongly, was reported lost in the morning only to be confirmed as completely held again by the evening. Further east, however, the Bluff and Spoil Bank were lost in the evening when the Germans were able to push forward along both banks of the Ypres-Comines canal.

By then Haig and Plumer had already decided to withdraw their main line of resistance to the so-called GHQ1 line, which ran south from Ypres ramparts to Shrapnel Corner and then on past Chateau Segard, Elzenwalle, and Ridge Wood to La Clytte, where it joined up with the French. By dawn the next morning the 21st Division's front line, which was now to be held only as an outpost line with supporting strong points at Vimy Post, Iron Bridges, and Bedford House, had been forced to withdraw further – this time to a line that ran east from the Brasserie round the southern edge of Voormezeele to Lock 8 on the canal and then on past French Farm and the western end of Zillebeke Lake to the Menin Gate.

Orders once more came through for the Pals after their return to camp on the second night. The 18th Battalion was told to return to its position of readiness at dawn the following morning: later that night it would take over the GHQ1 line on the right of the 19th Battalion down from Elzenwalle to the Brasserie and Ridge Wood. The 17th and 19th battalions meanwhile were held in camp but told to be ready to move at half an hour's notice. When no further orders came through the following morning Eric had time to write what would be his last letter home from the front.

Dear Father and Mother

I have received your letter of the 22nd and, this morning, your two parcels of foodstuffs. Just after my last letter to you our short period of so-called rest came to an end and there seems little hope of seeing any more for the present. I expect they will leave me out of the next lot for a rest if it is possible as I am the only officer at present with the battalion who has not yet missed a day of it. Although I don't like leaving the company I shall be glad of a little respite as it is now beginning to get on my nerves a little. Norman Winder is lucky as usual as he has gone on a course which lasts, I believe, nearly a month. Colonel Douglas has turned up here after two months in England but he is back at the transport lines as yet.

Best love to all, Eric

If Eric had really expected to be left out of the 'next lot' he would be quickly disabused. General Campbell, the commander of the 21st Division, visited the Pals' brigade HQ in the morning and issued verbal instructions that they were to relieve the 39th Composite Brigade in the line that night on both sides of Voormezeele. The village, which was less than two miles south of Ypres' Lille Gate, lay in the middle of a mile-wide natural funnel between the GHQ1 line in the west, which ran along the higher ground of the Segard Ridge, and the Ypres-Comines canal in the east. It was now virtually all that stood in the way of the Germans reaching Ypres. Lieutenant-Colonel William Weber, who was stationed on the ridge with the 2nd Brigade of the Royal Field Artillery and would later write of his experiences in an article for the Royal Artillery Journal entitled *A Tactical Study of a Field Artillery Group in Retreat*, realised that it was the place where the trouble would come.

At 2.15pm, an hour before the formal divisional order for the relief was issued, Eric, as the commander of A Company of the 17th Battalion, received his own orders from the battalion's adjutant.

You will please meet the CO at 39th Composite Brigade HQ at Walker Camp at 2.50pm today from whence you will probably proceed to the lines to reconnoitre. You will not be returning to your company and should therefore leave an officer in command and take a runner along with you.

The 17th Battalion's orders were to take over the eastern half of the Voormezeele sector from Convent Lane, 300 yards south-west of Lock 8 on the Ypres-Comines canal, to the north-west corner of the village. From there the 19th Battalion would take over the northern and southern 'switches' to Elzenwalle and Kruisstraathoek and the section of the GHQ1 line that ran between them. The 110th Brigade, whose three battalions of the Leicester Tigers had held the line north from Lock 8 to French Farm for the past fortnight, would at the same time extend its right flank to cover the sector from the canal to Convent Lane. After a year in England Brigadier Hanway Cumming had only returned to take command of the brigade a few days before the start of the Spring Offensive. Like so many other units they, and the 21st Division generally, had come out of the fighting, as he admitted, 'considerably knocked about and with greatly depleted numbers but with their morale and confidence unshaken'.[4] He would later write one of the more comprehensive accounts of the last few

---

4   Brigadier-General H. Cumming, *A Brigadier in France,* p. 129.

days of April in his memoirs, *A Brigadier in France, 1917 – 1918*. They would be published posthumously in 1922, a year after he was killed in an IRA ambush in Ireland.

The 17th Battalion's orders were to rendezvous with their guides at the northern end of Dickebusch Lake at 9.30pm: the 19th Battalion would follow on half an hour later. It was never going to be an easy relief but it was made worse by the fact that Eric had had no chance to reconnoitre. Only half an hour after his rendezvous with the CO at Walker Camp the Germans had attacked Voormezeele and, after heavy fighting, captured the chateau in the middle of the village. Although the 39th Composite Brigade recovered it less than an hour later, the Germans attacked again at 10.00pm and won it back. This time they held on to it and won a foothold in the village. By then Eric's relief was already under way.

What was even more worrying was the report, not finally confirmed until the early hours of the morning, that at 9.00pm a large German raiding party had also attacked and captured the 6th Leicesters' forward post at Lankhof Farm, just north of the canal near Lock 8. One of their officers and 20 men had managed to fight their way out but their company headquarters was lost and 70 men were missing. A counter-attack organised by the 7th Leicesters was unsuccessful and failed to dislodge the enemy. The result was that, although Lock 8 was still held, the Leicesters were unable to complete the relief between the canal and Convent Lane. As a result the battalion of the 39th Brigade which had been stationed there for the previous fortnight had no choice but to stay where they were. They had heard German voices north of the canal but, when they sent out a patrol to try to get in touch with the Leicesters, they were unable to find them. As they did not have enough men to make a counterattack they now formed a defensive line along the south side of the canal back to Iron Bridges, the point to which the Leicesters had withdrawn north of the canal.

In spite of the precarious situation on both its flanks the 17th Battalion still managed to complete its relief by 1.00am. Early the following morning, however, Eric received an urgent hand-written order from Major Pitts himself rather than, as was more usual, from his adjutant. His right flank, he was told, was not where it was meant to be: he was to try to get in touch with the 19th Battalion immediately or, if that was not possible, after dark. His left flank towards the canal would soon be of much greater concern. After a quiet morning the Germans were able to force their way into the defensive line there early in the afternoon. Lock 8 eventually had to be evacuated – but only after five hours of fighting. The 21st Division's subsequent summary of operations, which reported only local fighting between Voormezeele and Lock 8 on what was an otherwise uneventful day, belies Cumming's own more detailed account:

> The fighting on this day was carried on at close quarters with bayonet, bomb, and rifle, and was controlled and carried out chiefly by the junior officers of the battalions concerned with great dash and skill. The local situation was constantly changing and required individual action in carrying out the general scheme without waiting for definite orders; and the training which they had received for this purpose bore fruit here.[5]

Having tried unsuccessfully to bomb the enemy out the Pals were finally forced to withdraw 300 yards to a new line that ran from the northern edge of Voormezeele through

---

5   Brigadier-General H. Cumming, op. cit., p. 147.

The view from the northern end of Convent Lane towards the spires of Ypres. Vimy Post is beside the clump of trees on the left and Iron Bridges is on the extreme right in the line of trees that marks the Ypres-Comines canal. (Author, 2013)

The view south-west from Iron Bridges towards Voormezeele church with Convent Lane on the extreme left and Vimy Post beside the clump of trees on the right. (Author, 2013)

Vimy Post to Iron Bridges. One of their company commanders, 25-year old Captain Ronald Bloore, was killed at some point in the fighting. He is buried close to where he fell in one of Voormezeele's three commonwealth war cemeteries. It would be some time before his father, Charles, heard of his death: as the second officer on the Birkenhead-built sailing vessel Irby, he had been arrested and interned in Germany at the start of the war. By 6.00pm, when he received the following hand-written order from the adjutant, it would appear that Eric had assumed command of the battalion in the front line.

OC A Company
Please re-organise A, B, and C companies as much as possible and, at a time to be notified later, D Company will counter-attack.

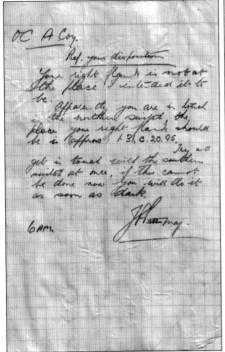

'Your right flank is not at the place
I intended it to be' – Major Pitts'
handwritten order to the officer
commanding A Company at 6.00am on 28
April 1918. (From Eric's cuttings book)

'Please re-organise A, B, & C coys. as
much as possible' – order to the officer
commanding A Company at 6.00pm on 28
April 1918. (From Eric's cuttings book)

Although the time for the counter-attack would be set for 7.45pm it had to be called off at the last minute when the Germans put down an artillery barrage only two minutes before it was due to start. It continued for almost three hours. As a result Major Pitts could do no more that night except organise the defence of his left flank as best he could.

Early the following morning the Germans threw their last reserves of men and ammunition into a final desperate attempt to take Ypres. It began at 3.00am with a deep and sustained bombardment along a 10-mile front from Zillebeke Lake down to the Scherpenberg, the hill south-west of la Clytte which would give its name to this last battle in the Lys offensive. Many who witnessed it, and not least those who had lived through Bruchmiller's hurricane bombardment at St Quentin, thought it the heaviest artillery barrage that they had ever experienced. Two hours of gas shells were followed by 40 minutes of large calibre high explosive. The casualties were heavy: many men were buried in the explosions. Then, as soon as it was over, the German infantry attacked with fixed bayonets – first at 6.00am, prompting an immediate SOS from Voormezeele when the advanced posts there were driven in, and then again in a second wave two hours later. By 10.00am the Leicesters holding the line east of the canal from Iron Bridges to Hazelbury Farm had reported that the troops on their right had given way and gone back beyond Voormezeele. Once the 19th Battalion had retired on its right the Pals' 17th Battalion had been left with no choice but to

The demarcation stone on the bend in the canal near Lock 8 with the bunkers at Lankhof Farm in the background. These stones were erected in the 1920s to mark the closest points that the Germans got to Ypres. In fact they managed to advance another 500 yards here up to Iron Bridges after they had captured Lankhof Farm on 27 April. (Author, 2013)

make a fighting withdrawal to the GHQ1 line, where they had firmly established themselves by 1.00pm. As a result they left a gap in the middle of the Voormezeele 'funnel' about 500 yards north of Vimy Post which Cumming had to race to fill, establishing a new flank from Iron Bridges across to Bellegoed Farm on the GHQ1 line.

Although fierce, and particularly so around Ridge Wood, the fighting further south and west had died down by early afternoon. Along the canal, however, it continued through the afternoon until dusk. By 2.30pm, according to Cumming, the enemy had bombed up the canal and were assembling to attack Iron Bridges.

> The attack was finally broken up and dispersed by combined artillery, machine gun and rifle fire, but not before a considerable amount of hand-to-hand bomb and bayonet work had taken place in the canal bed itself. Splendid work was done here by officers and men alike of the companies of the 6th and 7th Leicesters concerned, and they left their mark on the enemy to such purpose that the attack was not renewed.[6]

At 6.00pm a British defensive barrage put an end to any further fighting; and at 10.00pm the Royal Engineers and Pioneers were able to move forward to wire and generally improve the hastily-dug defences between Iron Bridges and Bellegoed Farm. Apart from periodic shelling by the German artillery the rest of the night was comparatively quiet along

---

6   Brigadier-General H. Cumming, op. cit., p. 149.

the whole front. It would remain so the following day.

Although it had been a close-run thing the enemy had once again failed to achieve their objective. Voormezeele would be the nearest that they managed to get to Ypres. With their backs to the wall the British had fought to the end just as Haig had asked. At 10 o'clock that evening, after three weeks of desperate fighting in Flanders and with nothing left to give, Hindenburg accepted the advice of his generals and called off the offensive. He later claimed in his memoirs that he had relied for its success on the British being left in the lurch by the French.

> Our own last great onslaught on the new Anglo-French line at the end of April made no headway. On 1 May we adopted the defensive in Flanders, or rather, as we then hoped, passed to the defensive for the time being ... Twice had England been saved by France at a moment of extreme crisis. Perhaps the third time we should succeed in gaining a decisive victory over this adversary.[7]

Haig summed up the final day's fighting in the Battle of the Lys in his later dispatch on the Spring Offensive:

> Very heavy fighting rapidly developed on the whole of this front, and ended in the complete repulse of the enemy with the heaviest losses to his troops. Throughout the whole of the fighting our infantry and artillery fought magnificently and in more than one instance our troops went out to meet the German attack and drove back the enemy with the bayonet. At the end of the day, except for a small loss of ground about Voormezeele, our line was intact and the enemy had undergone a severe and decided check.[8]

The 17th Battalion's own actions in the last four days of April are covered in just a page and a half of the battalion's war diary; and Pitts' entry for 29 April is as brief as it is bleak.

> At 3.30am heavy enemy bombardment opened, followed later by enemy attack, and our line was forced back to GHQ1 where I re-organised and held on to the position. The enemy got through on both flanks practically surrounding two of my companies. 'A' Company was actually surrounded and after severe fighting was captured.[9]

The relief of the battle-weary British troops began the following night. The Liverpool Pals' three battalions had to spend another day in the line before they too were relieved. After a night in camp at Ouderdom they were withdrawn to Brandhoek where a roll-call revealed that they were down to 27 officers and 750 men. For the second time in five weeks the brigade was re-organised as a single composite battalion under Colonel Rollo, with Major Pitts as his second-in-command. In the last four days of April the 18th and 19th battalions had sustained 150 casualties between them, 37 of whom had been killed. The 17th

---

7   Field Marshal Paul von Hindenburg, *The Great War,* edited by Charles Messenger, pp. 179-180.

8   Field Marshal Sir Douglas Haig, Despatch of 21 October 1918, recorded in the *London Gazette,* supplement no. 30963, 18 October 1918, page 12425 onwards, para. 68.

9   17th Battalion King's Liverpool Regiment War Diary, 29 April 1918, The National Archives, WO 95/2334/2.

Battalion, however, had sustained 282 casualties: 19 men had been killed in action, 82 had been wounded or gassed, but 181 were missing. The men of A Company, who Pitts said had been surrounded and captured in the final fighting, must have accounted for many of them. Among them was Arthur Ellis who had been the only one left of Eric's original complement of officers: he was now a prisoner of war. Stanley Ashcroft, who had been Eric's second-in-command when he joined the 17th Battalion in February but had subsequently been transferred to another company, was listed as wounded and missing: it was confirmed later that he died of his wounds while in German captivity. A keen rugby player, he had played for Cheshire against the All Blacks on their first tour of Great Britain in 1905. One of six brothers who had joined the infantry at the start of the war, he had been badly wounded at the Somme and had only returned to France at the end of 1917. His family had already paid a high price and were still in mourning. His youngest brother, Frederick, had been killed with the 18th Battalion on the first day of the Battle of Arras; and his eldest, William, who had also been badly wounded that day, had been killed only a month earlier while fighting with the 19th Battalion at Roupy on the second day of the Spring Offensive.

Nor was Eric among the Pals' 27 officers counted at Brandhoek. At some point in the final fighting he had been forced to leave the battlefield. On the day of the roll-call, and still suffering from the effects of gas, he wrote his first letter home from No 8 British Red Cross Hospital in Boulogne. His letter, written in pencil on cheap blue paper and in a shaky and inconsistent hand, is probably the least legible but most poignant of all that he wrote.

> Dear Father and Mother
> I am down at the above address sick but not wounded. I am not quite clear what has happened to me during the last two or three days. We had a very bad time on the 27th and 28th but I shall be able to tell you about it when I see you again. All my company are now gone save about half a dozen. I was buried twice on the 28th but was alright again. I saw the doctor the next morning and was sent to hospital. I was in a rather bad way as I had a temperature of 104 and a pulse of 130 so they sent me down telling me I had pneumonia.
>
> I am much better now and my temperature is down and all I have got is a bit of fever, the same as I had last year. I am living on a milk diet at the moment so am not exactly too strong. As soon as I can sit up I will try and write you a better letter. This is quite a nice place and one gets looked after very well. There are four of us in this room and the windows look out on to the harbour, the casino, the pier, and the shore. Ships of all sorts are passing, airships and aeroplanes flying round. In fact it is a very busy scene. Letters only take two days to come from London so I shall probably hear from you direct before the letters from the battalion are forwarded on.
>
> Best love to all, your ever loving son Eric

It would be some time before he heard that he had been awarded a bar to his Military Cross. His citation, which did not appear in the *London Gazette* until September, read as follows:

For conspicuous gallantry and devotion to duty during an enemy attack. After his company had been practically surrounded he re-organised and fought his way out, inflicting heavy casualties on the enemy. He showed fine courage and determination.[10]

His award would never be recorded in the battalion diary or in any history of the Pals or the King's Liverpool Regiment. By the time it was confirmed the Liverpool Pals had ceased to exist as a fighting force.

What, however, Eric's letters never make clear is exactly how and when he left the battlefield and found himself at hospital at Boulogne. He himself admits that he was unsure what had happened to him. What adds to the confusion is the reference in his letter to the Pals having 'a very bad time' on 27 and 28 April and to his seeing the doctor and being sent to hospital the following morning. The correctness of these dates – when the Pals relieved the 39th Brigade at Voormeeele on the first night and then took part in five hours' of 'local' fighting the following day – is open to question but appears to be confirmed both by the 'arrival report' that Eric had to complete when he left for England in May, in which he stated that he left his unit on 29 April, and by his having his Military Cross engraved with the words 'Bar – Voormezeele, 28 April 1918'. And yet by all accounts 'a very bad time' would seem to be a more appropriate description of the Pals' last two desperate days of fighting on the 28 and 29 April, when the Germans launched their final desperate assault along the whole line. We know from his orders to re-organise the battalion's three companies that Eric was still in the line on the evening of 28 April and, with the enemy launching their bombardment at 3.00am the following morning and following it immediately with two waves of infantry assault, it is difficult to see how he could have got away that morning to see the doctor. He was also clearly aware, when he wrote his first letter from Boulogne, that nearly all his men were gone. Indeed his medal citation, which was presumably written by his commanding officer, is, in its reference to his company being practically surrounded, almost identical to Pitts' entry in the battalion diary for 29 April.

There are other snippets of evidence as well which suggest that Eric may have got his dates wrong, and that he took part in the final fighting and did not leave the battlefield before the morning of 30 April. All this may not be of any great significance except inasmuch as I would like to believe that my grandfather was one of the few who fought throughout the 40 days of the German spring offensives at St Quentin and Ypres. His rare distinction of being awarded the Military Cross in both its opening and closing phases, as well as the brave sacrifice of so many brothers-in-arms, officers and men alike, in a series of often overlooked but climactic actions, deserves to be remembered in the annals of the Liverpool Pals and the King's Liverpool Regiment.

Indeed what other explanation can there be for two signals that Eric apparently received on the evening of 29 April? Although both are simply dated '29' without any month being given they are pasted in his cuttings book alongside his other orders at the end of April in what appears to be chronological order; and there is no other obvious month to which they could relate. The first signal, which is addressed to the officer commanding A Company, advises him of the counter-batteries planned for early the following morning; and the second, which is timed at 9.00pm, after the final fighting had died down, warns all company commanders of the likelihood of the enemy trying to work their way forward in

---

10 *London Gazette*, supplement no. 30901, published 13 September 1918, p. 10902.

'We are sending up rum now' – order to A Company – assumed to
have been issued on 30 April. (From Eric's cuttings book)

small parties during the night and of the necessity of keeping a very sharp look-out. Unlike
his earlier orders, which are written on cheap graph paper, these are written on pre-printed
army signals pads. A third and final signal, which is simply dated '30', would otherwise be
even more difficult to explain.

> We are sending up rum now – 1 petrol tin. The CO does not wish it to be issued tonight
> in case the men fall asleep.

14

Boulogne

May 1918

So, as the war dragged on, as the wear and tear of the trench life told, we came to think less of the gaudy act performed on the spur of the moment, to value more the worth of the man who was prepared to see the thing through.

Lord Moran, *The Anatomy of Courage*[1]

E ric made a slow but steady recovery in hospital at Boulogne. He would be there for almost a fortnight. Although he was suffering from severe headaches, which meant that for the first few days he had to write while lying down, he still managed to write eleven letters home over the next ten days.

The hospital had been a large hotel before the war. Eric's ward was on the fourth floor and, when he was finally able to sit up in bed, he could watch the hive of activity in the harbour below where there was a constant procession of troopships leaving for home under the escort of destroyers. He was envious of the 'lucky fellows' that he never imagined he would be joining. 'There are quite a lot of ships here', he wrote in a letter to his seven-year old brother Guy. 'I am sure you would like to be here to see them all.'

It is not a dirty, smoky place like Liverpool but more like Llandudno. I have just been watching a seaplane come down to the water after flying over the sea looking for German submarines. Do you know what a seaplane is? It is very much like an aeroplane only instead of coming down to earth on little wheels it comes down on the water on little boats which are called floats.

The traffic along the seafront brought back memories of his schooldays at Rossall although the constant noise and bustle got on his nerves. One thing at least for which he was grateful, so he told his sister, was the absence of shells and gunfire.

You have no idea how the incessant din gets on your nerves when you are a little out of sorts. Of course things get worse as the war proceeds. When I came out one was very rarely shelled when about five miles behind the lines. Then the Huns started bombing us every night and after a while we got used to that. Now he has a great number of long range guns, probably taken off his warships, and he shells our camps and dumps up to ten miles behind the lines. He does very little damage but it is distinctly annoying. Imagine each night as you lie in bed hearing a shell come regularly, say, every five minutes and land somewhere in the vicinity. Then, when you get up, you find your

---

1 Lord Moran, *The Anatomy of Courage,* London, Constable, 1945, p. 76 (with permission of Little, Brown Book Group Ltd).

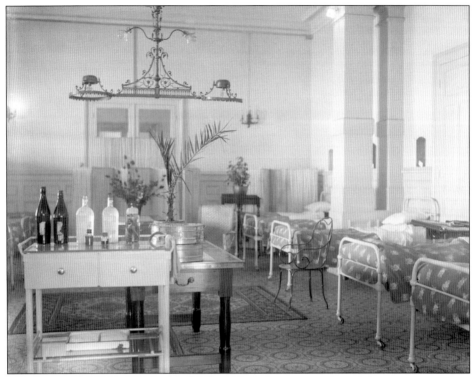

Officers' ward in a hospital in Boulogne, in this case No 14 General
Hospital, October 1916. (© Imperial War Museum, Q29136)

cookhouse gone or something like that. Believe me it is most distinctly annoying. Of
course a new one is soon built but that's not the point.

Eric's was suffering, at least in part, from a recurrence of the trench fever for which he
had first been hospitalised the year before at Arras. He never fully recovered from it. His
children would later claim that it was this rather than his heavy smoking, a habit which he
also picked up in the war, that caused the permanent rasp in his throat. At least, they said,
they never had any difficulty finding him in a crowded cinema foyer. Added to this now
were the effects of gas and the shock of having been buried alive. The former affected his
sight and voice, which only started to return a couple of days after his arrival. Eric believed it
was the cause of his appalling and persistent headaches which aspirin could not alleviate. He
had also strained his right arm which only made it more difficult to write. When he tried his
first game of billiards a week later he found that 'the pockets were too small or my arm too
shaky'. He had also come to believe that he had been discharged from hospital too quickly in
March, only a week before the start of the Spring Offensive. He was hoping now for a decent
rest before being sent back to the front although he was unsure whether he would be kept
where he was or transferred to an officers' rest-home.

They don't keep people here long these days. It is either Blighty or back to duty straight
away. It is rather a pity that they should have to rush one out. They are sending many

officers out who are far from being fit. This however doesn't appear to apply to doctors and padres with which this place is crowded. Many seem to have become permanent patients and they have a quite a good time.

And, as he told his sister, who was considering working as a nursing volunteer, or VAD, during her summer holidays, he did not appreciate the unsympathetic attitude of some of the nursing staff.

I think it is a very good idea for there is plenty to do in a hospital and I am sure they would be glad of your help. The VADs here seem to do all the work with the exception of some of the sisters who also work extraordinarily hard. Other sisters seem to prefer to sit and watch but at this last occupation I should say that the matron is the champion. She came round to me the first day I was here and saw me sitting up watching the room being cleaned and remarked that it was very nice for those who were able to sit and watch others work. Now I'd being doing a fair amount of work myself lately – in fact during the last 41 days I had only had my boots off for four nights – and I didn't quite like her tone so I said 'I suppose it is' and she hasn't been round here since.

After five days on a diet of milk Eric was allowed to get up and walk around the ward in his dressing gown. Although he was still unsteady on his feet his headaches had gone and his temperature was back below normal. All things considered he was feeling remarkably perky. 'A few days now and I shall be ready to go up the line again', he told his parents. His only worry was that his trench fever might return at any time. It would almost certainly mean, as his parents hoped, that he would be sent home on sick leave for up to six months. It was not what he expected: he was more concerned that his stay in hospital might mean forfeiting his turn for leave.

Much as I long for a glimpse of home again I don't want to leave this country yet. There is still a lot to do over here and many months more fighting yet, I am afraid. If one has the nerve to tell a convincing tale it seems an easy thing to get across the channel but, as I am feeling much better, I can't do that.

The following day he went downstairs for his meals for the first time but quickly got tired when he went outside for a short walk in the sun. On the day after that, however, he was able not only take a walk in the morning but also to stroll down to the harbour after lunch with John Whittle, another officer from the 17th Battalion. To avoid exerting themselves too much they hired a carriage to bring them back up the hill to the hospital in style.

As his appetite returned and his strength improved with the daily walks that he now took whenever the weather allowed, Eric grew increasingly frustrated by the strict rationing of his food. However his headaches also came back and he was unable to get rid of them. What he wanted most of all was news from home and his battalion. It was not until 8 May, after he had been in hospital for a week, that he received the first letters from his parents for more than a fortnight: they had been forwarded from the battalion. However, as he had given his parents his address in his first letter home from Boulogne, he now started to receive regular letters from them and the rest of the family. Their earlier letters continued to be forwarded haphazardly and, by the time he was discharged from hospital, Eric knew from his father's habit of numbering all his letters that only one of them had gone astray.

With the letters came Eric's usual requests for kit and clothing and now, in particular, for some immediate funds to tide him over. He had left the battle-field so quickly that he had been unable to take anything with him and was as a result 'rather on the rocks'. His batman, James Tatlock, was sadly no longer there to help him; and, although he had written to the battalion to ask them to forward his kit, he doubted whether it would ever arrive 'in these somewhat uncertain times'. It probably never did. What he needed most was some money to buy essential toiletries – 'a razor, tooth brush, and a few such odds and ends'. Within a week his parents had sent him a razor and a sponge along with some money. 'The razor you sent is A1', he wrote back: 'I suppose Father bought it as no-one else in the family would ever buy a gilt-coloured razor'.

As well as getting the local news from home Eric now also had access to British newspapers on their day of publication. He followed in particular the furore caused by the publication of General Maurice's letter on 7 May which challenged the honesty of Lloyd George's statements to the House of Commons on troop numbers. He also thought that the lack of any major stories meant that the German offensive had probably stalled. Nevertheless he still expected 'the storm to break out afresh' and was sure that he would soon be needed again in some capacity. As yet he had heard no news of the battalion. He was not even sure whether it still existed. There had been rumours before he left that it was to be broken up. When he heard that the battalion's medical officer and two other officers had been admitted to the hospital only a couple of days after him, he immediately tracked them down to get the latest news and to pass it on to his parents.

> They tell me that A Company is now only one man strong so perhaps you had better stop the cigarettes for a while. I am sorry to say that Ashcroft is believed killed: I don't know how he is officially reported so you had better be guarded in what you say. He was seen to fall and is certainly wounded and missing. I have little hope. What a terrible price the family have paid during the war! It is only a few weeks since his last brother was killed.

When his parents let him know that Colonel Campbell Watson was still in hospital in Boulogne receiving treatment for his shattered legs Eric was determined to track him down as well. On 11 May he told his sister how he came to find him.

> A rather curious thing has happened today that does not reflect too highly on my present mental condition. After I received Mother's letter telling me that Colonel Watson was still here I went to the Red Cross headquarters to find out which hospital he was in. The people there said Baltic House and described it to me. So I came back along the road looking for this place and to my amazement I found it was my own hospital. I then discovered the colonel quite near my own room. He is improving wonderfully but has had a very bad time and looks very ill indeed. He leaves for England tomorrow. He seemed very pleased to see me and was glad to hear what news I could give him of the battalion.[2]

---

2   The No 8 British Red Cross Hospital, which moved from Paris-Plage, near Étaples, to Boulogne in January 1918, was also known as 'The Baltic and Corn Exchange Hospital'.

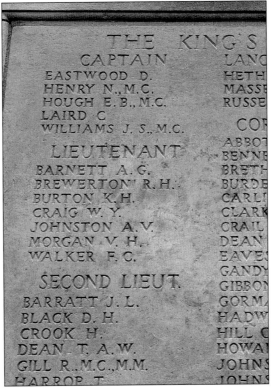

The names of Norman Henry, Harry Crook, and Rowland Gill on the
Memorial to the Missing at Tyne Cot Cemetery. (Author, 2013)

The two officers would not have known when they met that the composite battalion, which was now all that remained of the Liverpool Pals, had just seen its last action on the Western Front.

Once again the Pals had been given almost no time to recover after their withdrawal from Voormezeele. Within a few days they were in brigade reserve at La Clytte where the French and British sectors met. When the Germans broke through on their right on 8 May Colonel Rollo acted on his own initiative and sent forward two of his companies to help out the French unit which had been ordered to counter-attack but was without any other support. In what Rollo described as 'a very pretty piece of work, most gallantly done with very tired troops' the Pals managed to recover nearly all the ground that had been lost.[3] Sadly Eric's friend, Norman Henry, was killed leading one of the companies. It was still only seven weeks since they had shaken hands at Holnon Wood as they prepared themselves for what they thought would be their certain deaths. Henry's body was never recovered and his name, like those of Rowland Gill and Harry Crook, can now be found on the Memorial to the Missing at Tyne Cot cemetery.

When the Pals were relieved on 10 May their already weakened force had suffered another 250 casualties. Two days later at Buysscheure, just north of St Omer, the 89th

---

3   Brigadier-General F C Stanley, *The History of the 89th Brigade 1914 – 1918*, p. 285.

Brigade was disbanded and the last three battalions of the Liverpool Pals 'reduced to cadre'. A few officers were kept on for several weeks to act as instructors to the American forces now arriving in France. The remaining men, four officers and 216 other ranks, were sent back to the depot at Étaples. After two and a half years on the Western Front the Liverpool Pals were no more. There can probably be no better tribute to their final days than that which Field-Marshal Haig paid to all his troops in his despatch on the German spring offensives.

> The splendid qualities displayed by all ranks and services throughout the Somme and Lys battles make it possible to view with confidence whatever further tests the future may bring.
>
> On 21 March the troops of the Fifth and Third armies had the glory of sustaining the first and heaviest blow of the German offensive. Though assailed by a concentration of hostile forces which the enemy might well have considered overwhelming, they held up the German attack at all points for the greater part of two days, thereby rendering a service to their country and to the allied cause the value of which cannot be over-estimated. Thereafter, through many days of heavy and continuous rearguard fighting, they succeeded in presenting a barrier to the enemy's advance until such time as the arrival of British and French reinforcements enabled his progress to be checked.
>
> In the battle of the Lys many of the same divisions which had just passed through the furnace of the Somme found themselves exposed to the full fury of a second great offensive by fresh German forces. Despite this disadvantage they gave evidence in many days of close and obstinate fighting that their spirit was as high as ever and their courage and determination unabated. Both by them and by the divisions freshly engaged every yard of ground was fiercely disputed until troops were overwhelmed or ordered to withdraw. Such withdrawals as were deemed necessary in the course of the battle were carried out successfully and in good order.
>
> At no time, either on the Somme or on the Lys, was there anything approaching a breakdown of command or a failure of morale under conditions that made rest and sleep impossible for days together, and called incessantly for the greatest physical exertion and quickness of thought. Officers and men remained undismayed, realising that for the time being they must play a waiting game, and determined to make the enemy pay the full price for the success which for the moment was his.
>
> In the course of this report it has been possible to refer to a very few of the many instances in which officers and men of all arms and services have shown courage and skill of the highest order. On countless other occasions officers and men, of whose names there is no record, have accomplished actions of the greatest valour, while the very nature of the fighting shows that on all parts of the wide battle fronts unknown deeds of heroism were performed without number.
>
> The British infantryman has always had the reputation of fighting his best in an uphill battle, and time and again in the history of our country, by sheer tenacity and determination of purpose, has won victory from a numerically superior foe. Thrown once more upon the defensive by circumstances over which he had no control, but which will not persist, he has shown himself to possess in full measure the traditional qualities of his race.[4]

4   Field Marshal Sir Douglas Haig, Despatch of 21 October 1918, recorded in the *London Gazette*, supplement no. 30963, 18 October 1918, page 12425 onwards, para. 70 onwards.

Eric had a Military Cross and Bar to show for his gallantry. However he no longer had a battalion or even a brigade to which to return when he was discharged from hospital. He had told his parents, before setting out to find Colonel Campbell Watson, that he was scheduled to appear before a Medical Board after the weekend on Monday, 13 May. Although his health was improving he still could not get rid of his headaches. 'I may with a bit of luck get a few days sick leave', he told them, 'but I expect to get perhaps a week's light duty at the base and then back to full duty. By that time I should be quite fit again.' It must therefore have been a very pleasant surprise to find himself on the day after the Board walking down to the harbour to board a transport ship home for three weeks' leave.

15

Oswestry

June – November 1918

The message which I send to the people of the British Empire on the fourth anniversary of their entry into the war is "Hold Fast" … Having set our hands to the task we must see it through till a just and lasting settlement is reached. In no other way can we ensure a world set free from war.

Lloyd George, 4 August 1918[1]

Eric wrote only one letter home in the next two months; and everything about it comes as a surprise. It was written in Liverpool on the headed notepaper of The St John Ambulance Association's auxiliary hospital for officers in Princes Avenue; it is dated 21 June, or more than a fortnight after his home leave had expired; and its content is more concerned with the family business and his career after the war than with the war itself.

Dear Father and Mother

I arrived at Dale Street this morning soon after you had telephoned. I am sorry to hear that you have had bad weather but, as it has cleared up here this afternoon, perhaps you have been able to get out a little. I had lunch today with Uncle Jack and had a long talk with him about my going into the business eventually. I know Father wants me to go into it but I wanted to get Uncle Jack's idea of the thing first hand as well. I possibly led him to believe that I am not keen to do so, which is, of course, not the case. What I do not want is to have a job made for me there. As far as I can gather he wants me to go into it looking at it from a purely selfish point of view on his part.

I don't know what prompted me to go into this with him to-day especially as I have not spoken to you on the subject for so long. However I think that no harm, if anything good, has been done by it. I have been thinking about this matter for some time and must have a talk with you about it. I am not quite optimistic enough to foresee an immediate end to the war but things, though more critical than ever, seem brighter than they have been since the war started. At all events the end, when it does come, may be sudden and it is as well to have one's plans cut and dried. In other words, if I am not going into H & J, I should decide exactly what I shall do. Nothing would be quite as congenial to me as H & J but after the last three years I could settle down to anything with ease. There is nothing to hurry about and we can have a talk about it any time.

If you think that it is best for me to go into H & J and that my analysis of Uncle Jack's view is correct then of course the thing is settled for, as far as I am concerned,

---

1   Lloyd George's Message to the Empire was issued on the fourth anniversary of Great Britain's declaration of war.

206

nothing could be better. In this case I think it is apparent that I should not come straight back there. Do you think it is best to go back to Jackson McConnan and Temple? As far as I can make out this would be easily possible. If you think not, and that I might go elsewhere, I think it would be well to let Mr Temple know. I ought not to have written all this to take up part of your very short rest in reading it but, as there is nothing urgent about it, please don't do more than read it.

I had tea with Ju. We are taking Auntie Frieda to the Royal Court to-morrow afternoon to have a real good laugh: she has been working rather late the last night or two, Ju says. I suppose you know that Auntie Evelyn has been very ill with heart trouble but her condition is less critical now. I've had a letter from Captain Dickson of the 17th asking me to let them know when I am going back: their commanding officer, now Lt Col Pitts MC, is going to ask for me to join them. They are with the Yankees. I have written to say that I am trying to get back to the 6th. There are no 20th officers still left with 17th.

I have not been feeling very grand these last few days. They had been giving me strychnine but have knocked it off and are now giving me something else. Perhaps this change has caused it: however I feel much better now.

Best of love, your ever loving son, Eric

He would not write again for almost three weeks. His next letter, although headed just 'Tuesday afternoon', was almost certainly written on 9 July. Like those that followed it over the next few months it was sent from Park Hall camp near Oswestry on the headed notepaper of the 5th Battalion of the King's Liverpool Regiment. It was the camp where Eric had been based with the Liverpool Rifles before leaving for France in January 1917 and where the amalgamated third-line 5th and 6th battalions still formed part of the West Lancashire Reserve Brigade. Eric had arrived there three days earlier. A summary of his wartime service in his file at the Ministry of Defence records that he was finally considered to have left overseas service on 6 July. After 18 months with the Pals on the Western Front he had decided to re-join the Rifles rather than accept Colonel Pitts' offer. It was probably a good choice: the last of the 17th Battalion had returned to England by the time of his arrival at Oswestry.

We can only guess exactly where Eric was and what he did in the eight weeks between his discharge from hospital in Boulogne and his arrival at Park Hall. It is clear from his later letters that he spent at least some of his time at home; and it seems probable that he went there on his return from France before suffering a relapse which required his being admitted to hospital in Liverpool. Although highly toxic, strychnine was widely prescribed at the time both as a stimulant and as a tonic for those who felt run down; and, as he told his parents, he did not yet feel up to scratch.

I am afraid my being run down made me rather a nuisance at home. I feel so fed up with everybody and everything. I am glad, in some ways, to have something to do although I am going to give route marches and such a miss if I can for a while. As regards my position in the army I think it is obvious that, though perhaps not quite A1 at present, I shall soon be quite fit again. Of course discharge, I think, is absolutely out of the question. I should be only too glad to get out of the army tomorrow as I almost detest the life but, while the arrogant Huns, whom one can't help loathing a thousand times worse, are still at large I think it is plainly my duty to carry on as best I can. If I was unfit and altogether useless here I would of course take the first opportunity of getting out.

He was classified as C1, or fit for home service only, when he arrived at Oswestry. Although a second medical board examination passed him A1, or fit for active service, only a week later his classification on arrival meant that he might be kept there for six months.[2] He was still expecting to return to the front. The account of his conversation with his uncle Jack shows however that he was already thinking about life after the war. He was now only three months away from his 21st birthday and, even though his going into the family business must already have been discussed – and not least when he left school in 1914 and started working as an apprentice with Jackson McConnan and Temple, the time for a final decision was fast approaching. Everyone in the family, it seems, was walking on egg shells. Eric's decision to raise the issue independently and in private with his uncle, who was only 12 years older than him and had joined the company in 1901 when he turned 16, was almost certainly an acknowledgement of the difficulties that his father had faced a generation earlier. At the risk of appearing unsupportive Harry was keen to leave the final decision to his son. Robert Jones was still running his rival business in Dale Street. It was a continuing reminder of how he had fallen out with his older brothers, Henry and John, and with his nephew, Harry.

Of more immediate interest to Eric was the information that his father now confided in him, that he had been in discussions with Mr Temple about a possible amalgamation of their two businesses. Eric wrote back with his own thoughts on the matter.

It gives one a great deal of food for thought although I am not very surprised at most of the facts which are disclosed. My first impulse is to consider the proposed amalgamation as quite desirable and yours were, I expect, the same. It is however a very momentous occasion in the history of both concerns. I think your idea of allowing it to simmer, in Mother's usual happy metaphor, is the only thing for the present – especially as everyone is more or less upset and overwrought on account of the war. Often first ideas are the best and I expect that the amalgamation will come off eventually although at present, from the point of view of H & J, I can see more 'con' than 'pro'. Have you any idea as to how well Jackson McConnan and Temple have done of late? Do you know who the shareholders are? I feel certain that an amalgamation would be advantageous to them – but that is nothing to do with us at present.

It is very absurd for Father to say at the end of his letter that I should do as I think best without considering him. In the first place who am I – as yet at any rate? You know far more about what is best for me than I do. Then, if there is anyone I should consider in expressing my views, it is to you two, to whom I owe everything I have on the credit side of my life's account.

---

2   When examined or accepted for military service soldiers were placed into one of four medical categories from A to D. Category A meant that they were fit for active service; B that they were free from serious organ diseases and capable of serving overseas either on lines of communication in France or on garrison duties in the tropics; C that they were suitable only for home service; and D that they were currently unfit for service but might become fit within six months. Within category C itself a C1 was considered able both to march five miles and to see, shoot with glasses, and hear well; a C2 could march five miles but only see and hear 'for ordinary purposes'; and a C3 was deemed capable only of sedentary work.

Jackson McConnan and Temple and H & J Jones were both manufacturers of rope and twine. With a warehouse and offices at Goree Piazzas on Liverpool's waterfront and a rope works in Edge Lane, the Jacksons and McConnans had been in business together since 1825. Although it would appear that they were only joined later by the Temples, it was Tom Temple who was running the company by the time that Eric started his apprenticeship there in 1914. It was perhaps a sign that the company's problems, whatever they may have been, had started before the war and had then only been compounded by it. When his father, Charles, died in 1912, 32-year old James McConnan was summoned home after six years in Argentina to take his place as a director of the company. A gifted research scientist who had made his career in chemistry, latterly with the River Plate Fresh Meat Company, he took this opportunity to resume his research at Liverpool University and to join the staff of Lever Brothers' research department at Port Sunlight. It would suggest that he had been brought home primarily to protect his family's interests and that they were happy to leave the day-to-day running of the business to Mr. Temple.

Like so many others James joined up on the outbreak of war, serving first as a private in the 12th Battalion of the King's Liverpool Regiment and then as an officer with the Manchesters. He saw action at Gallipoli in 1915 before being sent to the Western Front where, less than three months after his arrival, he was killed on the Somme in September 1916. His cousin, George McConnan, a captain in the Liverpool Scottish, had been killed there only six weeks before him. James' death is likely to have been one of the reasons behind the recent talks of amalgamation. Many of the family businesses that still underpinned Liverpool's maritime economy suffered similar losses in the war and saw their future prosperity threatened by the sacrifice of their younger generation. Eric's parents must have thanked God that their son had not only been fortunate enough to survive but was also keen to join the family business. As Alice suggested, the talks were allowed to simmer. They were still simmering six months later at the end of the war; and there is nothing to suggest that anything ever came of them. Jackson McConnan and Temple would eventually be wound up voluntarily by Tom Temple in 1924.

Meanwhile Eric settled into his new and quieter life at Park Hall where he was re-united with Brocklebank and Goffey, his old friends from the Liverpool Rifles and members of two of the city's most respected shipping families. William Goffey, whom Eric considered his closest friend during the war, had arranged for him to share his room. However he was spending most of his time in and out of hospital. 'He seems to have had rather a bad time', Eric wrote home at the beginning of August: 'this time he has gone down with the Spanish flu'. In the meantime Eric had to put up with another room-mate: 'he is rather a curious individual and is very fond of relating to me his family history, past experiences and exploits so I get a trifle fed up with him.' He looked forward to having his friend back: he was 'someone to whom one can talk with a little freedom and compare notes together.'

Although Eric was kept busy life at the camp was relatively comfortable and the regime relaxed. Many of the officers were there on medical grounds. They had the use of a tennis court and croquet lawn and could play cricket when they felt up to it. Eric also managed to get home regularly for weekend leaves. When he was given command of F Company there was again confusion over his rank – and this time over whether he had automatically lost his acting captaincy when the Pals were disbanded and, if so, whether it had ever been restored. The matter did not come to a head until the following spring when Eric was already demobilised but was challenging the payments still due to him for his war service. Colonel

Caldwell, the camp's commanding officer, had to write to the authorities to confirm that he had more than once asked for Eric to be paid as captain and that Eric had continued to command a company when he returned overseas in November. Two weeks later another letter had to be sent, this time from Colonel Engleheart to the head of Western Command at Chester, in which it was confirmed that Eric had been appointed acting captain on 9 July and that he had not then relinquished the rank until his demobilisation. Even then that would not the end of the matter. When the Territorial Force, having been disbanded at the end of the war, was reformed as the Territorial Army in 1920 Eric applied to join. In August of that year he was finally promoted to the permanent rank of captain that he had never been able to achieve during the war. His application, however, had inevitably led to further disagreement and in the same month the *London Gazette* published a correction, confirming that he had after all relinquished the acting rank of captain in 1918 when he returned to France after the armistice. Perhaps it was not surprising. Commands and temporary, acting, and brevet appointments, where an officer was entitled to be called by a higher rank but without any increase in pay, could cause great confusion. When Brigadier Stanley was made a Companion of the Order of St Michael and St George in the King's birthday awards in June 1918 his rank and full title were given in the *London Gazette* as Captain and Brevet Lieutenant-Colonel (temporary Brigadier-General) the Honourable Ferdinand Charles Stanley DSO, Reserve of Officers, Grenadier Guards. No mention was made of his having commanded the 89th Brigade.

Eric's role at Park Hall was to supervise the training of new conscripts who would then be sent to replenish the battalions serving overseas. He tried to make their training as relevant and practical as possible, organising realistic rehearsals of night manoeuvres and lecturing new officers and NCOs on subjects such as 'the attack', but found it 'a terrible business to drag anyone here off stereotyped and very antiquated lines'. Although he was only 20, he was treated with the deference due to a twice-decorated officer who had fought in all the major battles of the previous two years; and on one occasion he found himself in front of the cameras when a news-reel was made of their training. He liked to keep himself busy: he could always find work to do. Much of his time was taken up with the inspections, paperwork, and general day-to-day administration that were a necessary element in the rapid turnover of new recruits now being dispatched to the front. His first company completed its training only four weeks after he arrived and, in one week alone, 19 officers left for the front. It only added to the burden on those who were left behind. Eric also found that the recruits' entitlement to a few days' home leave before going overseas could be a problem.

> I am very surprised to find how great a proportion of these boys overstay their overseas leave. I think it is agreed that the fault lies chiefly with the parents. It seems a pity that a clean record should be broken in such a way. I had a long talk with them before they went away and did all I could to ensure their return at the proper time; and of course they are all told the seriousness of the offence for which the maximum penalty is penal servitude. And yet a quarter did not return and many are still absent. I know it is not because they do not want to go abroad for they are all as keen as mustard.

Eric had hoped to be able to escort them over to Étaples but Colonel Caldwell refused to let him go. However another opportunity to return to France came up only a week later. With recruitment and training starting to wind down – his latest company would be discharged before completion of their training when boys of 19 and under were no longer needed in France – he was told that his staying at Park Hall would be a waste of his time. He was strongly encouraged to apply for a job as an instructor at Étaples: the post, with the rank of captain, offered good possibilities and would be a distinct step up.

Unfortunately the job never came off and Eric was left with little to occupy his time. He tried without success to wangle a trip in the brigadier's car to Prestatyn on the north Welsh coast to inspect the brigade's rifle ranges. He also started to explore the surrounding countryside on his bicycle. Park Hall was so large that Eric's men were billeted at some distance from the officers' mess and, as he had still been weak when he arrived, his parents had sent him a bicycle to get around the camp. He now used this for long rides with his fellow officers. They often stopped for a walk or to take tea at a hotel or with friends before, as seemed to be too often the case, they were caught in a shower on the ride back. These jaunts must have seemed idyllic compared to life at the front. However Eric had always been more concerned for his parents' well-being than his own; and his mother's health was now a worry. His father had found it increasingly difficult to keep the family business going during the war as it relied on imports for most of its raw materials; and both he and his wife over-stretched themselves by devoting most of their spare time to good works for the local church and community. They were both strong of heart but spare and wiry in body: and, although they no longer had to send food parcels to Eric at the front, the growing food shortages at home did nothing to improve their health.

It is not clear from Eric's letters exactly what was wrong with his mother. She was probably just exhausted. Eric agreed with his father that a change would be as good as a rest. In the middle of August Alice moved with Judy and Guy to Hoylake on the Wirral peninsula. Harry joined them whenever he could get away but for a while Eric wrote separately to each of his parents. However, after only a month apart, they were back together again at the Ruff and his mother was beginning to feel her old self. She and Harry had celebrated their 22nd wedding anniversary at Hoylake just before returning. Writing to congratulate them Eric added that 'with luck there may soon be some very good news in the papers to add to your happiness'.

Things had improved significantly on the Western Front in the four months since Eric's admission to hospital in Boulogne. He had been in no doubt at the time that the Germans would launch a third offensive, the only question being where and when. The German high command remained convinced that the defeat of the British Army in Flanders was the key to victory and that the failure of their two spring offensives had been due to the unexpectedly strong French support for their beleaguered allies. By the end of April, they reckoned, half of all French reserves were stationed between Amiens and the coast. They needed to draw them away if another offensive in Flanders was to succeed. Faced with a reduction in the quantity and quality of their own forces they were running out of time to win the war before the Americans finally took their place at the front.

On 24 April, the day before they took Mount Kemmel, the Germans made one final attempt to resurrect the offensive further south. It would be the first time that tanks lined up against each other in battle and, although the Germans captured Villers-Bretonneux, seven miles east of Amiens, they were beaten back again 12 hours later. By the end of the day both sides were back where they started. Only the casualty count had increased. Ludendorff however was already planning his third offensive – at Chemin des Dames, the long ridge east of Soissons where Nivelle's offensive had run aground the previous year. An attack there would force the French to move substantial forces east to defend Rheims.

Although it took six weeks to complete his preparations, resulting in a hiatus of almost a month after the abandonment of the Lys offensive, Ludendorff's assault on the ridge was another masterpiece of secrecy, tactics, and planning. The allied generals were again taken by surprise. The French, who considered the ridge to be an impregnable barrier, had discounted any possibility of it being attacked. As a result it was only weakly defended, and in part by exhausted British divisions who had been sent there for a period of rest and re-organisation. The British thought Arras a more likely target as it was the hinge between the first two offensives. Only the newly-arrived Americans, who relied on their own intelligence reports and a perceptive analysis of recent German strategy, had concluded that such a weakly-defended sector was the obvious target. But their allies chose not to take their views seriously.

When Bruchmuller launched another of his hurricane bombardments on the morning of 27 May he was unwittingly helped by the stubbornness of the French commander, General Duchesne, who, in direct contravention of his orders, had chosen to man his front line in strength rather than apply the new system of elastic defence in depth. Eighteen German infantry divisions were up against just four French and three British divisions; and, when they followed up Bruchmuller's bombardment, they found that Duchesne's forces in the front line had already been killed and that he had no more reserves on which to call. They were able to advance five miles by midday and another seven by nightfall; they went on to capture Soissons; and it was only on the banks of the Marne, famous from the battles of 1914, that they were eventually held up at the end of the month.

History however had begun to repeat itself. Beguiled by their success the German high command again failed to grasp that an offensive's success depended on knowing when to stop. Once more they were beguiled by Paris, only 40 miles away. Victory beckoned. The speed and depth of their advance had however created another bulge in their line which exposed their flanks to counter-attack. Tired and hungry German troops again fell greedily on the rich stores of equipment, clothing, and food that had been left behind. They were in champagne country and were able to toast their success in style.

The allies' defences hardened as once again they found their backs to the wall. For the first time American troops were among the reinforcements that were rushed to the area. Theirs would be a baptism of fire as they failed to grasp the harsh lessons that the French and British had already learnt in almost four years of war. Advancing steadily in massed ranks over no man's land in a counter-attack to take Belleau Wood, half of them were killed by raking machine-gun fire. There was no doubt however that their arrival marked a turning point in the war not just because of their numbers but also, and perhaps more tellingly, because of the morale-boosting fillip that their freshness and enthusiasm gave to their battle-weary allies. The enduring spirit of the British, French, and dominion troops meant that there was still a war to be won. Now, even though they had just conceded more ground, there was good reason for believing that they had the means to win it.

The Germans went on to launch attacks on both sides of the Marne salient to extend and protect their position. Their first attack was on their western flank between Noyon and Montdidier. A month later, on 15 July, they attacked Rheims on the eastern flank. The city was an important strategic target and a railhead that the Germans believed was essential to their continued occupation of the salient. However their offensive was again beginning to run out of steam. Each successive attack was less clear in its purpose and less thorough in its planning. The Germans' brief flirtation with an advance on Paris was abandoned. It was time for the offensive in Flanders to be renewed: it was now a month overdue. Bruchmuller's artillery was already loaded and on its way back to Flanders by train when the attack on Rheims was launched. Ludendorff started back shortly afterwards. He was forced however to scurry back on 18 July when he was told of a French counter-attack on the western flank of the salient. His new offensive in Flanders had to be postponed – this time, it turned out, for ever. General Mangin's counter-attack, spearheaded by two American divisions and 350 French Renault tanks, may not have been the overwhelming success and turning point that it was later claimed to be but it was nevertheless the first successful allied attack of 1918 and, as such, a dent in the enemy's morale. In two weeks of bloody and ferocious fighting Soissons would be recaptured and the Germans forced back almost as far as from where they had started.

Further north the British front had been relatively quiet in the three months since the abandonment of the Lys offensive. It was, in Haig's words, a period of active defence. Foch, anticipating a renewal of the German offensive there, pressed Haig to capitalise on Mangin's success by launching a pre-emptive strike. Haig, mindful of the high cost of his previous offensives and conscious of the need to use his limited resources effectively, argued instead for the relief of the continuing pressure on Amiens. Gough's replacement, General Rawlinson, agreed with him. With Foch's agreement they started to prepare for an assault in the first week of August on the German artillery that still threatened the city from the east.

Rawlinson, a general considered by many of his colleagues to be too clever by half, had learnt the lessons of the recent past and, most importantly, that surprise was crucial to success. He placed a cordon of absolute secrecy around his plans which he then maintained with sophisticated diversions and disinformation. Infantry and artillery were moved by night, their noise covered by aircraft patrols; false rumours were spread; and the traditional preliminary bombardment was abandoned, with the artillery's required range-finding concealed within the normal daily barrage. Above all else, however, his plan relied on the use of tanks. The Germans had no answer to them: they had recognised their potential too late and did not now have the time to catch up. Rawlinson assembled more than 600 tanks, almost the whole strength of the British tank corps, for an attack along a 14-mile front. They were supported by faster-moving armoured cars mounted with machine-guns.

His attack came early on the morning of 8 August. In a happy reversal of fortune the British were helped by a ground fog. Taken by surprise the German machine-gun crews were no match for the British tanks. Their emplacements were demolished or shot to pieces. By 8.00am Rawlinson had achieved all of his first objectives. Following on so quickly from Mangin's success on the Marne this was a body blow. The exhausted troops in the German front line could do nothing except surrender or flee. By the end of the day British and dominion troops had advanced seven miles along a 10-mile front to the north of the Amiens-Roye road. When progress slowed after three days Rawlinson and Haig called a halt. Foch disapproved but, unlike their enemy, they had learnt when to stop.

Germany would come to consider 8 August as the blackest day of the war. Although the British recovered only a small part of the territory that they had lost in March their blow was more psychological than territorial. The tank had sown seeds of doubt that would quickly germinate and flower. The demoralisation of the German Army, and the diminishing quantity and quality of its manpower, was, as Hindenburg realised, laid bare. The German generals were as shocked as their men. Ludendorff, believing that the war could no longer be won on the battlefield, offered his resignation: it was refused. When the Kaiser met his generals five days later it was agreed that the neutral Spanish or Dutch monarchies should be approached to put out feelers about peace negotiations. German expectations, however, that they might be allowed to keep Belgium and their other territorial gains or at least buy time to re-group under a temporary armistice, were unrealistic. In hindsight, as they would be reminded, they had been in a better position to negotiate when they still had the upper hand in March and April.

The war would now be over within 100 days. The Germans evacuated Montdidier immediately. Reports came through that they had also started to withdraw further north between Arras and Albert. Foch pressed the British to follow up but had to accept that it would take some time to organise. Although the fighting would be as fierce as ever when the attack was taken up again on 21 August British and dominion forces quickly built up a powerful momentum. Albert was taken on 22 August; the Canadians joined in north of Arras four days later; Roye was recaptured on 27 August; Bapaume was evacuated by the Germans on 29 August; Noyon fell to the French the same day; and Bailleul was recovered the following day. On the last day of the month the Germans evacuated Mount Kemmel and the Australians regained the bridgehead over the Somme at Peronne.

By the beginning of September the allies had recovered all the territory that they had lost up to the edge of the old Somme battlefield. The Germans were being forced back to the Hindenburg Line: it remained a daunting prospect. 'The news is still good', Eric wrote to his family at Hoylake at the end of August. 'One might imagine that the Boche, if his intention is to withdraw to the Hindenburg Line, is staying our pace sufficiently but the number of prisoners taken shows that he is being harried more than he likes.' Around 100,000 Germans were taken prisoner in August, 70,000 of them on the British front.

The allies' progress continued into September. Canadian success north of Arras exposed the German position to the south of Ypres. Lens, nine miles to the north of Arras, was captured on 3 September. Neuve Chapelle and Armentières followed on 9 September as the Germans withdrew again behind the Lys. Writing home on 14 September Eric reminded his parents that 'perhaps you have noticed in the news recently the names of places of which I brought home some picture post-cards. Things seem to be going very well.'

Determined to retain their independence the Americans had been given their own sector of the line. With the British intent on retaining control of Flanders to protect the Channel ports and the French the middle of the line to protect Paris, the Americans were given the right flank east of Verdun, where a German salient around the town of St Mihiel protected their railhead at Metz. It was the eastern terminus of all their transport and communication networks behind the front. Gung-ho to prove themselves in battle and with the Germans starting their evacuation the night before, the Americans were able to take the salient with the help of French forces within a day. However, rather than following on to take Metz, the Americans now agreed to move west to the Argonne Forest to form the right flank of a concerted allied assault on the Hindenburg Line. While most still saw the war dragging on into 1919 Haig was confident that victory could be achieved before the end of the year if Germany was given no time to re-group.

The Americans started off the assault on 26 September. It was taken up the following day at Arras and then, on the day after that, by Plumer at Ypres. Although the fighting was as desperate as ever, and would continue so for many days, Germany's world had started to collapse. Austria-Hungary had told her ally of her intention to surrender on 6 September but had been persuaded to hold back on the understanding that Germany herself would

German prisoners of war near Amiens, 9 August 1918. (© Imperial War Museum, Q9178)

sue for peace. Nine days later, with Germany having not yet honoured her commitment, Austria-Hungary approached President Wilson to negotiate peace terms. By now the allies were in no mood to accept anything less than unconditional surrender. Four days later, on 19 September, the Ottoman army was beaten decisively at Megiddo in Palestine: an armistice with the Ottoman Empire would be concluded within a month of the British capture of Damascus on 1 October. On 24 September Bulgaria requested a ceasefire after the collapse of the front at Salonica: within a week she too had signed an armistice.

Back in Germany the collapse of her allies only stoked the civil unrest that was already being fuelled by bad news from the front and conditions of near starvation at home. An increase in left-wing activism created fears of the same revolution against an autocratic government that had brought Lenin and the Bolsheviks to power in Russia the previous autumn. It was still less than three months since the Kaiser's cousin, Tsar Nicholas II, and his family had been executed in Ekaterinburg. Elements of the German Army continued to fight heroically, and often brutally, for the next six weeks but the war was already lost in the minds of many soldiers and civilians.

At a joint conference of Germany's military and political leaders at Spa on 28 September the decision was taken to seek an immediate armistice. Ludendorff collapsed at the conference and, by the time he recovered his nerve a month later, it was too late. Von Hintze, who had only become foreign secretary at the beginning of July, offered to resign but was asked to stay on. However the Kaiser accepted the resignation of Chancellor von Hertling, his senior minister. On 3 October he appointed in his place an unwilling and unprepared

Prince Max of Baden. At the same time the first hints were dropped that the Kaiser himself might have to consider his position: his abdication would bring to an end the 500-year rule of the House of Hohenzollern.

Major Freiherr von der Bussche, who addressed the Reichstag on 2 October to explain the conference's decision, made it clear that an armistice had to be concluded as quickly as possible.

> The High Command has been compelled to come to the enormously difficult decision that in all human probability there is no longer any prospect of forcing the enemy to sue for peace. Two factors have had a decisive influence on our decision, namely tanks and our reserves ... We can continue this kind of warfare for a measurable space of time, we can cause the enemy heavy losses, devastating the country in our retreat, but we cannot win the war.[3]

Hindenburg followed this up with a note to the new Chancellor the following day in which he made it clear that the High Command required the immediate issue of a peace offer in accordance with the conference's decision. Prince Max's first task on the day after his appointment was to send a note to President Wilson.

Back in England Eric's September was marked by two important events. The first – on Friday, 20 September – was his 21st birthday. He hoped to be able to get back from Park Hall in the evening so that he could join his family at the theatre in Liverpool. As well as getting the right to vote he would now also become a director and shareholder of H and J Jones. Any outstanding issues about his joining the family business had clearly been discussed further and resolved over the summer. However, late on Thursday afternoon he also received a telegram from the Lord Chamberlain which advised him that his attendance was required at Buckingham Palace the following week for the presentation of his Military Cross. Eric wrote immediately to tell his parents the news but warned them that, as he could not get hold of his commanding officer, he did not yet know whether he would still be able to get home for his birthday. It seems almost certain that he was and that, with his work at Park Hall now winding down, his leave was extended to cover his trip to London.

Eric and his father took the train down from Liverpool the following Wednesday to find their formal invitations from the palace waiting for them at their hotel. The following morning Eric was presented with his Military Cross and Bar by His Majesty King George V. It was perhaps appropriate that Eric's bravery in the desperate days of March and April was formally acknowledged on the day that the allies began their final assault on the Hindenburg Line.

As the fighting continued the politicians spent October negotiating the terms of an armistice. For the previous six months they had stayed in the background as the military endgame was played out. The war had gone on for so long that they had spent little time considering the terms on which it might be concluded. They now had to make some quick decisions. It had taken little more than a week in August 1914 for Europe to find itself at war. It would take five times as long to bring the war to an end.

President Wilson did not respond immediately to Prince Max's request for an armistice; and he chose not to disclose or discuss it with his allies. In many ways he reverted now to

---

3   Charles F. Horne (ed.), *Source Records of the Great War, Vol. VI,* downloaded from http://www.firstworldwar.com on 29 October 2015.

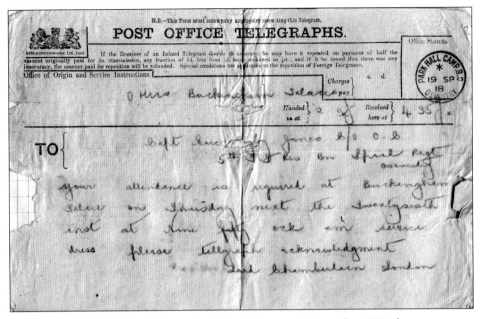

Eric's telegram from Buckingham Palace on 19 September 1918, the
day before his 21st birthday. (From Eric's cuttings book)

the role of self-appointed honest broker that he had assumed prior to America's entry into
the war. However, if Germany hoped that the American president might be more receptive
than his allies, she was quickly set straight. Wilson made it clear in his unilateral response
on 8 October that she would have to withdraw from all occupied territory. He also sought
clarification on a number of points, and in particular on the 14 points which he had outlined
to Congress at the start of the year as being the basis for any peace settlement and some of
which, he knew, remained totally unacceptable to his allies. Germany took only four days to
confirm her acceptance of Wilson's terms.

Meanwhile Major von der Bussche had been right to say that the German Army was
still capable of inflicting significant damage. As it fell back it applied the same 'scorched
earth' policy that it had used in the withdrawal to the Hindenburg Line in the spring of
1917. Eric would see the results at first-hand when he passed through the suburbs of Lille on
his return to the Liverpool Rifles after the armistice.

All the stations have been mined and most have been blown up or the explosives
removed. We passed through one station where Boche prisoners were working in fear
and trembling, trying to find a mine not definitely located but known to be overdue.
The Boche have done themselves very well here and we are now enjoying the fruits of
his labours. On the other hand the atrocities and destruction with which he is credited
are not at all exaggerated. I have just heard a few tales from some civilians: if rumour
is at all truthful the programme of our work in the next few weeks exceeds all my
expectations.

These tactics, combined with the senseless sinking of passenger ships, won Germany no

Admission card for Eric's investiture at Buckingham Place, 26 September 1918. (From Eric's cuttings book)

Captain Eric Rigby-Jones, MC, and Bar, Liverpool Rifles. (Author)

friends. Seen by the allies as the vindictiveness of a beaten nation, they served only to harden attitudes. On 14 October President Wilson advised the German government that the terms of any armistice would be set by the allies' generals rather than by their political masters. His responses grew stronger and terser as Germany squirmed to secure the most favourable terms. On 23 October he made it clear that any armistice would ensure that Germany was left with neither the territory nor the arms to resurrect the conflict at a later date and that, if she rejected these terms, the war would be prosecuted until her unconditional surrender. He also required, he said, the abdication of the Kaiser and the dismissal of the German high command. Ludendorff, his nerves now restored, argued for the rejection of Wilson's terms. However his recovery had been overtaken by events. In addition to the growing civil unrest there were now incidents of mutiny in both the army and the fleet. Germany was in danger of total collapse if the war was not now brought to an immediate conclusion. Ludendorff was forced to resign on 26 October; and, after another meeting at Spa on 6 November, a message was sent by wireless to Marshal Foch, as the allies' supreme commander, requesting a meeting to agree the final terms of an armistice.

The meeting was arranged for 7.00am on Friday, 8 November, in the Forest of Compiègne. The train carrying the German delegation was allowed to cross the front lines without interference. If the Germans still harboured any hopes of negotiating terms Foch made it clear that there would be no further discussion. What he offered was unconditional surrender in all but name. The German delegation asked for time to consider their position. They were given the weekend: the deadline for their response would be 11.00am on Monday morning. On Sunday evening, recognising that there was no further room for manoeuvre, they wired their acceptance of the terms. However, rather than agreeing an immediate ceasefire, the original deadline was allowed to stand. The fighting continued right up to the eleventh hour of the eleventh day of the eleventh month. The guns then fell silent after more than four years of war. By then the Kaiser had already abdicated. On Sunday evening he crossed into Holland by train. He would live in exile there for the remaining 23 years of his life. Europe would again be at war when he died on 4 June, 1941, a year after the British evacuation of Dunkirk.

Eric was still at Park Hall at the end of September. There was little left for him to do and, although he expected to be called for at any time, he would remain there until the armistice. He spent a week in October running a course at the brigade's musketry camp at Prestatyn and then was himself sent on a course for senior officers at RAF Worthy Down near Winchester. It was another one of those courses that combined instruction with relaxation. 'I was mistaken as to the nature of the school', Eric told his parents shortly after his arrival. 'It is an Air Force school which runs a week's course for infantry and artillery officers. Again I think I am mistaken: it is a pantomime.' There were only three mornings of lectures over the six days of the course at which 19-year old RAF officers with no fighting experience lectured colonels and majors on organisation, a subject of which they admitted they had very little knowledge. The rest of the time was taken up either with flying or with what Eric called 'recognised holidays'. It was a welcome break nonetheless. Eric found time to go sight-seeing in Winchester and enjoyed the thrill of being up in the air again.

Five days after his return, on the last day of October, he was told that, rather than being demobilised, he was to be sent overseas again. 'I shall be part of the army of occupation before long', he joked to his parents: 'Town Major of Cologne would suit me well'. He had to sit on a court martial for the first week of November before going home for ten days' leave.

Gobowen station near Park Hall camp: its main buildings are
largely unchanged from 1918. (Author, 2012)

However he still found time to brief his men on the armistice negotiations and to send his
father his best wishes for his 46th birthday on 4 November.

> At last I can look forward with more confidence to my spending your next, and I hope
> many more, birthdays with you at home. Good news is arriving so quickly that one
> hardly has time to grasp the significance of each particular item save that the end is
> drawing rapidly nearer each day. I am longing for the day when I shall be able to return
> to work with you. There is little chance, as Mother suggests in her letter of yesterday,
> of my becoming so enamoured of any post to which I am likely to be appointed in the
> army to cause me to be reluctant to abandon it on the first word of demobilisation.
>
> I see in to-day's paper a suggestion that the military faction may rally all Germany's
> forces for one last bid for a victory of sorts: in this case I shall soon be overseas again
> but not for very long. I shall be very disappointed if I am sent to Northern Russia
> which, other than France, I suppose is the only likely place to which I may be sent.

Park Hall was being rapidly emptied of troops. The camp, which already housed several
thousand enemy prisoners, was being converted into a prisoner of war camp. The 5th and 6th
battalions of the King's Liverpool Regiment were among the last to leave. Their destination
was still unknown when Eric left to spend his leave with his parents at Llandudno, where
they celebrated the armistice together as a family. Three days after his return to Park Hall,
on 16 November, the battalion was told that it would be moving to Milford Haven. It was,
according to Eric, a place considerably worse than Oswestry and one that he was glad to
avoid. His destination was France. He left the following afternoon, having arranged for the
London train to stop at Gobowen. For a second time he was on his way to join the Liverpool
Rifles on active service overseas.

16

Brussels

November 1918 – January 1919

Thus at eleven o'clock this morning came to an end the cruellest and most terrible war that has ever scourged mankind. I hope we may say that thus, this fateful morning, came to an end all wars. This is no time for words. Our hearts are too full of a gratitude to which no tongue can give adequate expression. I will, therefore, move 'that this House do immediately adjourn, until this time tomorrow, and that we proceed, as a House of Commons, to St Margaret's, to give humble and reverent thanks for the deliverance of the world from its great peril'.

Lloyd George, House of Commons, 11 November 1918[1]

When Eric arrived back in France a week after the armistice it seemed at first as if all was now right with the world. Although winter was approaching the weather was fine and the English Channel dead calm; a fleet of fishing boats bobbed peacefully in the harbour at Calais; and, most miraculously of all, the trains were running on time again. His high spirits were quickly brought down to earth however when, shortly after disembarking and while waiting for a train to Étaples, he saw 20 British prisoners of war returning from a camp in Belgium.

They were captured in March and had since been made to work but were almost starved. Last week they were given no food at all and a day or two later were turned out of their camp and told to make for the British lines. These few had sufficient strength to do it and, after walking eight miles, came across our troops. Many others were unable to leave the place through their weakness. Their condition was terrible. One has heard such tales of the treatment of our prisoners that perhaps one doesn't realise truly how miserable they are. They looked more like corpses than men walking. It makes one sorry that the war is over before the Boche has been sufficiently punished.

The British Army was still on a war footing. Eric had to go through the usual formalities at Étaples of testing his respirator and tin helmet. It would be another week before the rules were relaxed and he could tell his parents where he was; and, even then, he still could not tell them where he might be going. He was expecting to be held at the base for a few days before moving off to join the Liverpool Rifles. It was almost two years since his first arrival in France when, to his intense regret, he had been transferred to the Pals. Now he would be disappointed again when he found himself posted to the 5th Battalion. However, as the 5th and 6th battalions were stationed together near the Belgian border where, with the 7th

---

1   Hansard, *House of Commons,* 11 November 1918, vol. 110 cc. 2463-4.

Released British prisoners of war meet with liberating British troops
at Ath, 14 November 1918. (© Imperial War Museum, Q11444)

Battalion, they made up the 165th Brigade of General Jeudwine's 55th West Lancashire Division, he decided to do nothing until he reached them.

Having been stationed near Béthune throughout August and September, the 5th and 6th battalions had, by the end of October, advanced over 30 miles east to the Belgian border. On the morning of Friday, 8 November they entered Tournai to an enthusiastic reception from its mayor and citizens and, by the time the armistice came into force three days later, they had advanced a further 20 miles to the village of Meslin l'Évêque, just east of Ath and only 25 miles south-west of Brussels. When Eric joined them there on 22 November, he was relieved to be told that there would be no problem his getting a transfer. Three days later he was finally able to tell his parents that 'I am at last with the 6th Battalion after three and a quarter years of waiting'. It made up for the loss of his captaincy.

> I have reverted to lieutenant of course which is rather bad luck since I am really senior to three of the captains here: however I am quite satisfied and shall soon settle down. I am posted to D Company as second-in-command to Captain Childs, previously of the 8th Battalion. The other officers in the company are rather poor, which is the reason for my being sent here.

Eric's parents were not so stoical. He had to remind them several times of the rules of promotion in the Territorial Force and ask that they now address their letters to him as Lieutenant Rigby-Jones. The adjutant had assured him that his captaincy would quickly be

Road bridge over the Tournai-Ath line at Tournai station, destroyed by the Germans in September 1918. (© Imperial War Museum, Q47463)

restored. However, as time passed and nothing happened, the injustice of it began to rankle with him as well. With Captain Childs spending a lot of his time on administrative duties in Brussels Eric once again found himself in command of a company but without the rank appropriate to his responsibilities. He was reduced to observing just before Christmas that 'it is rather odd that I was commanding a company in France before my present company commander even received his commission'. Given that there were already enough captains in the battalion it is difficult to see why Eric's request for a transfer back to the 6th Battalion had been accommodated or even why it had been necessary for him to return to France at all. His own view was that 'it is worth anything to be here and to see the things that are to be seen.'

He was now allowed to take photographs and he asked his parents to send him as many rolls of film as they could lay their hands on. He wanted to keep a detailed record of what he saw. Unfortunately many of the rolls that he sent home to be developed were spoilt. It was still early days for the amateur photographer and Eric had a number of excuses including the rough treatment that his camera received, its loose catch, his changing films in daylight, and the lack of sun. None of his photographs appear to have survived. Although he must have been disappointed he was able to add to his collection of postcards and small souvenirs; and his long letters home paint a vivid picture of life in France and Belgium in the immediate aftermath of the war.

The inhabitants, especially the French, seem overcome with joy now that their liberty is restored. They have little left to them: all their animals of course have been taken as well as other things too countless to mention. They have been paid with imitation French notes or more often given a slip of paper which says that the English will pay after the war. On Saturday evening the people of the house where I am billeted told me all about the Boche when they were in occupation. They have had terrible times. They could not speak English but I can understand their French quite well. It is far more difficult trying to speak French oneself.

The roads are full of people returning to their homes. One meets hundreds trudging along carrying in a bundle all their worldly possessions. It is a strange sight. When I was last in France I saw them hurrying away from their homes, some of them already destroyed, having bundled together all they could carry into an old sheet. Now they come back with the same old bundle and, although they bear signs of terrible fatigue and often of hunger, there is a wonderfully cheery look on all their faces. Some are fortunate enough to have carts but they have no horses. Some of the carts are drawn by cows but mostly by the people themselves. Every British cart and lorry carries as many people on their way as they can.

Two days after Eric's arrival the 55th Division held its victory parade in Ath's main square.

The whole square was a mass of flags and on an elaborately decorated dais on the steps of the Town Hall sat the GOC and his brigadiers with the burgomaster and various

Civilian prisoners returning at Ath, November 1918. (© Imperial War Museum, Q3368)

civic dignitaries. In the centre of the square, which was kept open, were five flag poles. The bands of each battalion then entered the square in turn from different directions with the 6th leading. They were heralded by the regimental call and came in playing the regimental march. When all were assembled the divisional march, The Red Rose, was played and the divisional flag unfurled. Then the national anthems of Belgium, France, America and Great Britain were played while the flags of each were unfurled. The 6th Battalion's bugle band then played, then the massed brass bands of the other regiments, and then the Scottish pipes. The massed bands then played Schumann's Humoreske before all the flags were lowered to half mast and Chopin's Funeral March was played in memory of all the allies who had fallen in the war. The 6th band played the 'Retreat' and then the massed bands 'Land of Hope and Glory', 'Rule Britannia', and 'Auld Lang Syne'. The 6th then played the 'Last Post' and the show was concluded by the Belgian and British national anthems. The whole thing was most impressive and the sight of this old world square, gay once again after four years and crowded with thousands of civilians and men in khaki, is one which I shall never forget.

Two weeks later, on 7 December, the division was drawn up on both sides of the main road from Ath to Tournai for an inspection by King George V during his 10-day official visit to the front. It was still only 10 weeks since the king had presented Eric with his Military

King George V being greeted by troops of the 17th Division on 7 December 1918 at Thumaide, only a few miles from where the 55th Division greeted him on the same day. (© Imperial War Museum, Q3448)

Cross and Bar at Buckingham Palace.

We were closed up about eight deep on both sides so the whole division was in quite a small compass. His Majesty drove up in a car and the brigadiers were presented to him: he then walked down the road, loudly cheered by all. He was accompanied by the Prince of Wales and Prince Albert and a large suite. We then marched back to Ath and were dismissed there. I had a horse waiting for me so have ridden back here. Altogether we have covered 16 miles so I am nicely tired.

Between these two formal events the men of D Company of the Liverpool Rifles held their own private celebration with an armistice dinner and concert at the village school in Meslin l'Évêque on 29 November. The evening went off in great style. The sergeants waited on the men and then the officers on the sergeants. Dinner consisted of Lancashire hot pot followed by jam roll and cheese and biscuits and was washed down with tea, beer, and rum punch. Eric managed to borrow a piano from the house where he was billeted; and the concert afterwards – of songs, recitations, and comic turns performed by the men of the company with Sergeant Harwood at the piano – went on for almost three hours. According to the programme that Eric kept as a souvenir a final rendition of the national anthem was followed by 'service corps waggons' at 10.00pm. The programme had been made with paper and copying equipment salvaged from the wreck of a train, which had been derailed by the RAF while carrying the headquarters of a retreating German corps.

For the first week after the armistice all British units were ordered to remain where they were to enable the defeated German Army to complete its withdrawal to its own borders. The subsequent British advance, first to the German border at the end of November and then

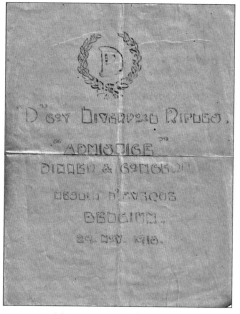
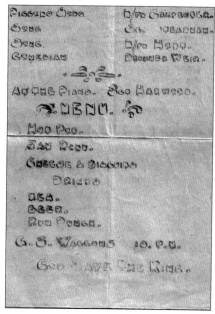

The programme for D Company's armistice dinner and concert at Meslin-l'Eveque on 29 November 1918. (From Eric's cuttings book)

on to the Rhine a fortnight later, was made difficult by shortages of supplies and the growing length of supply lines, by the thoroughness of Germany's scorched earth policy prior to the armistice and her destruction of the transport infrastructure, and by the congestion on the roads caused by returning civilians and prisoners of war. Haig quickly realised that he had to keep the forces required for the advance to a bare minimum. He handed the task to Plumer and Rawlinson and to their Second and Fourth armies. The 55th Division had been told of its participation on 15 November only to have its orders cancelled a week later on the day that Eric arrived. Like many other units it now found itself with time on its hands while it waited for demobilisation. It was a problem that Haig acknowledged in his final despatch of the war.

> In concluding this part of my despatch I desire to acknowledge with gratitude and pride the exemplary conduct of the troops both throughout the different stages of their arduous advance and since its successful completion.
>
> Among all services and in all armies, both those which took part in the advance and those which remained behind, the period following the armistice has indeed been one of no little difficulty. For those that went forward the real hardships of the long marches, poor billets, and indifferent food constituted a strange contrast to ideas which had been formed of victory. For all the sudden relaxation of the enduring tension of battle, and the natural desire of the great majority for an early return to civil life, could not but lead at times to a certain impatience with delays, and with the continuance, under conditions of apparent peace, of restrictions and routine duties gladly borne while the future of their country was at stake. Despite these disturbing factors, and the novelty of finding themselves masters in a conquered country, instances of misbehaviour have been remarkably few and chiefly of a minor character. The inborn courtesy and good temper of the British soldier have guided them in their attitude towards the inhabitants of the occupied districts. The spreading of a better understanding of the causes of the temporary shortage of supplies, of the difficulties of demobilisation, and of the continued necessity for keeping a strong army in the field has generally dispelled any incipient feelings of discontent.
>
> The discipline, self-respect and strong sense of responsibility which carried our men through to victory have in general been fully maintained amid changed conditions and new surroundings.[2]

The major challenge faced by the officers commanding those units that were no longer required for the advance was to keep their men fully occupied until demobilisation. Drill, route marches, and other military routines were quickly dropped from the daily schedule and replaced by sports, entertainments, and education. Divisional boxing matches and athletics competitions were arranged; the 55th Division's football team beat all-comers, including their own corps team and a local team from Brussels; and the divisional theatre company put on a 'peace pantomime' of Babes in the Wood, starring Baron Dugghoute and his wife. It was a hit not only with the troops but also with the many civilians and their children who were happy to pay the 10 cent entrance fee. Its printed programme, which Eric kept as a souvenir, included a number of humorous advertisements of the sort found in the

---

2   Field Marshal D. Haig, final despatch of 21 March 1919, recorded in the *London Gazette*, supplement no. 31283, 8 April 1919, page 4693 onwards.

trench magazine, the Wipers Times.

> MADAME ANGOSTURA'S "CRYSTAL GAZER" – Lectures on Spirit-ulism.
> Every evening at 8pm.

> LOST – truck no. 93151, containing turkeys, geese, and other necessities of war.
> Information gladly received by O.C. Divisional Canteen.

> LEAVE – do you want leave on compassionate grounds? If so then call on us!
> Thousands of satisfied customers! – Swingit, Slackum, Shirkit and Co.

> YOUNG LADY – with time to spare, wants washing. Apply Rusty Backs.

Education classes were established with English and elementary arithmetic as the main subjects. The classes, which were divided into three grades depending on ability, were attended by nearly all the battalion, including Eric and his fellow officers. In spite of his being in the top class for arithmetic Eric found it too simple and was keen to get on to stocks and shares and algebra. He also took up Spanish and German in preference to French, which he hoped to pick up in the course of his daily duties. However he opted out of shorthand even though he had won a prize for it at Rossall: he thought it would take too long to become proficient again and that without constant practice he would soon forget it. As someone who never did things by halves he asked his parents to send him some Spanish and German dictionaries as well as his old school arithmetic books. 'I think there is a Pendlebury among them and also a thick red one which are the best', he told them. 'It is difficult to do anything without books.'[3]

Eric thought that the 55th Division did more than most to keep its men busy. He also created for himself an informal role as tour guide and teacher of current affairs. Lloyd George had called a general election immediately after the armistice which was set for 14 December. Eric would be old enough to vote for the first time. More significantly the Representation of the People Act, which had received royal assent in February, now not only gave the vote to women over 30 for the first time but also, by abolishing property qualifications, enfranchised a third of the male population. The changes tripled the size of the electorate. Colonel Buckley, who commanded the 5th Battalion, was allowed home to contest, and win, the newly-created Liverpool constituency of Waterloo. When the results were announced just after Christmas Lloyd George found that, unlike Churchill a generation later, he had secured a resounding victory. Eric followed the election avidly. He even managed to find an army wireless station so that he could listen to the news as the results came through. Disappointed that his men showed so little interest he took it upon himself to brief them.

> I spent almost an hour this evening in the men's billet talking with them about the news in general – the election, the position in Germany, peace terms, demobilisation, and so on. I think it does a lot of good to point out the importance of these things to them and get them to think them over. There appears to be a latent spirit of bolshevism

---

3   Charles Pendlebury (1854 – 1941), who was born in Liverpool, was senior mathematics master at St Paul's School in London for 30 years. A prolific author of mathematics text books, his best-selling *Arithmetic* was first published in 1886.

in some parts of the army and it would be disastrous if it spread far. Unfortunately I cannot get other officers to do this sort of thing or take much interest at all, especially when the company commander is so indifferent. However he is going on leave shortly so I am looking forward to having things to myself for a while. I am afraid I have little news otherwise except for my grouses.

On Christmas Eve he took a party of his men to Brussels for a sight-seeing trip.

It is very difficult for them to discover the beauties of a place and, when they reach it, they perhaps do not realise its historical importance. I don't know whether it is quite the thing for an officer to walk round the place with a score of Tommies. However it was done and they enjoyed it thoroughly. I had read up on the history of Brussels and its architectural and other attractions and managed to give them a description of all the places we visited.

Word of the outing's success must have got around. In January nearly half his company signed up for a trip to the battlefield of Waterloo, just south of Brussels. Eric was keen to see as much of the country as he could. He made his first sight-seeing trip to Brussels at the end of November. It would be the first of many, both there and to other Belgian cities, all of which he described in long letters home to his parents. After getting two days' leave from his commanding officer he set off for the capital with a colleague called Lowe. They hitched a series of rides in lorries and staff cars and, after arriving in the early afternoon and booking into the Grand Central Hotel, they set off to explore the recently-liberated capital. The Belgian king, Albert I, had only returned the week before, making a grand state entry on horseback on 22 November beside his queen and the royal family and accompanied by the British Prince Albert, later King George VI, and Generals Plumer and Birdwood: they were followed by massed British, French, Belgian, and American troops.

We had a good look at the Bourse and then made our way to the Marketplatz, a most beautiful square in which stand the Hotel de Ville, the Maison du Roi and many old and beautiful houses. Everywhere was wonderfully decorated with thousands of flags. Here we were fortunate to come across a Belgian who offered to guide us round the city.

First we went up the hill to the cathedral and then on to the Park past the War Office and Theatre Royale to the Palais du Roi, to which the King has now returned. During the occupation this was used a hospital – not for German wounded but for Belgian soldiers wounded in the early fighting and for civilians from near the front. The red cross remains on all the windows but now there are Belgian sentries as at Buckingham Palace. Each alternate one presented arms to us as we passed in the usual sloppy style of all European soldiers.

Turning the corner past the palace of the Princess Caroline we entered the Place Royale in the centre of which, opposite the Chapel Royal, stands a magnificent equestrian monument. From here we had a splendid view of the Palais de Justice some half a mile away. Passing on our left the Palace of the old Duc de Flandre and the School of Music we came to the Palais des Beaux Arts. We looked round several rooms but there was not sufficient light to see properly the many magnificent pictures.

On we went as far as the Palais de Justice which stands on high ground whence one has a wonderful view of the whole city. It is, I think, the most magnificent building that I have ever seen and I understand that the interior is very beautiful but we did not go inside. The massive copper gates were taken down by the Boche and used for munitions. After he had left the city a mine was discovered beneath the building, as was the case with the stations and many big houses in the city. There are many beautiful houses in this quarter in which live many of the Belgian nobility and after a glance round these we returned on the car to the city where we took our friend to tea. During tea he told us many interesting tales about the Huns during their occupation such as the murder of Miss Cavell.[4] There is, by the way, a large monument erected to her by the Belgians and it was covered with wreaths. It was constructed in plaster for the day of the King's entry but will be finally made of bronze and marble.

After tea we parted from our Belgian friend and went to look at the shops. I doubt if I have ever seen such a display of goods anywhere. One could scarcely believe that there was, or ever had been, a shortage: but, of course, everything has been very dear and remains at quite a high price. Butter, for instance, used to cost eighteen shillings a pound and potatoes four shillings a pound. We were, however, able to obtain any amount of food without even any coupons. Lump sugar and pre-war cakes I had almost forgotten but here they were commonplace.

There has been no business or work carried on during the past four years and it is difficult to imagine how things were carried on. Most of the money in circulation consists of German mark notes and Belgian zinc coinage made under German control. I was rather disinclined at first to accept German notes in change and the people were quite indignant. The mark here is worth 1.25 francs whereas before the war I think it was only equivalent to about 60 cents. There are a great many of our returned prisoners in Brussels but hardly any other troops. There are also a great many Germans who have not yet left the place – but of course none of them are in uniform.

After seeing the shops we went to a cinema show as we saw advertised a film of the entry of the King and the army into the city. The pictures were excellent, so good in fact that one imagined oneself present at the time. The crowds in the city that day were immense and their enthusiasm indescribable. The entry of the army was very fine: the troops marched eight abreast and the guns in pairs. A famous French regiment was present and also some English troops headed by massed pipers. Afterwards photographs of the various allied kings, generals, and so on were shown. Of course King Albert was loudly cheered and Monsieur Max received a great ovation: but the longest cheers by far were for President Wilson.[5] There is a picture of Wilson in every shop in the place.

Afterwards we had dinner, incidentally a most excellent one. The city by now was very crowded and every band that could be raised was playing its hardest, leading all

4   Edith Cavell (1865 – 1915), a British nurse and matron of a hospital in Brussels, sheltered British servicemen in the first year of the war and helped them escape to neutral Holland. Arrested by the Germans in August 1915 and tried by court-martial, she was executed by firing squad in Brussels at dawn on 12 October 1915. After her death she became a symbol of German brutality and lack of humanity. A statue and memorial to her at Trafalgar Square in London was unveiled in 1920.

5   Adolphe Max (1869 – 1939) was Mayor of Brussels from 1909 to 1939. He was arrested by the Germans in September 1914 after he refused to co-operate with them and was interned for the duration of the war, latterly in Berlin.

BRUXELLES Palais de Justice, Panorama
Brüssel Justiz Palast, Panorama

Le Palais de Justice, Brussels. (From Eric's postcard collection)

sorts of processions. We went then to the Coliseum and got back to the hotel sometime
after 11.00pm. The streets were still crowded and the noise seemed to continue for
hours with people singing national anthems. The streets were lit up with a brilliance
equal to London before the war. This morning after breakfast at 9.30am we wandered
round for a while and then left at 11.30am.

If Eric thought that his parents would want an account of all the major sights it was his
obvious enjoyment of the novelties of life on the continent that he chose to share with his
sister, Judy.

I hope you will be able to visit the continent some time: everything is so very different
to England. There is something quite indescribable about a place like Brussels. Of
course you find people of every race under the sun and one cannot fail to remark on
several features of the place so unlike our towns. One is struck most, I think, by the
boulevards which in summer must be very beautiful and by the many open places with
their statues and fountains.

The business life of the city seems very slow and one misses the hurry and bustle of
people in our towns. In a great many ways the Belgians are years behind the times. The
cars are always a source of amusement since they still use single-decked trams with from
one to three trailers which give them the appearance of a small train. The conductor,
instead of being provided with an electric bell, blows a little brass horn. There is no
apparent restriction as to the number which may be carried on a single car although
its alleged capacity is marked. One is allowed to stand on the platforms at each end
– even where the driver is – and it is remarkable how many Belgians can be packed
into these places whose size is not more than three square yards: I should think that
twenty is about an average number. Of course one cannot breathe but then one does

not expect these little comforts when travelling in France and Belgium. In the centre there is probably a very fat Belgian smoking a terribly vile cigar. At the far end there are three people who want to get out at the first stop. Their place is taken by six others. At the next few stops no one gets out – they couldn't even if they wanted – but another dozen get on. The car is now nearly full and you will find two people on each buffer and four people on the steps on which they have one foot and they are clinging like leeches with their teeth, eyebrows, etc as the car jolts round the curves.

The ordinary railways only run between the big towns but a small-gauge line links up the smaller places. This as a rule runs at the side of the road but often in the centre. The line from Hal runs right into the centre of the city. It is rather a terrifying sight at first to see the train rushing down the street, rocking from side to side and whistling like a siren. What happens when anything gets in the way I cannot say for I am sure they cannot be stopped easily.

The police and all the railway officials appear to have walked straight off the pantomime stage. The police are well armed but would be more effective if made of wood since they couldn't then run away. Of course they don't control the traffic – it would be too much trouble. There are a great number of street vendors in the main streets. I came across one yesterday singing the praises of his wares (bootlaces – bad ones) to the tune of the national anthem. Then one sees a big dray drawn by three cows in front of the Bourse. Imagine this in Threadneedle Street!

With what he described as 'the desire for mementoes of an American tourist' Eric picked up souvenirs as he went – a German postage stamp over-printed for Belgian use, a German one-mark note that was still being used as Belgian currency, and an embossed envelope from the Belgian parliament. By the end of December, he said, he knew Brussels better than Liverpool and had left everyone else miles behind in the sight-seeing stakes. Other officers asked if they could join him on his trips or wanted to know what to see and how to get there. 'I almost think I could qualify as a guide to Cook's tourist parties', he told his sister. Given his obvious enthusiasm it is perhaps surprising that he never went back to France or Belgium. It was a part of his life that he tried to put behind him. Like so many other servicemen he chose never to discuss his wartime experiences with his wife or children.

Although the Rifles had been expecting to move from Meslin l'Évêque since the beginning of December it was not until the middle of the month that they found themselves settled in comfortable but draughty billets among the palatial mansions of Uccle, an affluent suburb of Brussels three miles south of the city centre. It reminded Eric of Liverpool's Sefton Park. They expected to be there for three months. It was now easier for him to go sight-seeing, to ride in the nearby Bois de Cambre, which he described as the Hyde Park of Brussels, or to visit the cinema whenever he was bored or the weather was bad.

By now he was thinking about Christmas. It would almost certainly be his first away from home; and he was homesick. He read and re-read his letters from home each evening and wished that he could be with his family who were planning to spend their Christmas at Llandudno. Although his parents sent him a Christmas present along with their usual parcels, a recurrence of his trench fever prevented Eric doing any shopping himself. For three days he was, he confessed, in rather a bad way. He had a temperature, the pains in his back and limbs had returned, and he was unable to eat; his hands were too shaky to write and he had to tear up every attempt at a letter. He recovered quickly by dosing himself with quinine

1918 Christmas dinner menu for the officers of the 6th Battalion. (From Eric's cuttings book)

but then found nothing that he could afford when he went on a last-minute shopping trip to Brussels on 21 December. He had wanted to buy some Brussels lace for his mother but nearly collapsed when he was told that a veil cost 2,000 francs. Instead he bought souvenirs to bring home later, including a much smaller piece of the same lace for his mother. 'I think she prefers a little of the best,' he said, 'to a larger quantity of the inferior article.'

Eric planned to keep himself busy over Christmas and New Year to avoid feeling home-sick. On Christmas Eve, after paying his company and finishing off his chores, he took his men on their sight-seeing tour of the city. He returned for dinner in the mess where the battalion's commanding officer, Lieutenant-Colonel John McKaig, gave one of his famous performances on the bagpipes. By then it had been snowing for several hours and the snow lay thick on the ground. Although they were far from home it felt like Christmas.

After church on Christmas morning Eric took himself off to see the Royal Armoury Museum at the Halle Gate. In the evening he joined the other officers in the Liverpool Rifles as they celebrated their first peace-time Christmas for five years with a slap-up feast of eight courses. He kept the printed menu which he got all those present to sign: unfortunately he glued it into his cuttings book so their signatures can no longer be seen. Oysters, consommé a la victoire, and fillets of plaice were followed by the traditional roast turkey and plum pudding before the meal was rounded off with meringues and ice cream, a savoury of grilled anchovies, and dessert and coffee. To drink they had a choice of cocktails, champagne, whisky, port, vintage cognac, and Benedictine. How very different it must have seemed from the diet of Maconachie stew, bully beef, and hard biscuit that they had grown used to in the trenches and from the time, only nine months earlier, when Eric had gone hungry for a week in the great retreat.

Sadly the men were unable to have their Christmas dinner that day. The only hall big enough to accommodate them all at one sitting was not available until Boxing Day. Eric did however distribute the cigarettes that he had been sent from home but had kept back until then. The cigarettes available in the Belgian shops at the time were terrible – even worse, Eric said, than those from the army canteen – and he thanked his parents for choosing the men's favourite brand which, while not to Eric's taste, were widely preferred to the ubiquitous Woodbines. 'Just then there was a famine in cigarettes', he told them, 'so they were especially welcome. Even one or two during a famine are more acceptable than hundreds when there are plenty.'

On Boxing Day Eric went to Waterloo for the first time. 'I had read up the account of the battle and studied the map previously', he told his parents when he gave them a detailed account, 'so was able to go straight round the places of interest without the humbug of a guide.' In spite of the poor weather he managed to see everything before catching the 4.30pm train back to Brussels where, that evening, he helped his fellow officers serve the men their Christmas dinner.

Eric went back to Brussels the following afternoon, this time to have a proper look at the paintings in the Palais des Beaux Arts. Perhaps it was not his area of interest or perhaps he had already seen too much in too short a time: either way he was less impressed by the paintings than he had been by the architecture of the city. 'Rubens' works are all very fine', he said, 'but the Flemish painters can't compare with our own. One gets tired of the same religious theme in nearly all the pictures.' That evening he had organised a trip to the opera for himself and his fellow officers. Colonel McKaig and his brother, who was the battalion's transport officer, together with the adjutant, the doctor, the chaplain, and Captain Childs were among the party of eleven. They met for dinner at 6.00pm before going on to the magnificent Theatre de la Monnaie where they had seats in the front row of the dress circle to see Eric Audouin and Lucien van Obbergh in Gounod's Faust. 'The orchestra and staging were superior to anything I have heard or seen', Eric reported home. 'The performance was excellent and it is marvellous that they should be able to produce such a show after four years of war during which the theatre has been closed.' The only dampener on a wonderful evening was that, with the performance going on for so long, they missed the last tram home and had to walk the three miles back to their billets.

As teetotallers Eric's parents may well have disapproved of the celebrations in the officers' mess on New Year's Eve. It was a very late night and the following morning Eric missed the early and only train to Malines, the medieval city 14 miles north of Brussels which was the seat of the country's only archbishop. As it was New Year's Day there were almost no cars on the road to give him a lift. However, rather than giving up, he walked most of the way there and back. It did not leave much time for sight-seeing. 'There is very little to see', he wrote home, 'or, at any rate, I saw little as I did not arrive until 4.15 pm and then left less than an hour later.' By the time he got back to Brussels he was so exhausted and hungry that he treated himself to a large dinner before catching a car back to his billet. By now he had seen almost as much as he reasonably could. He rather hoped that he might be able to get further afield – to Antwerp, Ghent, and Bruges – but for that he would need the permission of his divisional commander, General Jeudwine.

Everyone's thoughts had turned to demobilisation by the time education classes resumed on New Year's Eve. It would be an enormous task to bring all the British forces home and to assimilate them back into civilian work and society. Eric had started to work on it at the beginning of December by finding out and then classifying the former occupations of his men. He told his parents how the process was going to work.

> The rate of demobilisation is worked out and also the rates at which various districts can absorb men. A commanding officer then receives a certain allotment of men to go back to, say, the Liverpool district and a statement that, say, engineers are to receive preference. He first takes 10% from the men with the longest service regardless of all other considerations; next all men for whom he has a release slip ('pivotal men'): and then he takes engineers giving preference to married men.

Men in key professions or with definite jobs to go to were given priority. As Eric was now a director of H and J Jones both he and his father were keen that he start work there as soon as possible. Harry had already made his own enquiries to what he thought were the appropriate authorities in Liverpool. Just before Christmas, however, Eric learnt more about the process from a friend who had just returned from leave. He told his father that he had to complete a 'guaranteed employment certificate', get it authorised by a Major Duncan at the Ministry of Labour's Appointments Board in Brunswick Street, and then send it on to him: he would then hand it to his commanding officer who would take it from there. Even with such a certificate he did not hold out much hope of an early release. By Christmas the only man in the battalion to have been demobilised, apart from miners, was an accountant.

King Albert I of Belgium reviewing 55th Division in Brussels
on 3 January 1919 (© Imperial War Museum, Q3504).

The process began to gather pace in the new year. On 3 January General Jeudwine issued a Special Order of the Day to mark the third anniversary of the formation of the 55th West Lancashire Division. In it he summarised the division's achievements and praised his men for all that they had done. Eric must have felt mixed emotions when he read it. The general's message appealed to a divisional camaraderie of which he had not been part. His war had been fought with the Pals rather than the Rifles – and the Pals, as he remembered them, were no more. However, when Jeudwine paid tribute to the many men who were no longer with them – 'there are some still suffering from wounds', he wrote, 'and some whose graves we have left on hard-fought fields and behind grim trench-lines where they faced the enemy with such splendid courage and determination: they are not forgotten' – Eric's thoughts must have turned to the many friends and colleagues who had been less fortunate than himself – to his batman, James Tatlock; his chess partner, Rowland Gill; the bishop's son, Aidan Chavasse; the three Ashcroft brothers; his friend, Norman Henry, with whom, so he thought, he had faced certain death in the spring; his men in A Company who had been surrounded and taken prisoner in April; and Colonel Campbell Watson, who had lost his legs. He had had many close escapes but somehow he had managed to come through unscathed.

'Peace, we believe, will now soon be firmly established and then we shall all be scattered', Jeudwine concluded. 'As, owing to the manner in which demobilisation is to be carried out,

Lord Derby reviews 55th Division during the Brussels review on
3 January 1919. (© Imperial War Museum, Q3508)

I may not have another opportunity I wish everyone now in the division, or who has been in it, success and happiness in whatever he may undertake.' That morning he inspected the division for the final time in the Bois de Cambre before it paraded past King Albert in front of huge crowds on Avenue Louise. Lord Derby who, as ambassador in Paris, was already hard at work preparing for the peace conference at Versailles which would start a fortnight later, also found time to attend. Eric watched a newsreel of it at the cinema the following week and found it amusing to see himself and his friends on film. On his return he updated his parents on how things stood.

With regard to demobilisation things are proceeding very slowly although some 60 men have already gone – these are chiefly miners and agriculturalists. There is a shortage of Z15 demobilisation forms and I have not yet filled one up. Since no papers are to be sent forward until the whole battalion is completed it would make no difference if I myself was able to get an odd form now. A list of the priority of classes to be demobilised is frequently brought to our notice on which I see that men in possession of a guaranteed employment slip stand quite high. It was such a slip that I thought you could perhaps get for me.

In view of the likely developments at about the end of February which you mention in your letter it does not seem to me that it is desirable for me to leave the army before then. On the other hand it will, I presume, be some time before anything definite with Jackson McConnan and Temple is agreed upon. I understood from you when I was at home that you wanted me to go to them if any amalgamation takes place but to go to Ormskirk if it does not come about. Is it therefore worth my while going back to Ormskirk first if I then have to go to them later? I doubt that there will be enough for me to do if I came home immediately though I should have plenty to learn.

Of course I am anxious to get home but it seems ridiculous for me to leave the army and be doing nothing or practically so for a few months. I am afraid I am not too well acquainted with the situation and what I really want to know is whether you want me to try and get away at once or what time to try for. I am afraid it will take some time for me to get my head working properly since during the last three and a half years it has had little enough to do of the nature that will be required of it later.

Eric was again unhappy with his lot. 'I am getting more and more fed up with being under a company commander who has so little interest in his men,' he had told his parents at the beginning of January. 'He appears to be one of those people who manage to hold on to their jobs by sheer bluff.' He never made clear the precise cause of his discontent but he had to persuade his father, who was even more aggrieved on his behalf, not to write to the War Office to complain.

Naturally I am also very fed up about things but I am trying to take a philosophical view of it. The present state of affairs in the company is such that I dare not put it on paper and I have a very difficult job. If there was any more fighting to be done I should most certainly complain but since there is not it matters much less. I am continually being told by others that I would have the company if the CO was not so kind-hearted in not wanting to break a man at this stage. Anyway I will say no more about it here. I shall make every endeavour to get home unless I hear from you that you do not want me back yet. For this reason I am not trying to get any jobs that are going although there are now several vacancies that I have the opportunity of going in for. There is one, Railway Transport Officer of Brussels, which would be quite a good job. At present only one officer has left this battalion while I hear that in other battalions and divisions demobilisation has been proceeding much faster.

At least Eric was able to get away for a long weekend after he finally got permission to visit Antwerp. He left on Saturday, 18 January. As usual he had read up on what he wanted to see, having purchased a Ward Lock guide-book in Brussels. He would give his parents another detailed account of all that he saw, including the cathedral with Rubens' Descent from the Cross, the Palais des Beaux Arts, the Hotel de Ville, the zoological gardens, the docks, and the Church of Saint Paul 'which is more rich in works of art than any building I have yet seen'. Unsurprisingly he thought that he had managed to see almost everything and was particularly taken with both the Plantin Moretus Museum and the Folklore Museum where 'an old hemp rope and a collection of medicines, especially one which was supposed to cure toothache, attracted my attention. I should also have liked to have walked away with a very fine old copper wind vane'. On his two evenings there he went to the cinema and to the Theatre Royale to see a production of the opera, Manon.

Things moved quickly when he arrived back on Monday evening. The following morning he received the guaranteed employment certificate that his father had completed and passed it on to the Demobilising Office. Three days later, on Thursday, he wrote what would be his last letter home as a serving officer.

Dear Father and Mother

I hope to be home almost as soon as this letter reaches you. An allotment for two officers was received today and, as I was first on the list as the result of the guarantee certificate you sent me, I was asked if I wanted to go. No other officers have yet got papers through for release as pivotal men: hence my being top of the list. If I miss this chance it may be quite a long while before I go and, as I have got no job here and there is little chance of my getting one at this stage of the war, I agreed to take the vacancy. I leave here on Saturday morning and will perhaps be home by Wednesday but I don't know quite whether I shall be detained at a depot either here or in England. I hope that I have done the right thing but of course I have had no chance of consulting you.

Love to all, your ever loving son, Eric.

His departure was delayed a week as he had undertaken to bring the mess accounts up to date before he left. He did not arrive back in England until 31 January; and on the same day he was formally disembodied from the Territorial Force at No 2 Dispersal Unit at Prees Heath, 15 miles east of Oswestry. His army pay was stopped immediately but he was allowed to continue wearing his uniform for another week. On 17 March the London Gazette duly reported that he had relinquished the acting rank of captain on ceasing to be employed on 31 January 1919. His war was over. He took a month off and then started work with his father at H and J Jones.

17

A Triumph of Brain and Effort

Eric Rigby-Jones

20 September 1897 – 20 July 1952

It would take another book to do justice to my grandfather's life after the war. He had achieved a lot by the time of his death in 1952 after a long and painful struggle with cancer. He was only 54. He would almost certainly have achieved a lot more if had he lived longer. He died only a week after his father. Harry had sold the rope works in Ormskirk in 1939 shortly after the outbreak of the Second World War, thereby bringing to an end several hundred years of rope production in the town. He continued however to run H and J Jones' wholesale business in Liverpool throughout the war before finally selling up and retiring with Alice to the Lake District in 1946. By then he was 75. Alice would live for another 11 years after the deaths of her beloved husband and eldest son. She died on my eighth birthday in 1963: I remember her well. Brief appreciations of Harry's and Eric's lives appeared only a few days apart in the *Ormskirk Advertiser*. However it was left to an Irish newspaper, the *Leinster Leader*, to publish a full obituary of Eric on 26 July 1952, six days after his death, under the headline, 'Leading Industrialist's Death'.

Mr Eric Rigby-Jones, of Morristownbiller House, Droichead Nua [Gaelic for Newbridge], whose death occurred on Sunday, had been managing director of Irish Ropes Ltd since the foundation of the industry at Droichead Nua in 1933 ... Mr Rigby-Jones, whose organising ability and technical knowledge played a major part in the success of the industry he founded, was a very popular and respected figure, and was particularly esteemed by his business colleagues and by his factory workers. By his death Irish industry has sustained a grievous loss, and his passing is widely and deeply regretted.

... Having left the army Mr Rigby-Jones was appointed director of H and J Jones and Co Ltd, the family cordage business at Liverpool. Married in June 1922 to Sarah, youngest daughter of Dr John Charles and Annie Davies of Rhos, Wrexham, North Wales, he had two sons, Peter and Michael, and a daughter, Ann. In 1925 he became a member of the Liverpool Rotary Club and in the following year paid his first visit to Ireland, spending a fortnight on business in the west. In 1927 he visited the United States; in 1928 he was appointed to the College of Stewards of Liverpool Cathedral. He was mainly responsible for the welcome of 10,000 boy scouts at Liverpool Cathedral for the great Jamboree of 1928.

In 1933 Irish Ropes Ltd was established and Mr Rigby-Jones came to Droichead Nua as managing director of the factory. At the time of establishment the factory was no more than the dilapidated riding school of the old military barracks. The floor was of mud and it is on record that there was not one whole pane of glass in the windows. With characteristic zeal and thoroughness Mr Rigby-Jones set to work to build up his industry. First the premises were renovated, then the machines were installed, and a small staff was engaged and production began. In the beginning business was slow but the managing director's great organising ability and business acumen were very much in evidence as he pushed ahead with his plans to cater for the home market and to explore the markets of the world. He instituted the shorter working week as his staff expanded and, contrary to general expectations, this novel idea worked successfully from the outset. When the Minister for Industry and Commerce, Mr Sean Lemass, inspected the new factory on its first anniversary in 1934 it was obvious that the industry had come to stay and was sure to expand. It was the beginning of Droichead Nua's recovery; the town had been stricken but Irish Ropes, and the mounting volume of employment it offered, set the town on the right road to recovery.

Through the years Mr Rigby-Jones continued to be the guiding spirit behind the factory's remarkable progress. He instituted new insurance and welfare schemes among his workers and saw to it that the fullest payment was made for their services. The deceased had little interests outside his home and the factory; the industry was his life-work, and so great was his interest in it that he visited Africa on two occasions in order to develop relations between the manufacturers and the growers of the raw material, sisal. During a fuel crisis in the town some years ago Mr Rigby-Jones very generously made available to the townspeople a stock of fuel. Although he took little public interest in town affairs he was always keenly aware of the town's requirements and in many ways behind the scenes, as it were, he was responsible for a number of improvements in the town.

As a manager and organiser of industry Mr Rigby-Jones had few peers; in his dealings with his workers he was known as a straightforward, firm, and generous employer. They recognised him as one who had their welfare and security sincerely at heart and at all times gave to him the co-operation and service he so fully deserved. His widely-mourned passing will be a major loss to Droichead Nua and to Irish Ropes Ltd. A fitting memorial to his life-work will be the magnificent factory premises which he raised from a dilapidated building to the imposing present-day status as the hub of a thriving Irish industry.

The funeral, which took place at the new cemetery on Wednesday, was fully representative of industrial, business, and social life. Chief mourners were Mrs SD Rigby-Jones (widow), Peter and Michael (sons), Ann (daughter), Mr Guy Rigby-Jones (brother), and Mrs J Forshaw (sister). All of the factory premises closed on Wednesday as a mark of respect.[1]

The decline in Liverpool's prosperity after the war, the death of his grandfather, John Rigby-Jones, in 1926, and the world economic crisis at the end of the 1920s had all forced Eric and his father to consider some radical solutions to protect their family business. Among them was its possible relocation to the newly-created Irish Free State: it had been their main export market since the turn of the century but was now threatening to impose

---

1   *Leinster Leader*, 26 July 1952.

Eric marching in the victory parade in Ormskirk. (Author)

punitive import tariffs in order to protect and develop its own native industries. Eric was still a captain in the Territorial Army when he leased part of the old cavalry barracks in Newbridge, Co Kildare from the Irish government in 1933. The barracks had lain abandoned since the British Army's evacuation of Ireland in 1922. It was also only a year since Eamon de Valera, who had once been sentenced to death for his part in the Easter rising in Dublin in 1916, had been elected Ireland's prime minister. He had already joined battle with the British government in his goal of achieving his country's total independence from the British Empire.

For Eric, who had already spent most of the previous three years away from his wife and young family researching possible sites in Ireland, the chances of making his factory a success looked slim. He brought a small team with him from Liverpool and, to save money, they camped out in the barracks with Eric using the camp bed and leather jerkin that he had had with him on the Western Front. Somehow they managed to open the factory within six weeks of arriving, using a single machine that his father had sent over from Ormskirk. Life was tough at first – his family would not join him permanently in Ireland until 1937 – but, by the outbreak of the Second World War, the family was reunited and Eric had built up the business so successfully that Ireland, having previously been wholly dependent on British imports, was now almost self-sufficient in rope and twine. Eric was even able to diversify

Eric as managing director of Irish Ropes, late 1940s. (Author)

into the weaving of sisal carpets under the brand name of Tintawn.

The war, or the Emergency as it was known in neutral Ireland, brought new and even greater problems for Eric, his family and his business. His elderly parents chose to remain in Ormskirk and endure the blitz in Liverpool while his sons, now in their teens, followed him first to Rossall and then into the British armed forces. Mail was censored and travel between the two countries was difficult and often dangerous. His children could not always get home for their school holidays – they stayed instead with their grandparents at The Ruff; and, when his wife's father died in Wales in 1942, they could not get home for his funeral.

Eric and his wife, Dorothy, now found themselves in the same position as his parents in the previous war. Eric also had a business to run, and one that was vital to Ireland's policy of agricultural self-sufficiency. The strain came close to breaking him. When petrol imports dried up he had to resort to using peat to heat the factory and run his spinning machines and to gas produced from homemade charcoal to power his car. When he could no longer obtain sisal from East Africa or other hard fibres from the Far East he had to turn to growing flax on an industrial scale. It was largely due to his perseverance that Ireland never ran out of the agricultural twine that was essential to the gathering of the annual harvest and so to the policy of self-sufficiency. And yet, however sincere were his affection for the Irish and his commitment to his business, Eric also kept in touch with the British representative's office in Dublin, and not least in the summer and autumn of 1940 when it looked as though Germany might to use Ireland as a back door for the invasion of Great Britain.

In spite of a fire at the factory in 1940, which threatened to destroy almost all the stocks of raw material that he had carefully built up, Eric and his family somehow managed to pull through. By the end of the war he was even selling flax to the British government for making into parachute harnesses. Within a year of the war's end Irish Ropes was listed on the Dublin and London stock exchanges: and, by the time that it celebrated its 21st birthday in 1954 – two years after Eric's death when it was being run by his younger son, Michael – it was employing more than 400 staff, producing more than 350,000 miles of agricultural twine a year, and was a major exporter for the Irish economy, trading in over 50 regions across all five continents. Annual sales, which reached £1 million for the first time that year, were split equally between Ireland, the United Kingdom, and the rest of the world. Sales to the United States had grown in two years from £10,000 to £50,000 after the company had found a niche market for its high-grade lassoos and lariats.

One of Eric's first investors and a driving force behind the new company was Arthur Cox, the Dublin solicitor who founded the leading Irish law firm that still bears his name. As the chairman of Irish Ropes he would pay his own tribute to his friend in his annual letter to the company's shareholders at the end of 1952.

Irish Ropes has suffered a grievous loss in the death on 20 July of our founder, Mr Eric Rigby-Jones, who from the start was managing director of the company but even more so its mainspring ... He worked and planned tirelessly. He worked with his brain but did not disdain to work with his hands also. He instructed local unskilled labour and soon converted it into men skilled in an old but modernised craft. He employed new methods and modern machinery. He was a man of exceptional ability with unlimited energy, a clear foresight, and the single-minded purpose to establish this industry. As a result of his labours there arose a factory which may well claim to be one of the most up-to-date and efficient rope factories in the world. His life was devoted to the success of the company. It is the fruit of his efforts that today we proudly enjoy a high reputation not only in Ireland but in many parts of the world. No-one realised better than he how essential modern machinery and the most modern methods are but his thoughts never turned from the men who worked the machinery and carried out the methods. He never ceased to think of our employees. No possible effort was spared to institute every possible scheme for their benefit. He realised the importance of making direct contact with the producers of sisal, the raw material of the factory. Through his visits to East Africa and his friendships with growers and producers he became a leading authority on the fibre.

He created and fulfilled much in his comparatively short life. The years since 1933 have been difficult years and to have achieved so much was a triumph of brain and effort. The place of Mr Rigby-Jones in the history of Irish industry must always be a high one. His loss is mourned by this company and by the cordage industry in many lands. It is mourned also by us who had the honour to be amongst his many friends.

Eric's eldest son, my father Peter, was at his bedside when he died and, at the request of his nurse, read him the 23rd psalm – 'The Lord is my shepherd: I shall not want' – as he slipped in and out of conscience. His mother, Dorothy, would later ask him to pin his father's set of miniature medals to his chest before his coffin was closed. She also placed simple notices in the Times and Daily Telegraph. They made it clear that, although Eric loved Ireland and had made it his home for 20 years, he had died an Englishman, and a proud man of Lancashire at that.

RIGBY-JONES – on 20 July 1952 at Morristown, Newbridge, County Kildare, Eric, much loved husband of Dorothy. Funeral Newbridge 3pm Wednesday, July 23.
'They win or die who wear the rose of Lancaster'

Appendix

The Infantry Battalion and Its Place in the Structure of the British Army

The battalion

For most infantrymen the battalion was their home: it was the unit for which they felt the most loyalty and esprit de corps. A numbered unit within a named regiment, such as the 20th Battalion of the King's Liverpool Regiment, it comprised about 1,000 men when at full strength although it often ended up with many fewer. It was under the command of a lieutenant colonel with a major as his second-in-command. As well as its four infantry companies a battalion had a headquarters staff which included an adjutant, quartermaster, medical officer and padre together with supporting units of signallers, pioneers, transport staff, cooks, medical orderlies and stretcher bearers.

Smaller units – company, platoon, and section

Each of the four companies in a battalion, which were differentiated by the letters A to D, comprised around 200 men when at full strength and was commanded by a major or captain with a captain as his second-in-command. Each company was in turn split into four platoons of around 50 men: numbered one to four, they were commanded by a lieutenant or 2nd lieutenant with a platoon sergeant as his second-in-command. Platoons were themselves split into four sections of 12 men each and were usually commanded by a corporal or other non-commissioned officer (NCO).

Larger units – brigade, division, corps, and army

A brigade, such as the 89th Brigade of Liverpool Pals, was originally composed of four battalions with a brigade headquarters staff and was commanded by a brigadier-general. With a total of 4,000 men and 250 horses a brigade stretched for over two miles long when properly formed up. The number of battalions in a brigade was reduced from four to three at the start of 1918.

An infantry division, numbered like the 30th Division, was a self-sufficient fighting force comprising three infantry brigades alongside artillery brigades, units of Royal Engineers, transport, medical and veterinary, and labour and pioneer corps, a machine gun company (from April 1917), and a divisional headquarters. Usually commanded by a major-general, a division totalled around 18,000 men and 5,000 horses when at full strength and stretched for almost 15 miles when formed up. Great Britain had 20 divisions in 1914 – six regular and 14 reserve: by the time of the armistice in 1918 there were 75 divisions – 12 regular, 30 territorial, 30 new army, one naval, and two home service.

An army corps, such as Maxse's XVIII Corps, was identified by Roman numerals and at the start of the war comprised two divisions under the command of a lieutenant-general. A corps was often increased later to three or four divisions, and not least when large forces were required for an offensive. Unlike divisions, which moved regularly and were frequently transferred from one corps to another, a corps tended to remain in one place.

The British eventually had five armies in the field on the Western Front, each of which usually comprised three or four army corps. These armies included Allenby's Third Army, of which Eric's 20th Battalion was a part during the battle of Arras in 1917, and Gough's Fifth Army, of which his 17th Battalion was a part during the German Spring Offensive of 1918.

The five armies came under the overall command of General Headquarters (GHQ). General Sir Douglas Haig took over from Sir John French as commander in chief of the British Expeditionary Force in December 1915 and was subsequently promoted to Field Marshal in January 1917.

Select Bibliography

Official Records and Papers Held by Public Institutions
Historic England (National Heritage List text entries)
The London Gazette (Haig's despatches and medal citations)
The National Archives (battalion, brigade, and divisional war diaries)
Parliamentary Archives (*Hansard*)

Newspapers
Leinster Leader
Ormskirk Advertiser
The Times

Published Sources
Anon., *De Ruvigny's Roll of Honour,* 1914–1924.
M. Barber, *A History of Aerial Photography and Archaeology,* Swindon, English Heritage, 2011.
J. Buchan, *Mr. Standfast,* London, Hodder and Stoughton, 1919.
R. Churchill, *Lord Derby; 'King of Lancashire',* London, Heinemann, 1959.
A. Clayton, *Chavasse – Double VC,* London, Leo Cooper, 1992.
Reverend J.O. Coop, *The Story of the 55th (West Lancashire) Division,* Liverpool, Daily Post Printers, 1919.
G. Corrigan, *Mud, Blood, and Poppycock,* London, Cassell, 2003.
Brigadier H. Cumming, *A Brigadier in France,* London, Jonathan Cape, 1922.
Brigadier-General Sir James Edmonds, *History of the Great War: Military Operations, France and Belgium, 1918, Vols. I–V,* The Naval and Military Press in association with The Imperial War Museum Department of Printed Books.
General Sir Hubert Gough, *The Fifth Army,* London, Hodder and Stoughton, 1931.
Field Marshal Paul von Hindenburg, *The Great War,* edited by Charles Messenger, London, Frontline Books (an imprint of Pen and Sword Books), 2006.
T. &. V Holt, *Major and Mrs. Holt's Battlefield Guide to the Ypres Salient,* Barnsley, Pen and Sword Military, 1996.
Charles F. Horne (ed.), *Source Records of the Great War, Vol. VI,* New York, National Alumni, 1923.
T. Jones, *Lloyd George,* London, Oxford University Press, 1951.
T. Jones, *Welsh Broth,* London, W. Griffiths & Co, 1950.
D. Lemmon, *Johnny Won't Hit Today: A Cricketing Biography of J.W.H.T. Douglas,* London, George Allen & Unwin, 1983.
H. McCartney, *Citizen Soldiers: The Liverpool Territorials in the First World War,* Cambridge, Cambridge University Press, 2005.
H. McPhail & P. Guest, *Battleground Europe: St Quentin, 1914–1918,* Barnsley, Leo Cooper, 2000.
G. Maddocks, *Liverpool Pals: A History of the 17th, 18th, 19th, and 20th (Service) Battalions, The King's (Liverpool) Regiment, 1914–1919,* Barnsley, Leo Cooper, 1991 .

H. Marshall Hole, *The Jameson Raid,* London, Philip Allan, 1930.

M. Middlebrook, *The Kaiser's Battle,* London, Allen Lane, 1978.

Lord Moran, *The Anatomy of Courage,* London, Constable, 1945.

J. Nicholls, *Cheerful Sacrifice: The Battle of Arras 1917,* Barnsley, Leo Cooper, 1990.

P. Oldham, *Battleground Europe: the Hindenburg Line,* Barnsley, Leo Cooper, 1997.

B. Pitt, *1918, The Last Act,* London, Cassell, 1962.

P. Reed, *Battleground Europe: Walking the Salient,* Barnsley, Leo Cooper, 1999.

P. Reed, *Battleground Europe: Walking Arras,* Barnsley, Pen and Sword Military, 2007.

G. Rose, *The Story of the 2/4th Oxfordshire and Buckinghamshire Light Infantry,* Oxford, B H Blackwell, 1920.

S. Sassoon, *Memoirs of an Infantry Officer,* London, Faber and Faber, 1930.

W. Shaw Sparrow, *The Fifth Army in March 1918,* London, John Lane The Bodley Head, 1921.

R.C. Sherriff, *Journey's End,* London, Victor Gollancz, 1929.

Brigadier-General F.C. Stanley, *The History of the 89th Brigade, 1914–1918,* Liverpool, Daily Post Printers, 1919.

W.H.F. Weber, *A Field Artillery Group in Battle: A Tactical Study based on the Action of 2nd Brigade RFA during the German Offensive 1918, the 100 Days' Battle, and the Battle of Cambrai 1917,* Royal Artillery Institution Printing House, 1923.

Frederic William Wile, *Explaining the Britishers,* London, William Heinemann, 1918.

L. Wolff, *In Flanders Fields,* London, Longmans Green & Co, 1959.

E. Wyrall, *The History of the King's Regiment (Liverpool), 1914–1919,* London, Edward Arnold & Co., 1930.

Electronic Sources

Commonweath War Graves Commission (http://www.cwgc.org/)

Firstworldwar.com (http://firstworldwar.com/)

Old Front Line Battlefields of WW1 (http://battlefields1418.50megs.com/)

The Great War 1914 – 1918 (http://www.greatwar.co.uk/)

The Long Long Trail, the British Army of 1914–1918 – for family historians (http://www.longlongtrail.co.uk/)

Wikipedia

World War One Battlefields (http://www.ww1battlefields.co.uk/)